... a page-turner and a tonic for tired souls. It affirms the wisdom, values, optimism and belief in America's promise which Tom and his eleven siblings absorbed from their extraordinary immigrant father.... By his clear precepts and strong example, the Hom children learned that honesty, discipline, hard work, and education can overcome discrimination and transform opportunity into high achievement and personal fulfillment.... It should be required reading for middle schoolers, college freshmen, and New York Times *subscribers.*

Pete Wilson, former Mayor of San Diego and former Governor of California

Reading Tom's powerful story brings to life the journey of a remarkable family and the lessons one man can teach all of us. It was mesmerizing, deeply moving, and inspiring.... I look forward to sharing his memoir with the next generation.

Gil Ontai, American Institute of Architects, American Planning Association, Campus Director, Springfield College, Tustin Campus

Tom Hom brings to life a slice of San Diego's rich and diverse history in a way that embodies the many facets of the human spirit. From the struggles to the triumphs, and from disparity to equality, his is an American story that once you start, you won't want to put it down.

Tom Karlo, General Manager, KPBS

... contains plenty of fresh insights into the cultural, political and business experiences his family has had in San Diego since the late 1800s. Few others can write with such authority about the evolution of our region....

Supervisor Ron Roberts, San Diego County Board of Supervisors, Fourth District

I am so excited about this book. Just like the Chinese name given to him by his parents, Hom Cheuck Ngee, Tom Hom has "excellence" and "manners." Just like the title of this book, Tom Hom, the rabbit, has indeed traveled on a bumpy road. As a life-long learner, I can say that Tom's unique voice will undoubtedly inspire and transform many who read his story.

Li-Rong Lilly Cheng, Managing Director of the Confucius Institute at San Diego State University

This is the fascinating story of Tom Hom, a path breaking pioneer and leader in politics, business, and community service. Through his family life, and deep involvement in city activities, he offers an insightful account of events over the past eight decades in the San Diego city and region.

Leland Saito, Associate Professor of Sociology, University of Southern California

Historians and readers seeking personal inspiration will enjoy the gentle Tom Hom's memoir. He writes with humor and self-deprecation about many important chapters of San Diego's history in which he was involved as a produce distributor, real estate agent, city councilmember, state assemblyman, and key player in the development of such San Diego landmarks as Qualcomm Stadium, Gaslamp Quarter, Petco Park, and the Chinese Historical Society and Museum.

Donald H. Harrison, editor, *San Diego Jewish World*

... provides a first-hand account of one of San Diego's most important civic leaders of the 20th century.... This is an attention-grabbing book that is hard to put down.

Adrienne Vargas, Gift Giving Officer of San Diego Foundation

... is a brilliantly orchestrated composite of memories and experiences of a well-respected individual and one of the greatest community leaders of our time. From his early childhood years in San Diego, building of a successful business, to his honorary position as city councilman, Tom Hom continues to demonstrate the importance of dedication to family, heritage, and passion for a bright future for our citizens.

Hal Sadler, Chairman of the Board, Tucker Sadler Architects, Inc.

Tom Hom has a story that needed to be told. He broke the barrier that stood between the establishment and the Asian community, first as a City Councilman and later as a member of the State Assembly.

Murray K. Lee, Curator of Chinese American History, San Diego Chinese Historical Museum and author of *In Search of Gold Mountain, A History of the Chinese in San Diego, California*

... his journey may have been bumpy, but without it Asian Americans…would not appreciate the endurance, the courage and the leadership of someone who is so loved and honored ... by all communities. Now his story is here to share with everyone. It is inspirational, challenging, informative — and an endearing benchmark for all of us to aspire to as Americans. And, by the way, it is as well-written as any biography I have ever read.

Leonard Novarro, Pulitzer Prize nominee, journalist and co-founder Asian Heritage Awards and Asian Heritage Society

In Rabbit on a Bumpy Road, *Tom Hom portrays the life of his family that originally came from another country and culture and developed a strong and creative American life while overcoming the impediments that were then in the path of those of non-white racial origin. It is a fascinating book. I could not stop reading it.*

Leon L. Williams, Retired San Diego County Supervisor

What a wonderful book! Tom Hom weaves historical events throughout his life. I found myself totally captivated as I read along. A wonderful experience! What a life!

Sally Wong-Avery, President, Chinese Preschool, School, and Service Center of San Diego

Tom Hom, a living legend in San Diego, offers three valuable story lines to readers: The American immigrant family's work-hard-and-make-good story of success; the young politician's story of victory over conventional wisdom; and the story of a business, built from the bottom up with the usual triumphs and letdowns.... This memoir will help future historians piece together the story of San Diego in the post-World War II era....

Roger Showley, Staff Writer at *UT San Diego*

TOM HOM

Rabbit *on a* Bumpy Road

TOM HOM

一只兔子崎岖的心路历程

Rabbit *on a* Bumpy Road
A Story of Courage *and* Endurance

Sunbelt Publications, San Diego, California

Tom Hom: Rabbit on a Bumpy Road
  ...A Story of Courage and Endurance

Sunbelt Publications, Inc.
Copyright © 2014 by Sunbelt Publications, Inc.

Edited by Barbara Villasenor, First Reads
Cover and book design by Michael Schrauzer
Project management by Deborah Young
Printed in Korea

Sunbelt Publications, Inc.
P.O. Box 191126
San Diego, CA 92159-1126
(619) 258-4911, fax: (619) 258-4916
www.sunbeltbooks.com

17 16 15 14   5 4 3 2 1

Library of Congress Cataloging-in-Publication Data

Hom, Tom, 1927-
  Rabbit on a bumpy road : a story of courage and endurance / Tom Hom. --
First edition.
     pages cm
  ISBN 978-0-932653-44-4 (alkaline paper) 1. Hom, Tom, 1927- 2. Chinese Americans-
-California--San Diego--Biography. 3. Businessmen--California--San Diego--Biography.
4. Real estate developers--California--San Diego--Biography. 5. Legislators--California-
-Biography. 6. San Diego (Calif.)--Officials and employees--Biography. 7. Chinatown
(San Diego, Calif.)--Biography. 8. San Diego (Calif.)--Biography. 9. Community
life--Calilfornia--San Diego. 10. San Diego (Calif.)--Ethnic relations. I. Title.
  F869.S22H69 2014
  328.73'092--dc23
  [B]
                              2014004074

Photo of Tom Hom by Melissa Jacobs, Photographer, San Diego Photo
Title translation to Chinese calligraphy by Li-Rong Lilly Cheng, Managing Director of the
Confucius Institute and Professor at San Diego State University

To
Father
Mother and Ah Nuing
Dorothy and Loretta
my six children
my siblings
and the many kind souls who
guided and mentored me
to be true to myself and to others

Table of Contents

PREFACE

W HEN I WAS IN ELEMENTARY SCHOOL I READ THE AUTO-
biography of Benjamin Franklin. I was impressed enough to
have read the memoirs of many other people afterwards, some
famous and not so famous. Each and every one of them had a story to tell
and it gave me an outlook as to how broad, interesting and inspiring life
can be in each of the various and totally different, backgrounds.

That is perhaps the reason why, at this advanced age, I have decided to
write my memoirs, joining the crowd. Conceivably, my late wonderfully
intuitive wife had a lot to do with this. In 1957, after we were married for
five years, Dorothy insisted that I start writing a diary. She kept a diary
and periodically would share from her diary some of the times we spent
together before and after our marriage. Many times, in trying to have me
start a diary, she would playfully say something like, "Besides, you could be
famous one day!" I doubted that! I did, however, start my diary and kept it
up ever since, for 55 years. It provided much of the material for this book.

I grew up in a large family with 11 siblings in the 1920s and 1930s. It
was a time when it was not too unusual to have large families. Now, two
generations later, my five daughters each have only two children, and my
one son has three. Small families are not uncommon today. With family
structures changing, the social issues are changing as well.

IN MY FATHER'S TIME, PRIOR to World War II, employment opportunities were not readily available for minorities. For this reason, the Chinese
made their living by going into businesses they could own: hand laundries,
produce and small grocery stores, and restaurants. With large families
and rather limited income, the normal priorities had to be something like
this — live modestly, eat well, and save money for the kids to go to college.

In many ways, I have been given the opportunity to see the great transformation of these changing times. From the social and economic restrictions of my father's time to mine, many legal and *de facto* barriers have
been eliminated. This is especially true for my children's generation where
opportunities are unlimited. This speaks well for the American people. I
have always felt that in America there were enough good people to be

aware of the need to make these changes in order to rectify some of the injustices of the past.

In writing my memoirs I know there will be some differences of opinion on how various scenarios played out. I found this happening when I was writing and describing an event and noticed that someone else had described the same event differently. I understand this, for there can be many perspectives. I took all these viewpoints advisedly and with respect. I take the responsibility for what I wrote, knowing that I can possibly be wrong, however, it is still the way I saw and analyzed it. As I see it, there can be many shades of any one color.

On some occasions, I have changed the names of people in order to protect the individuals and their families from possible embarrassment. With some of the actual names that I used, if I felt it was sensitive, I asked permission for that usage. All and all, in seeking verification and help in describing the events in the book, people have been more than helpful and kind in lending me their knowledge.

IN WRITING THIS BOOK, I WANT to acknowledge the many people who have encouraged and helped me along the way. Of course, the earliest supporter was my late wife, Dorothy, who believed in me, and my present wife, Loretta, who was indirectly chosen by Dorothy. My six pro-active children, Nora, Gayle, Phyllis, Jennifer, Cindy and Winthrop, provided constructive critiquing, especially in helping me to keep "my voice" in the writing. Periodically I turned to my siblings for verification on various subjects and events, and I thank them for their support.

There are the people who helped put this memoir together, such as editing, design layout, artwork, scheduling, advisory, production and all else that it takes to produce a book. I especially give thanks to Diana Lindsay, Lowell Lindsay, Debi Young and the rest of the team at Sunbelt Publications, including Michael Schrauzer for excellent design work, and to my editor Barbara Villaseñor of First Reads.

I also want to thank Murray Lee for his wise counsel and encouragement and to Dr. Lilly Cheng of Confucius Institute at San Diego State University for the beautiful translation of the book's title into Chinese calligraphy.

1. A Rabbit

AGES 0 TO 4

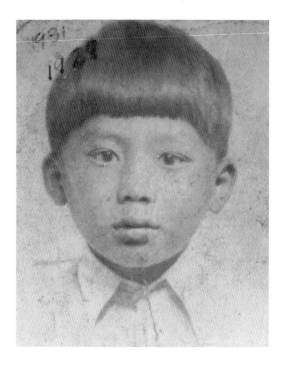

一只兔子崎岖的心路历程

Tom Hom, age four.

CHAPTER 1

Chinatown

IT WAS THE YEAR WHEN THE COURAGEOUS YOUNG MAN, 26-YEAR-OLD CHARLES A. LINDBERGH, FLEW SOLO ACROSS THE ATLANTIC FROM NEW YORK TO PARIS IN 33 HOURS, PRESIDENT CALVIN COOLIDGE SURPRISED THE NATION BY ANNOUNCING THAT HE WOULD NOT RUN FOR RE-ELECTION, AND THE GREAT YANKEE BABE RUTH HIT HIS RECORD 60TH HOME RUN.

IT WAS THE YEAR I WAS BORN, 1927.

I was born on the 15th of February under the sign of Aquarius, according to western astrology. Those born under this zodiac sign are said to have a strong social conscience, are humanitarians keenly interested in making the world a better place, are unwilling to follow the beaten path, and treat people from all walks of life as equals.

Also, by the Chinese calendar, I was born in the Year of the Rabbit. Those born in the Year of the Rabbit are creative, compassionate, amiable, modest, and cannot bear a dull life. They like to communicate with others and enjoy learning, and are said to make excellent diplomats, politicians, and writers.

And then to top it off, my parents named me Thomas Edward Hom at birth and shortly after gave me a Chinese name—Hom Cheuck Ngee. The meaning of my name, according to the Chinese characters, is "excellence" and "manners." Imagine that!

Doctor Lillian Wentworth, whom the Chinese community greatly loved because she took good care of so many of us, delivered me. After a swift slap on the rear, I howled loudly and clearly to make sure everyone knew that I was a survivor. After all, fatality rates in childbirth then were quite high.

I was born at home in Chinatown, San Diego, California just three blocks from where, in the 1890s, the famous Wyatt Earp had his saloon and gambling hall. Today my home site is the location of the San Diego Chinese Historical Museum, exhibiting the history of the Chinese in San Diego, situated adjacent to the well-known Gaslamp Quarter downtown.

My father was Hom Chong and my mother was Yee Kam Yuep. I was their third child and their third son, which made my dad pop a few buttons. According to Chinese tradition, sons are the ones who carry on the family name and bring fame and great honor to the family. Between being a son, and all the positive attributes of being an Aquarian, a Rabbit, and my Chinese name, I felt a lot of pressure to be good, study hard and succeed. I'm still trying to figure out if I ever made it.

Chinatown covered about four square blocks in the downtown area near the harbor, adjacent to Japan Town and a small Filipino town. Because the Chinese were the ones who built most of the railroads and also did most of the commercial fishing for the fish markets from 1860 to 1900, most Chinatowns in the western part of the United States, especially those in California, Oregon, and Washington, were generally located near the railroad terminals and close to the bay, if there was a bay. Needless to say, ours was not a silk stocking area, but it was an exciting part of town.

The Chinatown houses were mostly one story, wooden and brick. Some houses had two stories with businesses operating on the street level and living quarters on the second floor. Our home was upstairs in a brick building that stretched almost a whole block, with a balcony stretching the same length, along J Street. The merchants would start early in the morning and work late into the evening. No one ever heard of a 40-hour work week then. It was probably more like a 70-hour work week, which was pretty typical for new immigrants at that time. Most of the streets were paved, and many sidewalks were made of wood planks. I remember some of the boys would look between the planks searching for dropped coins. When they found one, they would put some gum at the end of a chopstick and fish it out. Come to think about it, it's almost like our forefathers scavenging for gold in the Gold Rush days in northern California.

With the merchants doing their hustling and bustling businesses, and the large families in the apartments, life was never boring. Since many of the families in Chinatown were related one way or another, I grew up in a very large extended family environment. We freely ran in and out of different families' homes and always felt welcomed, and we would often be given treats. There were a number of lottery houses, herb stores, grocers who handled exotic stuff like shark's fin, bird's nest, thousand-year-old eggs—which were not really a thousand years old, but just looked like they were—dried seahorses and squid and hundreds of other things that made it a fascinating neighborhood to just wander and explore.

In a way, Chinatown was pretty much a self-contained community; just about everything we needed was available. However, if we wanted something more American, we would go shopping at the department stores on upper Fifth Avenue. Marston's, the largest and best known department store, covered half a square block in a huge, imposing white four-story building. To my mother, Marston's was grandiose. And it was. Especially when it was decorated throughout the store with flowers of the season: poinsettias for Christmas, tulips for spring, and so on. Even as a young child, its fairyland atmosphere always amazed me.

When I was four, Mother took me there to buy a pair of shoes. After looking at several, I picked a Buster Brown pair with a strap overlapping on top. I thought I looked neat in my new shoes. When I got home I proudly showed them off to the rest of the family, until brother number two, Allen, told me that they were girls' shoes. I was so deflated and disappointed that I cried for half an hour, until I heard Allen get a good scolding from Mom. Then my crying stopped.

MY MOTHER WAS A KINDLY PERSON, always caring and considerate. I cannot recall when she was ever mean to us or to anyone else. She was a disciplinarian, though, and she did it in a reasoning way.

Mother was born in China in a district outside of Canton called Toishan, and was matched up with Dad, who was from the district of Hoiping in the Canton area. My aunt arranged for them to meet in the village store accompanied by their parents, under the pretense of shopping. My Dad and Mom knew beforehand the purpose of the shopping trip. This gave both the youngsters a chance to see and get a sense of each other, while the old folks shopped and gossiped. Naturally, it wasn't long before they fell head over heels for each other, and they married when Mom was 18.

Sadly, at age 29, Mother passed away from appendicitis complications at Mercy Hospital. She had so much to look forward to and she was so young, it was a shock to the family. In the 11 years of their marriage, she gave birth to five children, all boys. I can imagine she and Dad were probably the talk of Chinatown, having fulfilled the Chinese tradition of desiring sons. In later years I often thought Mom must have had a handful coping with five rambunctious and probably not-too-well-behaved boys so close in age.

I was a little less than five years old when Mother passed away. For me, that was the first time in my short life that I experienced some confusion. Mother was no longer around and I didn't know why. Shortly afterwards, my Aunt Ah Moo told me that Mother went to China to visit her family and would be back, but she didn't know when. At that young age, I guess dying was just not part of my awareness, and the adults wanted to keep it that way, except I do remember seeing Dad cry and I didn't know why. That was the first and last time I ever saw my father cry.

CHAPTER 2

A Bible Story

IN THE YEAR 1884, THE UNITED STATES STARTED CONSTRUCTION ON THE PANAMA CANAL AND MARK TWAIN PUBLISHED HIS PERENNIALLY FAMOUS NOVEL, THE ADVENTURES OF HUCKLEBERRY FINN.

IT WAS ALSO THE YEAR MY GRANDFATHER, HOM FUNG, FIRST came to America, arriving in San Francisco on the *S.S. Korea.*

Two years earlier Congress passed a special law, known as the Chinese Exclusion Act, the first and only law passed by the federal government to exclude a certain ethnicity or race of people from entering the United States. Chinese laborers were not permitted to come to America. The law made one exception. A limited number of Chinese individuals could come into the country if it were proven that he was of a non-labor profession, such as an adequately financed business merchant, student or teacher.

This 1882 Chinese Exclusion Act was initiated, and influenced by the labor unions whose workers were in the states along the Pacific coast. The given reason for the law was to halt the immigration of the Chinese laborer class, such as cooks, farmers, and railroad workers, as they represented a group that was willing to work harder and longer for less money. In actuality, it was to protect the American workers.

Grandfather managed his own grocery store in China, and as such, he came to America immigrating as a merchant. When Grandfather Hom Fung arrived, he first had to prove that he was a businessman and not a laborer. He was intensely interrogated and cross-examined by the immigration officers for three months before he was finally allowed to enter America. Grandfather's responses to some of the questions included information about my grandmother, who had bound feet and remained in China to care for the family.

Grandfather Hom Fung's first stop was San Francisco, where he visited with friends from his home district of Hoiping and the Tom family clan. The surname Hom and Tom share the same Chinese character, which makes us relatives.

Upon arriving in San Diego, Grandfather formed a partnership with seven others to establish the Hong Far & Company, a Chinese merchandise store, at 220 J Street, in Chinatown. He stayed in America for 11 years. During that time he visited his family in China four times before he returned permanently to retire in 1895. Grandfather had three sons and two daughters. My father David was the fourth child and the youngest son.

FOURTEEN YEARS LATER, ON JUNE 14, 1909, Dad came to America, arriving in San Francisco on the ship *S.S. Manchuria* at age 15. He arrived with only 16 cents in his pocket. Being the son of a merchant, he was processed by immigration onboard ship instead of at Angel Island Immigration Station. One of the first places he went was the Chinese Presbyterian Mission in Chinatown. There they fed him and gave him a set of American clothing and taught him Bible stories. He was so impressed with the story of David and Goliath that he adopted David to be his American name. He was small in stature, about 5′4″, so the name David fitted him perfectly for his new life in America. As the years went by, every enterprise he engaged in he named David, such as the David Produce Company, a wholesale produce firm he started in 1920. He also had a brand established for packed produce named the David brand. He later even had packaged jarred jams and jellies under the David brand.

He was proud of his adopted first name. However, it did cause a bit of confusion. For years people outside of the Chinese community thought our last name was David. My siblings and I were often referred to as the David kids, and many called me Tom David. I remember once a customer asked me, "How in the world did your family end up with such a biblical name as David, and not a Chinese name?" I straightened him out on that. It wasn't until many years later when I became involved in politics that people realized our family's surname was not David, but rather, Hom.

Dad stayed in San Francisco for several weeks with relatives, and eventually worked his way down to San Diego, where there were many Hom

On board the Manchuria, San Francisco, June 16-09.

141, Hom Chong.   Inspr. McChesney.

Merchant's Son.   Intr. Gubbins.

SS Manchuria, June 14-09.   Sten. JPB

                    Applicant   Sworn

Q What are your names?
A Hom Chong; no other name.
Q Are you married?   A No.
Q Have you ever been married?   A No.
Q Have you any children?   A No.
Q Have you ever had any?   A No.
Q How old are you?   A 15. (officers are of the opinion that applicant is about the age claimed; identity O.K.)
Q When and where were you born?   A K.S. 21-8-15 in the Gew Wook village, H. P. district, China.
Q How large is that village?   A 60 to 70 houses.
Q Where was your house located?   A 1st house 4th alley.
Q Who lives in the 2nd house?   A Hom Hing Mow.
Q Any children in that house?   A 1 boy and 3 or 4 girls.
Q Who lives in the 3d house?   A Hom Soo Hin.
Q Any children in that house?   A I know he has 1 boy; don't know how many girls he has.
Q What is the name and distance of the nearest market place?   A See Sun market and the Gow Mee market about 2 or 3 li away.
Q Do you cross any water to reach them?
A Yes, you cross water to go to the Gow Mee market but not to the other. You cross on a boat to get to the Gow Mee market.
Q Are there any mountains about your village?   A Yes.
Q What have you been doing in China?   A Attending school from age of 7 until end of last year.
Q Where did you attend school, in the ancestral hall?   A Yes, in the ancestral hall.
Q Have you any brothers or sisters?   A 2 brothers and 2 sisters:
      Hom Yuen, 29, in business in the Chung Shar market, China.
      Hom Yen, 20. Left China for this country K.S 33-7; don't know the steamer. He is in San Diego.
      Hom Wan, sister, 11, home in China.
      Hom Ho, sister, 9, home in China.
Q Did you ever have any other brothers or sisters then these you have mentioned?   A No.
Q What is your father's name?   A Hom Fung, 58. He is a merchant with the firm of Hong Far & Co., San Diego, Cal.; don't know the street.
Q What is your mother's name?   A Yee Shee, bound feet, 53, still living in China.
Q Did your father ever have any other wife besides Yee Shee? A No.
Q Did you ever see your father?   A I was 7 or 8 years old when my father returned to this country.
Q Has your father any brothers?   A 4 brothers, no sisters.
Q Where are they?   A One is dead and the others are in China.
Correctly identifies photos of alleged father and alleged brother Hom Yen and self.
Q Who is there in the U.S that knew you in China besies your brother?   A I know a certain Hom Jing Mow who is a member of the firm of Lun Chong & Co., San Francisco.
Q Is he going to be a witness for you?   A No.
Q Have you anything further to state?   A No.
Q Have you understood the interpreter?   A Yes.
(sgd) J.B. McChesney; J.H. Gubbins.
(sgd) in Chinese:
6-18-09.

This immigration interview of Hom Chong (David Hom) aboard the SS Manchuria, June 16, 1909, was recently discovered by Judy Yung. Prior to her discovery of this document, it was not known that my grandfather, Hom Fung, was a merchant in San Diego for a period of time.

relatives, including his second oldest brother, Hom Yen. Dad gravitated into working in the fresh fruit and vegetable business, and then later started his own business by peddling fresh produce door to door. Succeeding in that, he later established his wholesale produce firm, the David Produce Company, located on lower 6th Avenue in downtown where all the produce houses were then located. It was a marketplace that consisted of many different races and ethnic groups from just about everywhere in the world, with many different languages and accents. It was a real United Nations.

Before going into business for himself, Dad went to public school for two years, along with attending night classes at Chinatown's Chinese Congregational Mission, to continue learning to read and write English. He was a serious person, but a friendly one, who made friends easily.

In later years, after establishing his David Produce Company, he worked long hours, starting at 4 a.m. to about 6 p.m. In spite of these long hours, Dad always made a point to have dinner at home together with his family. He felt it was a sacred time when his wife and his children could share the day's activities together and exchange thoughts. I remember the occasions he would take time to teach us the rights and wrongs of life and

how to conduct ourselves. He would often emphasize to us boys, "Always be a gentleman … be a gentleman!" That was important to him. In hindsight, while young, I can't say being a gentleman was always easy. But later, as I got older and I wanted to become more like my dad, it became easier.

My father, Hom Chong (David Hom), who arrived in America from China in 1909.

CHAPTER 3

The Immersion

IN THE FALL OF 1931, I STARTED SCHOOL AT LINCOLN ELEMENTARY, where most of the Chinese kids went, located at 12th and F Streets downtown. It was in a hustling and bustling part of town where there were all sorts of retail stores and many residences. I entered kindergarten without speaking a word of English. Well, maybe I knew "yes" and "no", but that was about it.

On my first day in class the teacher gave us all small garden tools of hoes and shovels to dig in the large sandbox. While digging, the boy next to me dropped his shovel, and when I bent over to pick it up, another boy was hacking away with his hoe and accidentally hit me in the head. It hurt a little bit until I rubbed where the hoe had hit me and I saw blood on my fingers. Then I really started to bawl, for at least half an hour. The teacher put some medicine on the wound and tried to stop me from crying, but without success, until she reached into her apron for something and said, "Candy?" I stopped crying and also realized I just learned a new English word, "candy." English by immersion was working already.

In those days, schools didn't have programs such as English as a Second Language so immersion was how most kids from Chinatown learned English. It must have worked pretty well because most of us went on to college and became successful in many fields.

11. A New Mother

AGES 5 TO 10

New Mother Ah Nuing.

CHAPTER 4

Mother

A FTER MOM PASSED AWAY, WITH FIVE OVERLY ACTIVE LITTLE boys on his hands, Dad decided he needed to marry again. In the interim, we were being taken care of by our kindly aunt and uncle, whom we called Ah Moo and Ah Bock. They had a laundry business so they could only do so much, especially when it came to keeping us from getting into mischief. In spite of that, they were always patient and caring. I have always remembered them as special people in my life.

Ready to remarry, Dad notified his mother and father at the village in China that he would like them to find a nice wife for him. He gave several criteria that he wished for in a wife. In a short while, his parents replied that they found someone that they believed would be suitable for him. He would, however, have the final say, after getting acquainted with the proposed bride. They also told him that the proposed bride also had the right to refuse to marry if she decided the compatibility did not agree with her. It was an open ended proposal.

After two weeks of getting acquainted Dad and the young woman found that they both had something good to offer to each other. Dad could offer her a new life in the great country of Gold Mountain, as the Chinese called America. And she would be a new mother to his five children, and in the future have additional children of her own.

Dad married and came back with my second mother who we were told to call Ah Nuing. She was attractive, twenty years old, and, as part of the new movement of young people that was taking place through the efforts started by Sun Yat Sen for a new Republic of China, she was well educated.

I remember there were a number of times ladies in Chinatown brought letters that they had received from their home village for Ah Nuing to read and write a reply. In her spare time, she often read Chinese classic literature. She also had a large Chinese-English dictionary to learn English words. In later years, I looked in the book and found it most confusing and challenging.

It wasn't long after Dad and Ah Nuing married that we moved from Chinatown to a larger house in Logan Heights, a working class neighborhood, with a United Nations makeup. Shortly after we settled in, Dad and Ah Nuing started the second round of David Hom children: four more boys, again a jackpot, and three girls, which was a Godsend, bringing a balance of grace and tranquility to a household full of rowdy boys. Dad stuck to the tradition of using all-American names like Albert, Helen, George, John, Margaret, Beatrice, and Paul. With so many kids, the older ones were assigned to take care of the younger ones and were responsible for their wellbeing, like diaper changing, which sometimes we made a game as to who could change them faster and neater. Brother number two, Allen, was the best.

As we got older, 12 to 14 years, our main responsibilities of taking care of the younger ones got passed onto the next batch of younger kids. Relieved of these responsibilities, Dad would take us to the David Produce Company warehouse to do what we called "fun work," like packing and sorting fruit and vegetables, and sweeping the floor and stacking boxes. Another treat was when Dad gave each of us a quarter to eat lunch at one of the restaurants in the produce district for what we called true American food. It was a treat because at home we always ate Chinese food. My favorites were Italian spaghetti with meatballs, Irish beef stew, and hash brown potatoes.

Because of our move, I changed to another school, Sherman Elementary. Unlike Lincoln where there were a number of Chinese kids, there was only a handful at Sherman. With this new mix of kids, I began my cultural immersion experience. It was an experience that taught me there is good in every race and culture. It is just a matter of accepting it.

THE 1930S WERE A TIME WHEN the whole world was in the grips of the Great Depression following the 1929 stock market crash. It was also when

Franklin D. Roosevelt was elected president, and Adolf Hitler defeated President von Hindenburg for control of Germany. During this period the FBI finally caught and killed the murderer and notorious bank robber John Dillinger in a shootout in Chicago, and the 18th Amendment was repealed to end Prohibition after 14 years. On the lighter side, in California, McDonalds opened its first hamburger stand.

Father's business, like most others, was affected by the slow economy. He had to lay off a good part of his employees. In so doing, he brought crates of fruit and vegetables home for us to sort, recondition, and pack. Knowing that our company's restaurant customers needed to save on labor as well, he would have us shell sweet peas in great volume. This was before the age of frozen foods. He probably sold more shelled peas than anyone in the state of California. Like we kids often did, we made a game as to who worked the fastest and produced the most. We often ended up shooting peas at each other with our pea shooters, which were like blow guns. When we got too volatile, Ah Nuing would put us back to work.

In the fourth grade I was seated near the rear of the classroom, where we were seated alphabetically. At that time I didn't know that my eyesight was nowhere near 20/20 and I had a hard time reading the blackboard. Invariably, I would need to walk up to the blackboard to make out the written words and then return to my desk to do my work. The teacher, Miss Cole, a very caring person, noticed that and subsequently moved me to a front desk. A few days later, she sent me to the nurse's office for an eye examination. Two weeks later I was fitted with glasses. The glasses were great, enabling me to see distance clearly. I wore them home and when Dad saw me, he was puzzled. "Tom," he said, "how come you have glasses?"

"I couldn't read the blackboard," I said, "so the nurse gave them to me so I could see better."

"How much will it cost?" he asked.

I replied, "Nothing, Dad, the nurse said it was free." Dad was amazed. He was not used to having things like expensive glasses given free.

The next day, to show his appreciation for this touch of kindness, he had two crates of produce delivered to the principal's office.

III. Sweet Bread

AGES 11 TO 12

一只兔子崎岖的心路历程

CHAPTER 5

Spanish Lesson

I ENJOYED SCHOOL, ESPECIALLY NOW THAT I COULD SPEAK ENGLISH fluently. English by immersion worked pretty well. I even learned a few not so proper words, too. I had an older friend, Sal Gonzales, who was eager to teach me. One day Sal said, "Tom, do me a favor. Here is a nickel; run over to the Mexican store and get me two sweet breads. Tell them to give you the *puta* kind." So at the store I told the lady clerk I wanted two *putas*. She looked at me with a stunned look, and then laughed. She called over two of her co-workers and asked me to repeat what I wanted. I did, and they laughed even louder. I then pointed to the sweet bread case and said two of those. When I got back to Sal I told him what happened. He was laughing so hard he could hardly get out the words. Finally, when he told me that *puta* really meant "whore," I was terribly embarrassed. Even at that young age I knew what a whore was, because I knew of the Red Light District, called the Stingaree, where a lot of sailors went. It was located next to Chinatown. Well, anyways, I chalked that up as a part of my Spanish immersion lesson. I also learned that the correct Spanish word for sweet bread was *pan dulce*.

Thinking back, my favorite teacher was my third grade teacher, Miss Wade. She was soft spoken and had the ability to make learning fun in that she made each one of us feel like we were someone special. About 30 years later, I was surprised to receive a letter from her congratulating me on winning the election to the San Diego City Council. I couldn't believe she had remembered me after all that time. Wow! Was I that outstandingly bad … or that good? I wrote back and thanked her profusely. She was still as kind and thoughtful as I remembered her to be. Later I learned that she taught for over 40 years and married late in life. Lucky man!

With so many kids in the family, we didn't have anything like an allowance. Whenever we wanted some spending money, which was like five or ten cents, we'd ask either Ah Nuing or Dad for it. Times were very tough then, so money was always tight. Ah Nuing was tighter and Dad a bit looser.

In order to create some spending money, some of the boys did different things to earn money. Number one brother, James, sold *The Liberty* and *The Saturday Evening Post* magazines. He did quite well, selling the most in town. Number Two brother, Allen, had a paper route delivering the *Los Angeles Times* across the bay in the rich residential area of Coronado, where he also made good tips.

As for me, Number Three, I sold the *San Diego Union* newspapers at the thriving business area of 12th and Market Streets, until about two weeks later when two big guys came by and told me to "get lost" because this was their territory. Later I asked the newspaper agent whether there was such a thing as an exclusive territory. He said no. So I moved a few blocks away and set myself up on an island in the middle of the street where there was a four-way stop sign. From this new location I sold more papers, according to the agent, than those two thugs put together. This was my first wonderful experience in the Free Enterprise system. Just be innovative and be better.

The Chinese Congregational Mission had always been a big part of our family's life. As I said earlier, my dad took some of his English lessons there. When my new mother, Ah Nuing, came from China, she took lessons there as well, until she became too occupied running the household and giving birth to the younger seven kids. In spite of having no more formal English classes, she did pretty well communicating with us older boys. She would talk to us in Chinese and we would normally answer back in English. Sometimes we would answer back both partly mixed English and Chinese. In no time she picked up a lot and was able to talk with our non-Chinese neighbors quite freely and go shopping, although she never really lost her Chinese accent.

Our church was first established in 1885 by the large First Congregational Church through its missions program working with the Chinese immigrants. The church that I grew up in was at its third location, 645 First Avenue, downtown. The land for the church was donated by George Marston, a well-to-do gentleman who owned the Marston Department Store, the largest department store in San Diego. The church had a multi-purpose chapel, classrooms, lounge, kitchen, and a beautiful little garden with a fish pond made of rock. It also had about 15 dormitory rooms. These rooms were rented out at a nominal rate to single men who were recent Chinese immigrants. At that time, being part of a minority group, it was not unusual to find it difficult to find a decent place to rent. So the dormitory rooms were a Godsend for these bachelors.

At the ripe old age of 12, I realized I would be graduating from the 6th grade moving on to the 7th grade at Memorial Junior High, a school that was about four times bigger than Sherman Elementary. Rumor was going around that the new "Peagreen Boys," that's what the new incoming students were called by the older students at Memorial, would be subjected to being "de-panted" by some of the older and rowdier boys. When we finally got there, we Peagreens hung together for protection, but nothing happened. There were some playful shouts and threats, and that was the extent of it.

I learned something from that. Believe very little of rumors. But I also had my best running shoes on, just in case.

iv. War Clouds

AGES 13 TO 15

一只兔子崎岖的心路历程

Old City Hall, 1938. Photo courtesy San Diego History Center.

CHAPTER 6

Rocky Ramirez

THE LATE 1930S WAS THE BEGINNING OF DRASTIC CHANGES FOR THE WORLD. JAPAN INVADED CHINA, HITLER'S NAZI GERMANY INVADED POLAND AND DENMARK, THEN WENT TO WAR WITH GREAT BRITAIN AND FRANCE. THE GIANT GERMAN DIRIGIBLE, THE HINDENBURG, EXPLODED IN FLAMES IN NEW JERSEY, AND PRESIDENT FRANKLIN D. ROOSEVELT WAS RE-ELECTED BY AN OVERWHELMING MAJORITY. THE WAR CLOUDS ERUPTED AND WORLD WAR II BEGAN.

ON THE HOME FRONT WE CHILDREN DID NOT FEEL THE INtensity that was building up over the war issues, but we did hear talk by grownups about how our country was trying to stay out of it, but might get dragged into it anyway. As kids, we were preoccupied with school, homework, helping out at home, and, at times, we older boys worked part-time at the David Produce Company helping Dad.

Working at the produce warehouse was fun and a great training ground for all of us kids. It taught us tolerance in understanding and appreciating the many different ethnic groups that were in the produce market. We learned to eat different kinds of foods as well. We also got to know the different kinds of characters that hung around the marketplace, like the homeless and winos. One important thing I learned was that they were neither necessarily dumb nor bad. Some were quite intelligent and I learned a lot about life from them. They would tell me where they came from and how they got into their present situation. It gave me insight as to what I needed to do as well as what I needed to avoid doing in my growing-up years.

Many of my lessons came through observing my dad. Dad had a tolerance for these men. At times he would give them some money to buy a taco or hamburger, which cost 10 cents. He would extract a promise from them that the money would be for food and not for anything else. At times, when he was short-handed, Dad would hire one of them on the condition the man would stay sober. When sober, these men were very good workers. Unfortunately, their sobriety lasted only about three to four weeks at most, before going on another binge.

One of the smartest people I have ever known was a middle-aged, red-headed Irish guy, Wino Charley, who graduated from the University of Illinois. Wino Charley occasionally worked for Dad mostly packing produce. He was good at it. Sometimes I packed alongside him and talked with him for two to three hours at a time, asking a million questions about everything. He was like a walking encyclopedia and taught me a lot about people and the world. Throughout the years I have occasionally thought of old Charley and wondered what had become of him.

In 1932, we moved from the Chinatown apartment into a single family house, which gave the family much more living space. We moved to 16th and K Streets in the Logan Heights neighborhood about 12 blocks from Chinatown. It was a rather quaint area with drug stores, grocers, gas stations, and most services needed in a neighborhood. The ethnic makeup was mixed and, as far as I can remember, people just got along fine, except for an occasional dispute over an issue that had nothing to do with race or ethnic background. One of my best friends was Mike Nagem, whose family was Syrian. Over at his house his mother fed me pita bread, lamb shish kabob, cheese, and olives of all kinds. Mike, in turn, liked to come to my house to eat, and Ah Nuing fed him his favorite Chinese food, soy sauce over rice. We each thought we were getting the better deal.

A block from us, around the corner, lived a nice Mexican family who made good tamales, and had several kids with whom we often played and socialized. There was an uncle named Rocky Ramirez in their family. I think Rocky was his professional name as he was a professional boxer. Rocky, when he was not training, would take time to teach us kids the art of boxing. He had six to eight pairs of gloves and had us learn how to hold our guard up, weave, duck, give the 1-2-3, upper cut, counterpunch and so on. He said boxing was good training for us, both for protection, and good exercise, so we took to it with enthusiasm. After about six months a lot of us got pretty proficient in the art of boxing.

At Memorial Junior High, boxing was part of its athletic program. We did not have the designation of boxers like flyweight, lightweight, middle-weight, or heavyweight, but in its place the boxers were placed in weight categories. The gloves were the oversize type that would soften the blows, but if a good hard punch was thrown, one could make the opponent pretty woozy. The judging was done by the point system. I signed up for the boxing program and fell into the 120 to 125 pound category, which had about 20 fellows in it. We would fight each other to establish ranking. After about two months of pounding each other, lo and behold, I became the number one ranked in our weight category. With that, I quietly thanked Rocky.

After word got around that I was number one, there were some challenges from other heavier weight categories. There were about six of these challenges from higher and lower categories, and again, low and behold, I won four of them and had draws on two. I don't recall if I ever lost a match. Again, thanks to Rocky.

Funny thing, all of a sudden I began to have more guys coming up to me wanting to be friends, putting their arms around me and having lunch with me. I even got invited to a couple of birthday parties. Yes, all of a sudden I got respect. Thank you, Rocky!

I can't say that I was an outstanding student, but I did do fairly well considering I was involved in so many activities both inside and outside of school. I always did well in art and math classes, getting As and Bs. I loved history and science and did fairly well there, but in English and literature I never did better than a C. I began to think that girls had a natural grasp for English and literature and boys excelled more easily in math and science. Nowadays, I don't see any disparity at all. I can see that gap has closed as witnessed through my six children who are now grown, as well as through my thirteen grandchildren.

One of my best teachers was Miss Arnold, my 8th grade English teacher. She was probably in her late twenties or early thirties, attractive, and ran a very efficient classroom. I would say about half the boys in her class were in love with her, she was that attractive. She also had two Chinese girl students that were smart, well mannered, and were the teacher's pets. They helped grade student test papers and had certain privileges others did not have, like not having to do certain homework because the teacher was confident they already knew the subject matter to perfection.

It so happened that one day Miss Arnold had to leave the classroom to go to her car for something and while she was gone some of the boys started to throw spit balls at each other. One hit me, and then I too got into the spit ball throwing game. Just then, after I was in the fray for less than 30 seconds, Miss Arnold walked in. Instantly, the room became quiet. She walked slowly to her desk, looked around the room left and right, and when her eyes settled on me she said, "Tom, stand up!" I stood, thinking there would be other boys she would be calling. She did not call anyone else. She spoke to me in a firm voice, "Tom, why is it that the other Chinese kids are so well behaved and you are not?" All of sudden, I realized, according to her, I had let my race of people down. Not only that, I had disgraced my dad, who constantly preached to us boys, "Always remember, be a gentleman!"

I didn't appreciate it then, but I must say I did thereafter. Later I settled down and studied harder and didn't cause any further problems. My grades even got better. Even though I hate to think what the school board today would say about what Miss Arnold said to me in 1939, as time went on, she turned out to be one of my best teachers ever. And, yes, I was one of the boys who fell in love with her, too.

By the way, one of the teacher's pets, a Chinese student named Evelyn, ended up becoming my sister-in-law; she married my older brother James. After about 70-plus years, Evelyn still remembers that incident and occasionally teases me about it. Yep, sometimes a put-down can be uplift.

CHAPTER 7

City Hall

THE AGE OF TWELVE MUST HAVE BEEN AN IMPRESSIONABLE period of my early life. It was on two occasions that started me thinking about government and politics and how our democratic system worked.

The first occasion happened when I was helping Dad at the David Produce Company, when he got a call from a customer that needed some produce that afternoon to take care of a party that evening. I went with Dad to make the delivery, and on our way back our little truck broke down at the corner of 5th and G Streets. City Hall was located on the southwest corner. While we were waiting for the mechanic to come help us, Dad pointed to the four-story building and said, "Tom, here in America the kind of laws that come out of there depend on the kind of people the voters put in there!" That impressed me because I never really thought of Dad being interested in how our government ran. He always thought that when it came to government, he was on the outside looking in. Right then and there I thought to myself, "Gee, wouldn't it be nice if I could one day be inside looking out and making laws, too?"

During that same period, at Memorial Junior High we had a principal by the name of William J. Oakes, a very steady, caring, and respectful man, who seemed to make a point of knowing hundreds of the students by their names. It would not be unusual for him to stop us in the hallway and ask how things were going and if we had any needs or problems, come to see him. Whenever he spoke, either in the classrooms or in the auditorium during student body assemblies, he would give us a brief talk on Americanism, encouraging us to be involved in building a better society. Because our student body was a racially mixed group, including many kids from immigrant families, he would always emphasize that we were all Americans and that we could be whatever we wanted to be. It depended on how hard we are willing to work for it.

After hearing him talk like that for three years, I thought, even then, that I might have a chance one day to run for public office and be the guy inside, looking out.

In later years, when I think of people who have left the greatest impressions on me as a role model, Principal William J. Oakes ranks way up there.

It was still at the height of the economic depression when my friend Billy Richardson, a tall blond-haired boy with a flair for getting in trouble, told me and a few other friends that we could make some quick money to go to the movies.

His scheme was to raid several boxes of fruit from his next door neighbor, a produce peddler, who shared the same backyard fence. The plan was for us to climb the fence and steal the fruit that the peddler had stored in his shed. Billy said, "With the fruit that we get, we'll sell it to a small grocery store telling the grocer that the fruit came from our families' backyard fruit trees." I must have been about thirteen and dumb. The other three guys and I went along with the scheme. Billy was one of those guys who had a certain charisma and could convince others he could do just about anything right, including talking himself out of trouble.

A couple of nights later, we raided the fruit peddler's shed. In so doing, one of the guys accidentally knocked over a big stack of empty crates, making a loud shattering noise. All of a sudden, a flood of lights lit up the yard and like a bunch of scared rabbits we made a beeline for the fence, hopped over, and disappeared.

That was not the end of it. The next day the fruit peddler went to Billy's house to tell his parents what their son had done. He also wanted to know who the other boys were.

When I got home from school, on the porch was my dad and his good friend, Mr. Leo Ying. Dad had a serious look and Mr. Leo Ying looked very embarrassed. The first words from Dad were, "Did you go last night with a bunch of boys and break into Mr. Ying's yard to steal some fruit?" I hemmed and hawed, and confessed. I never saw my dad so red in the face. He just apologized over and over to Mr. Ying for my stupidity, saying he could not understand why I would do such a reckless thing as we had our own produce company and, besides, I knew better than that. To my surprise, Mr. Ying came to my defense saying that I was misled by that bad boy Billy. That only made my dad more mad, my being so stupid as to allow someone so bad to mislead me.

Needless to say, I think that was one of the worst lickings I ever got from Dad. I learned something from that episode, though, and that is to tread cautiously before committing to people who are fast talkers and seemingly have a lot of charisma. The saddest thing about the whole event was that I humiliated my dad terribly, especially when I knew he took such great pride in all his kids.

AS I SAID, ONE OF MY FIRST JOBS was helping Dad at the produce company. Being down there in all the excitement of the wholesale produce markets was so much fun, it never seemed like work. Most of the businesses would start at about 3 a.m. and peak normally at about 11 a.m. After that, the businesses either started winding down or closed down.

During those peak hours, truckloads of fresh produce would arrive from local farmers and from as far away as Mexico and all different regions of the western United States. Buyers came to check the quality of the merchandise and haggle over the prices. In the marketplace you could hear many different languages aside from English, such as Greek, Italian, Chinese, Spanish, Japanese, and seemingly everything else. The atmosphere was upbeat, extremely competitive, noisy, and very colorful.

With such a diversity of so many ethnic and cultural groups, I do not recall any real issues because of racial or ethnic differences. Friends were made right across the board. It would not be unusual that friends would call each other a derogatory ethnic term with fondness and a smile. That was part of the colorfulness in the produce market's atmosphere.

After being raised in this type of diverse cultural atmosphere, my brothers and I were better prepared to understand people of different backgrounds in a positive way. Not only that, we also learned a lot in the art of negotiation. Since produce was a perishable item and arrived daily, knowing how to haggle and negotiate was an important part of the business. I also learned that the true art of negotiation is to produce two winners, both the buyer and the seller leaving satisfied. Two winners was the key.

CHAPTER 8

Flea-ana

IN THE LATE 1930S WHILE THE WAR CLOUDS GATHERED OVERSEAS IN EUROPE AND ASIA, MANY NATIONS ALIGNED THEMSELVES EITHER WITH THE AXIS, CONSISTING OF GERMANY, ITALY, AND JAPAN, OR THE ALLIES, CONSISTING OF ENGLAND, FRANCE, RUSSIA, CHINA, THE UNITED STATES, AND A NUMBER OF LESSER POWERFUL COUNTRIES.

A T THAT TIME THE UNITED STATES WAS NOT ACTIVELY IN-volved in combat, but it did get very much involved in a lend-lease program that provided war supplies of planes, tanks, ships, guns, and other materials to the Allies.

From deep depression, the total economy began to boom. A number of aircraft factories and ship building yards headquartered in San Diego. To supply the labor for all these new industries, a great influx of men and women from all parts of the country migrated to San Diego to work. New military bases were established in the county of San Diego: Camp Callan, which today is the site of the University of California, San Diego in the La Jolla area; Camp Elliot, where the community of Tierrasanta is located; plus the enlargement of the Naval and Marine Training Stations near Point Loma by the San Diego Bay.

Even at that young age I felt everything was rapidly changing. With so many new people in town, the streets and neighborhoods were getting crowded, particularly in the downtown area along 5th Avenue where most of the department stores and other businesses were located, along with several movie houses.

In those days, at least in our family, we kids did not have any regular allowances. We generally worked at the produce company for Dad and he would give us some spending money if we did a good job and didn't fool around too much. Occasionally, I would get a quarter, which was plenty enough to go to the movies at our favorite Casino Theatre. Generally we got to watch two to three main features, a serial chapter on the Lone Ranger or other heroes of ours like Flash Gordon or Tarzan, a comedy feature of the Three Stooges, and the World News. To see the complete matinee took about four hours. A quarter went a long ways, because kids paid only a dime to get in and still had enough left for a hot dog or hamburger.

One day with my quarter I treated my friend Mike Nagem to the Casino Theatre, and had enough change to buy a 5 cent foot-long hot dog to share with him. My friends and I liked the Casino Theatre the best, in spite of the fact that across the street was another theatre called the Diana, which sometimes had good features for only 5 cents for kids. What we didn't like about the Diana was that it had fleas. Every time we went there, we ended up scratching throughout the show. One time we even saw a huge, and I mean huge, rat running on the stage in front of the screen that stopped in the middle, looked around for about a minute, and then scurried off. Whenever we fellows talked about the Diana, we always referred to it as the "Flea-ana." We only went there when we were desperate.

Next door to the Casino Theatre was a shoeshine stand with about six chairs manned by three African-American brothers. They were always cheerful and good natured and charged 15 cents a shine. With the influx of new people in town, especially military, they were always busy. They had people standing by, and some even made appointments for a shine. They were fast and would snap the shine cloth with a cracking sound in a rhythmic manner, almost like making a musical tune, often singing along as they polished. Watching them was real entertainment.

One day while some of my friends and I were watching the brothers do their shining, one of them turned to us and said, "Hey, you boys seem to like shoe shining! You ought to go into it! You could make some good money!" While walking home, we talked about what he'd said. By the time we got home several of us decided to do some of that "good money" venture, and the next day we built ourselves shoeshine boxes from the wood of fruit lug boxes. I asked Ah Nuing to advance me 30 cents to buy the shoe polishes, black and brown, which were a nickel each, and two brushes at a dime each. For cloth, she gave me an old diaper. I painted on the sides of the shine box the words "10 cents." I was ready to go into business.

The next day Mike Nagem and I paired up to go into this new venture. We started to walk towards downtown by way of Market Street, a busy commercial thoroughfare with stores, restaurants, bars, and other businesses. By the time we got downtown, we had each made 70 cents. That wasn't too bad because it paid for all the cost and some profit. My first day profit/loss statement looked pretty good.

Since it was getting dark, Mike and I decided to call it quits and go home. I gave all 70 cents to Ah Nuing; she gave me back 30 cents and she kept 40 cents. I didn't mind, that's how we handled money in the family. We kids gave our earnings to our parents and they in turn rewarded us with some of it back. I can understand that, with a family about 10 then, we learned to share a lot. There was an open door to this approach though. Whenever any of us wanted something, like a special book, even a bicycle or whatever else, we would ask Dad for it. He listened to our request, considered it, and then made a decision. In most cases, if it were reasonable and affordable, he would agree.

After about a couple weeks of shoe shining with some of my friends, my dad asked me where I did most of my business. "In the bars, where the sailors and soldiers hang out," I told him. It didn't take him long to decide that hanging out in bars was not a good atmosphere for a young 13 year old. So I had to quit going to bars, and business dropped by 75 percent. Like any good businessman, I decided to close shop and quit the shine business. Besides, it wasn't as fun anymore.

It so happened at that time my brother Allen had an early morning *Los Angeles Times* paper route across the bay in Coronado, where I sometimes would go with him. His boss asked me whether I was interested in taking over a delivery route from one of the guys that was moving out of town. I said yes, but before I could take it, I had to have a bike. I told my dad about the great opportunity of having my very own paper route, but I needed a bike. He thought that was a good reason, so he took me to the number one bicycle store in town, Gilmore's Bicycle Shop located at 8th and Broadway downtown. Dad bought me a brand new red and black Excelsior bike. I got the paper route and serviced it for about two years.

It was then that I was beginning to learn that when one door closes, others will open.

CHAPTER 9

Peach Bully

MY DAD HAD A JEWISH FRIEND BY THE NAME OF SAM LAZAR, who owned a bakery/deli/grocery store on 5th Avenue, a busy part of downtown. Sam had a thriving business, but because he was getting along in age, he wanted to rent out his produce department as it took a lot of time away from the main part of his operation, the bakery and deli.

Sam bought his produce from Dad and had trusted him in their business dealings. One summer he asked Dad if he was interested in leasing the produce department from him. Dad, forever the entrepreneur, immediately thought how it would be a good opportunity to make a profit as well as become a training ground for us boys to learn the retail business and deal with the general public.

So Allen and I were designated to operate Lazar's produce department. We were the bosses aside from Dad. At that time, Allen and I still had our *L.A. Times* paper routes but since our paper routes started early in the morning at 5 a.m. and finished at 7 a.m., we still had time to get the produce stands ready for the day's business. Being young and energetic, it was no problem. Besides, to take on this new challenge would be fun and exciting, along with the ambition of making a profit.

Allen was talented in improvising and was quite artistic. He directed the rearrangement of the produce stands, set up the fruits and vegetables in a way where the colors would enhance each other, and rotated the items so there would always be freshness showing. We did good business right off. According to Mr. Lazar, we were doing at least twice the business that he had been doing when he ran the produce department. Yes, that summer was profitable and Dad was proud of us for being so innovative and diligent in our work efforts.

Not everything, however, went smoothly. One morning after Allen and I had completed the display of the fruit stands, which was in the open air front part of the store, three teenagers came by and stood before the well stacked fruit. They looked it over and the bigger of the boys picked up a large, juicy peach, bit into it, and said, "Hmm, good peach! I think I'll have another one!" and stuck it in his pants pocket and, with a bit of arrogance, started to walk away.

"Hey," I said in a strong voice, "aren't you gonna pay for the peaches?"

"Hey, man, these are samples! I'm doing you a favor by sampling these crummy peaches!"

From there we got into an argument, and when it became obvious he wasn't going to pay, I reached down to the outside of his pants pocket and squeezed the peach hard, making the peach juice ooze all over his pants. Stunned and mad, he yelled, "Why you four-eyed bastard, if you didn't have glasses, I'd beat the shit out of you!"

Strangely enough, one of his buddies offered to hold my glasses, and more strangely, I gave them to him. As soon as I handed the glasses over, the peach sampler took a swing at me, which I quickly ducked, and I punched him hard in the stomach and followed through with a left on his nose, and then a hard right on his mouth. He fell back and landed on his butt, then rubbed his nose and mouth, and seeing blood, he cried out and said, "Hey, hey, that's enough! I didn't mean anything!" One of his buddies helped him up, the other handed me my glasses and they scooted off. Again, thanks to my friend Rocky Ramirez, the professional boxer, for his pointers in the art of boxing.

Later, Mr. Lazar told me that the peach sampler was the same guy that stole from him previously. After that, it was interesting that whenever the three boys walked by our place they would self-consciously do a half wave and half smile to me. And I'd respond likewise.

As I grew older, I became inclined to think that bullies, like the peach sampler, were happier when someone put them in their place. I liked to think they became happier by not living that pretense of being bully-tough.

After summer was over, Allen and I finished our paper routes as early as possible and made a beeline down to the produce stand to put on a fresh display of fruits and vegetables, and then rush off to school. We had a person take over while we were in school. After a while, things did not work out, as it was difficult in tracking the flow of the cash receipts while we were gone. When we came in after school, it seemed that much of the merchandise was gone and there was not enough cash to show for it. We figured that the merchandise was either stolen or sold and the money pocketed.

All in all, with our paper routes and school work, Dad decided that it was best to turn the produce department back to Mr. Lazar. We gained some good work experience in being bosses and also learned something about the retail business.

v. Declaration of War

一只兔子崎岖的心路历程

The USS California sinking, Pearl Harbor, December 7, 1941.

CHAPTER 10

Day to Remember

ON SUNDAY MORNING, DECEMBER 7, 1941 JAPAN ATTACKED PEARL HARBOR IN HAWAII. THE NEXT DAY, WITH OUR NATION IN SHOCK AND FULL OF REVENGE, PRESIDENT ROOSEVELT AND CONGRESS DECLARED WAR ON JAPAN AND THE REST OF THE AXIS NATIONS, THOSE BEING HITLER'S GERMANY AND MUSSOLINI'S ITALY.

DECEMBER 7, 1941, IS A DATE VERY FEW OF US WOULD EVER forget. The radios, starting about 10:30 a.m., broadcasted continuing news of the brutal sneak attack by Japan that Sunday. Those of us who were old enough remember, to almost the exact moment, when we heard about it and what we were doing. I was carrying my 3-year-old second sister Margaret and visiting with my friends half a block from our house. My friend from junior high, Mike Nagem, came over and told us that Japan had just bombed Pearl Harbor. Our first question was, "Where is Pearl Harbor?"

That afternoon several of us boys went to the San Diego Balboa Stadium to see the San Diego Bombers professional football team play an out-of-town team. We all had tickets from the All American Cleaners, who gave tickets to kids under 16 if their parents brought in their clothes for dry cleaning. One of the kids, Johnny Ortega, whose parents were in the entertainment business, took a lot of their clothing there for cleaning, and got lots of free tickets.

The announcer interrupted the game with an urgent message from the Commandant of the 11th Naval District and the General of the Army. They ordered all military personnel to immediately return to their ship or camp base. Following the announcement, the Star Spangled Banner played and everyone stood up. At the end of the song, sailors, marines, and soldiers filed out of the stadium with everyone applauding. It was an emotional moment. It made a number of us boys feel that if we were only older, we'd join the fight. After that, it was hard for us to focus on the game itself; our minds were wandering all over the place, especially recounting the touching scene of the servicemen suddenly leaving to fight the war.

That one day, so many things were happening. Major newspapers in town all had EXTRAS! Some twice that day. Groups of young men all over the city were going downtown to the military recruiting stations to enlist in order to fight.

Today as I write this, after seeing America in several wars since World War II, I cannot recall there were any protestors against that war once we got into it. From the very ordinary person on the street to the highest official in government, the nation as a whole was unified in fighting and winning.

At one point before Pearl Harbor, however, there was a segment of the population that opposed getting involved in the war as they felt it was none of our business. Charles A. Lindbergh was one of them; but after Pearl Harbor he enlisted in the U.S. Army Air Corps, commissioned as a colonel, and was very much involved in the war effort. After the sneak attack on Pearl Harbor all opposition evaporated and the country became very cohesive to win the war.

Our world started to change rapidly. War Bond rallies were held throughout the country to raise funds to finance the war and United Service Organizations (USO) were springing up all over to support servicemen and women. War plants were going full blast with three shifts around the clock making planes, tanks, ships, and other war necessities.

CHAPTER 11

The Proven Patriots

ONE OF THE REPERCUSSIONS OF THE PEARL HARBOR ATTACK was fear, panic, and resentment of all Japanese. This included people of Japanese descent who were born and raised in America and had lived here all their lives. Many were farmers and in the wholesale produce business like my dad. He did quite a bit of business with them. Because of the hysteria in the country, many Americans not only resented the Japanese living here but also felt many of them were spies feeding Japan all kinds of secret information about America's military bases, including its defensive and offensive strategies.

A short time after the attack on Pearl Harbor there were a lot of rumors of Japanese spies directing an imminent bombardment of the west coast of the mainland United States, and that hoards of spies were already in operation. These rumors provoked greater fear and resentment toward all people of Japanese descent.

In a very short time, due to public fear and political expediency, President Franklin D. Roosevelt enforced Executive Order 9066, demanding the removal of all people of Japanese descent. This included men, women, and children, regardless of age and citizenship, from the west coast states, namely California, Washington, Oregon and the southern part of Arizona. With very little notice, whole families were moved to remote areas of northern Arizona, Nevada, Utah, Colorado, and other inland states. Barbed wire relocation campsites were quickly erected, with machine gun towers surrounding the campsites to house the Japanese.

With the stroke of the pen, 130,000 people were moved just like that, leaving their homes, businesses, and most of their personal belongings behind. Each person was allowed to take whatever personal needs and clothing they could carry in two suitcases. All this had to be done within a few short days.

During this traumatic time of questioning the loyalty of people of Japanese descent, a group of patriotic Japanese Americans worked tirelessly and diligently to prove otherwise. In time, the Japanese American Alliance League, an organization of Japanese American citizens, petitioned President Franklin Roosevelt to permit the formation of an army-fighting unit to defend America in the war. In the process of working with the political body in Washington, D.C. and the U.S. Army, President Roosevelt finally approved such a unit to be formed in February 1943, 13 months after the beginning of the war.

The Army formed the Japanese American unit known as the 442nd Regimental Combat Team. In a short time it fought and won many heroic battles in France and Italy, becoming the most decorated unit of fighting soldiers in America's history. The 442nd averaged about 3,000 men that earned an astounding 18,143 individual decorations, including 9,486 purple hearts. It suffered 680 dead.

With the impact of the Japanese American 442nd army unit, much of the American public's fear of disloyalty by the people of Japanese descent was somewhat alleviated. As time went on, three presidents, Harry Truman, Gerald Ford, and Jimmy Carter, expressed regret and stated that Executive Order 9066 was not necessary.

After the war ended on August 15, 1945, there were a number of Congressional hearings pertaining to the war. Included was the issue of why the United States was not prepared ahead of time regarding the surprise attack on Pearl Harbor. Japanese espionage was one of the issues. After lengthy studies, there was conclusive evidence that there were not any—not even one case—of a Japanese American taking part in spying or transferring military secrets to Japan.

CHAPTER 12

Farmers by Circumstance

D URING THE TIME OF THE JAPANESE RELOCATION, ONE OF my dad's Japanese friends, Mr. Yamashita, came to see him and urged him to take over the operation of his two farms, both in the Mission Valley area. One covered 25 acres, part of where Qualcomm Stadium is now located, and the other 20 acres were about a quarter mile away. They were both in full bloom, with crops ready to harvest: celery, tomatoes, cauliflower, string beans, lettuce, radishes, carrots, turnips, and much more. He wanted to turn everything over to Dad, including tractors, horses, dogs, the use of the house and other facilities, for a very reasonable price and a low deposit. The deal was made.

Needless to say, operating a farm was not a snap, especially in wartime. Labor was extremely difficult to find. Supplies and parts for repairs were hard to obtain. Some of the older Hom boys, namely Allen, Wellman, Herb and me, were recruited to do some of the harvesting, planting, and weeding. I never knew farming was so hard. It was backbreaking work in the hot sun, and it was often muddy, rife with bugs and snakes, and the hours were long. On school days, we worked after school and came home after dark.

In the earlier part of working there, Dad would tell us kids to pick as much of a certain vegetable as we could. And then he left. The irony of it was that we kids would often end up playing by tossing vegetables at each other and sometimes would run down to the San Diego River, about 300 yards from the farm, and swim or set traps to catch rabbits. With all this playing around, only a small amount of the crop was harvested when the truck came to pick it up and Dad would be disappointed.

Later, Dad devised a method on how to get better production from us. For Allen, he would put a stake at the beginning of a row, let's say at lettuce, and put another stake way down the row, which Dad would estimate would produce so many crates of lettuce. For me, he would do likewise, but the furthest stake would not be quite as far. He did the same for Wellman, not quite as far as mine, and even less for Herb.

Then he'd say, "Once you boys pick the lettuce to the end of the far stake, you will be free to do whatever you like. You'll be finished working for the day!" We were amazed how productive we were that day, finishing in about half the time we ordinarily took to do the same amount of work. Dad did that in weeding, planting, and other things as well. It was fun and challenging. Most important, we got the work done.

In later years, with my six children growing up in a two-story house with six big bedrooms and a full basement, chores and housecleaning were always in need of upkeep. My wife Dorothy and I devised a checklist of chores to do, with assignments for each of the kids. This would be done mostly on Saturdays or on days before having guests. It worked great as it did with Dad. The reward? Freedom! Free time!

In 1942 the war environment was rapidly gearing up. It was the year I graduated from Memorial Junior High, and moved on to the big stage of San Diego High School. As a freshman, I noticed that there were military recruiters for the U.S. Army, Navy, and Marines on campus. A number of the seniors joined. They would receive their graduation diploma in advance and be acknowledged at the school assembly, with the school marching band honoring them with a rousing send off for their patriotic service.

CHAPTER 13

San Diego High School

S AN DIEGO HIGH WAS THEN KNOWN AS THE GREY CASTLE, FOR it was built along the lines of a castle, sitting on a knoll at the lower portion of the 1,500-acre Balboa Park, in the heart of San Diego. The school covered over 20 acres, with a student body of about 2,000, the largest in San Diego, of which about 100 to 125 were Chinese American students. I felt I was now in the big leagues: high school football games, going out for sports, and starting to notice girls.

Many years before my arrival, some Chinese students started the Mai Wa Club for social purposes and for doing worthy causes. The advisor was Miss Mary Walker, one of the much beloved teachers.

Whenever a Chinese student enrolled in San Diego High, the club would send a personal invitation for him or her to join. I was flattered by the invitation, and I joined paying dues of one dollar a year. I was able to afford that. I met a lot of new kids and learned to dance at the social events. The jitterbug was the rage then. That, plus learning the fox trot, waltz, and rumba made me feel pretty groovy. I can't say I was popular, but I was trying to get there.

One thing stands out clearly in my mind even after all these years. It was my science class, taught by Mr. Wise, a scholarly man, not very big in size, a bit pudgy with a whole crop of white hair. He looked like an Einstein, without a mustache.

One day Mr. Wise told the class that one of the great challenges of mankind was to one day be able to fly to the moon. He said, "Theoretically, we know what we must do to get there, which includes knowing that we must be able to launch a rocket ship that would fly at least 17,000 miles per hour to get out of the earth's atmosphere!" Planes then were flying at the average speed of 250 miles per hour. So he went on to say, "Even if we should find a way to jet propel a rocket 17,000 miles per hour, there is not any material known to man to build a rocket ship that could withstand the heat that would be generated by the atmosphere's friction. It'll flare up and explode!" He went on to say, "The problem has been pinpointed, a finite problem; therefore, man can now work toward resolving it!"

Mr. Wise went on to ask the class, "What are the brakes in a car for?"

The class answered loudly in unison, "To stop the car!"

He said, "True! That's partly right, but the finite answer is to stop the wheels from turning."

Today, of course, we all now know that particular finite problem for the rocket ship has been solved.

That really taught me a lesson. In every problem, the true finite problem must first be identified. After identifying that, you can then go about solving it. It has helped me in my family life, business, social situations, and elsewhere.

DURING THE WAR YEARS LABOR was short, with the defense plants going full blast, and other businesses shorthanded. High school kids were encouraged to help wherever they could, like picking crops, working in restaurants, and any other type of work wherever needed. Housewives were leaving their housekeeping duties to pitch in by working in the defense industries.

Likewise, I was also busy with two jobs: my morning *L.A. Times* route before school and working at Dad's farm after school until sundown.

Then a high school buddy asked me if I was interested in working where he worked, at the Pacific Square Ballroom, in downtown near the bay. Everyone knew about the Pacific Square Ballroom, because that was where the big bands came to play, such as Glenn Miller, Tommy Dorsey, Benny Goodman, Harry James, and singers like Frank Sinatra, who was not quite super famous yet, the Andrew Sisters, and other well-known entertainers.

It didn't take me long to decide that it was a great opportunity with all the famous people coming and going, so I decided to quit my paper route. My friend took me down to the Pacific Square Ballroom to meet his boss, and through his recommendation I was hired on the spot. My duties were to help keep the ballroom area clean of debris, pick up the soda bottles and take them to the storeroom, clean the ash trays, mop up any liquid spills, etc. The bathrooms had their own maintenance crew. Lucky me! The ballroom did not allow any hard liquor, so I was to be on the lookout for any violation and report it to the bouncer guard. It was a pretty easy and fun job. I also helped supply the orchestras with refreshments and got to meet some of the celebrities like Harry James, Benny Goodman, Frank Sinatra, Tommy Dorsey, and many others.

During this war economy, defense plants were going fulltime, 24 hours a day, with three shifts. And with the military training camps, Camp Elliot, Camp Callan, the Marine Training Station, and the Naval Training Station, all in San Diego proper, there was a great demand for entertainment. To try and meet that demand, the ballroom was open from 8 p.m. to midnight, with the second shift from 1 a.m. to 5 a.m. Both shifts were always sold out, with people lined up hours before opening.

I worked the first shift only, on Thursdays, Fridays, and Saturdays, and generally would get home via my bike or bus about 1 a.m. My dad didn't especially like my working so late, but he understood I liked working there. And when I told him they did not allow liquor at the ballroom, he thought it was all right so long as I got enough rest in between my school work and farm work.

The boss always rewarded us with some free tickets whenever he thought we did a good job, and I never knew I could be so popular. I had so many friends, even girls wanted my attention, and it didn't seem to matter that I wasn't even a bit dashing. They would be extra friendly, and then they'd ask me to get them tickets for the Pacific Square Ballroom.

After working for several months at this fun place, I was promoted to the soda fountain where I helped serve and kept the inventory list as to what we needed to order for the next day's business. My boss thought I did such a good job, he wanted me to work the two shifts. I tried it for about four weeks, getting home at sunup. I found myself falling asleep in the storeroom at work as well as nodding off in the classroom, and my grades were going downhill. It didn't take me long to agree with Dad that I should quit and tend to my schoolwork. I wasn't really the scholarly type, but my dad thought I should be, for education was the top priority with him.

Because I no longer worked there, I no longer had access to free ballroom tickets, which made me realize how quickly a guy could be de-popularized by "good friends." That's okay; episodes like these teach us how to keep our balance in life.

AS THE WAR CONTINUED TO ESCALATE, with much of the young men being drafted into the military, there were also a great number stepping up to volunteer rather than waiting to be drafted. In 1942, my brother James, along with several of his Chinese American buddies, was among them. As a group they joined the U.S. Army Air Corp, the predecessor of today's U.S. Air Force. There was much publicity over this in newspapers and radio—there was no television back then—as China was part of the Allied Forces that was at war with Japan. Actually, China's war with Japan started five years prior to the Japanese attack on Pearl Harbor. The enlistment of Chinese Americans was a good morale builder for our side. Dad had mixed feelings, proud and sad at the same time, to see his first-born son go off to war.

During this period, my dad and Ah Nuing had their last child, brother Paul, which made 12 kids in the family. There were seven total from second mother, Ah Nuing, consisting of four boys and three girls. This, plus my first mother's five boys, meant that we always had a full house. The bigger kids would double up on beds, smaller ones triple up, with bunk beds crowded in the single rooms, and even sofa beds in the living room.

One thing Dad harped upon a lot was that we must make a point to eat dinner together. It was important, as that was the one time where we could share the meal and share each other's events of the day. He felt it was good family bonding time. That's when he would philosophize with us older kids, like how important it was that we did well in school, respect the elders, be a gentleman, help each other, and always learn to share whatever we have.

Whenever Dad would cut a melon, like a watermelon or cantaloupe, or a pie or cake, he would cut them up in different sizes. After the cutting, we would serve ourselves, by picking the piece that we were taught to pick. The youngest picked first, he would pick the smallest piece, the next youngest would pick the remaining smallest one, and so on with the next smallest, and finally the last to pick was the eldest, James, who was left the largest piece. It was the pecking order lesson. The youngest respects the older ones by leaving the larger pieces for them; the older ones protect and care for the younger ones by seeing that they are taken care of first.

Yes, that pecking order worked pretty well, and as we got older, married, and had our own families, the pecking order loosened up quite a bit, as it should, since our first obligation now was to our own family. Today much of that pecking order still remains among the siblings, in a camaraderie way.

We all had Chinese names, but all the children were given westernized names as well, with many named after famous people or as suggested by or named after Caucasian business friends. We were, starting from the eldest, James (after a friend) Eric (Eric the Red Viking explorer); Allen Ernest (a friend); Thomas (Edison) Edward (a friend); Wellman (a friend) David (after Dad); Herbert Hoover (the President); Albert Henry (a friend); Helen Alice (doctor's choice); George (a friend); John Phillip (Sousa); Margaret Ann (doctor's choice); Beatrice Violet (doctor's choice); and Paul (Revere) Francis (Scott Key).

As the years went by, I surmised that we were given these very American-ized names because Dad envisioned that one day the family would become part of the American fabric, and these names would help us maneuver more freely to achieve higher goals in the greater society.

That was Dad, always preparing and having high hopes for us.

CHAPTER 14

Changing Times

T HE YEAR 1943 WAS A MAJOR TRANSITORY YEAR FOR OUR whole family. With Dad working 14- to 15-hour days for so long, his health began to deteriorate, and he contracted tuberculosis, becoming weaker and weaker as time went on. His typical working schedule was waking up at 4 a.m., going to the produce company, working until about 4 p.m. in the afternoon, home for a short nap, dining with the family, and then returning to the produce company at 6 p.m. to receive produce arriving from the farmers, and calling customers for their orders to be delivered the next day. He would come home about 9 p.m. With produce businesses open six days a week, he worked fulltime six days a week and also part time on Sundays.

As time progressed, Dad's health continued to get worse. In his weakened state he had to cut back his working hours and left much of the management of the business to the hired help. Because the produce business was a perishable business, with the need for constant turnover of fresh produce coming in all the time, and the need to sell the prior shipments first, the operation without Dad's hands-on management began to falter. Within six months much of the business was lost and funds mismanaged. My brother Allen and I, being the two oldest at home, would eventually come to help after school.

In Dad's final days, he wanted to spend some time at the farm in Mission Valley. He enjoyed sitting on the porch at the farmhouse, with fresh air, spring sunshine, looking at the new crops growing and occasionally spending time talking to his loyal, long-time employee, Joe Flores, who served as foreman of the farm operation.

The last time I saw Dad alive was the day before he was moved to Mercy Hospital. The evening before he left for the hospital, the family was gathered together at the farmhouse in the living room. Dad was lying on the couch and all the children were present except for James who was in the service. The 11 of us kids, ranging in age from 17 to baby Paul, along with mother Ah Nuing and Joe Flores, gathered around Dad.

It was sad, for we knew the end was near. That evening he shared with us his philosophy of family and how important it was to stick together and help each other, the older ones must take the responsibility of bringing up the younger ones, and that the younger ones must pitch in and help wherever they can. It was very much the pecking order that he had instilled in us many times in the past. Except this time it seemed so much more meaningful.

He also gave instructions to Joe Flores as to what needed to be done at the farm, and which crops would be good for the late spring planting, instructing him to plant several acres of hard shell squashes, like acorn, butternut, and banana squashes, as they held up well after picking and would keep for several months when the prices would then go up. That was Dad, a good father and an astute businessman down to the last minute.

IN MAY 1943, ABOUT A MONTH before Dad went into the hospital, Allen and I got permission from Principal Dr. Aseltine to leave school early. The school year was almost completed, and we were needed to work full time at the produce market to help support the family. Allen, a senior, got his graduation diploma early, and I would be moving into the 11th grade in the fall semester.

By the time Allen and I started working full time at the produce company, the business had dwindled down quite a bit with only three employees. Although Allen and I were brought up in the produce business, we never really had any experience in the management of older people. Here we were, a couple of teenagers, taking over and trying to save the business. The employees understood our family's dire situation, and Allen and I understood that we could learn from experienced people, so we all got along pretty well. Besides, only Allen and I could sign the payroll checks and that helped. Through Allen's direction, who had a knack for figures, we cut out the customers with bad credit, went after many of the late paying accounts receivables that had been neglected for so long, credit checked new customers, and spent time balancing the books each week.

It was only two days after Dad entered the hospital that I answered the phone at the produce company, and a lady from the hospital gave the expected bad news. Dad had just passed away. Expected, yes, but not quite prepared. I handed the phone to Allen, and after he hung up, we both cried. I think at that moment we both matured by several years, knowing that we now had very serious responsibilities before us.

In order to build the business back up, Allen bought a small hand operated mimeograph printing machine. We printed our own flyers with pictures of fruit and vegetables that I would draw, and mailed them out to grocery stores and restaurants soliciting business by quoting quality and low prices. I must say, the response was excellent, to the extent that it ruffled the feathers of some of our produce friends and competitors in the market. All and all, the produce business was very competitive, and this kind of competition was expected.

As the business started to improve, I needed to help make deliveries. I wasn't a licensed driver as I only learned how to drive at the farm, taught by Allen. In order to get a license, if you were between 16 and 18, you had to have your parents sign your application. Because Ah Nuing was a full time mother with a houseful of small kids, she did not have the time to go down to the Department of Motor Vehicles to sign the application. Since Allen and I looked very much alike, we decided that I would use his driver's license. I was such a small guy I had to sit elevated on an extra cushion in order to see over the steering wheel. Luckily, I never got into an accident nor was I ever stopped by a cop. I did that for two years, and then got my own license when I turned 18.

After several months of us managing the business, Allen heard from "Uncle Sam," notifying him that he was being drafted and had to report at a certain time and place for his medical examination for induction.

When Allen got his draft notice, my first thought was, "Does that mean I'll be in charge of running the company? Wow! No way! I'm only 16, and I'm not that smart!" I didn't have to worry after all.

When James was notified of Allen's draft notice, he applied to be relieved from the service in order to support the family and to run the two essential businesses that were necessary for the war effort. That was food distribution at the produce company and food production on the farm. It took several months for the honorable discharge to come through. Shortly after James arrived home, Allen left for his army training at Camp Roberts.

James, who had worked closely with Dad in the company since he was young, took the operation in stride. In time, which took a number of years, the family built the company into one of the largest produce companies in southern California.

I enjoyed working at the produce company, for it was beginning to grow and profits were coming in. I took a year off from going back to school in order to continue to help grow the business. When I started back the following year, I was one year behind my former classmates, but made new friends in my junior year. That was okay because I was beginning to learn that in life one needs to adjust constantly, and the way to do that was to remain flexible.

Adjusting to the major crisis of Dad's passing away, taking over the business, and returning to school a year behind, quickly matured me by a few years.

CHAPTER 15

Back to School and a New Direction

W HEN I RETURNED TO HIGH SCHOOL AND WAS READY TO sign up for new classes, my homeroom counselor, Mr. Ernest, suggested I take drama as one of my elective courses. With surprise and reluctance, I said, "Why drama? I'm not interested in being an actor!"

He told me, "Because, Tom, I find that most of my Chinese pupils are smart students, but they're generally too reserved and have a tendency not to express themselves freely. I think drama will help you in the future in accomplishing what goals you might have in mind. Drama will help you be more convincing in expressing your thoughts and ideas!"

Apparently, Mr. Ernest had taken drama himself and he convinced me. So I took Miss Lois Perkins' drama class. I think I surprised Miss Perkins because when I first attended class, she said with a pleasant smile in front of the whole room, "Why, Tom, it's wonderful to have you with us. You're my first Chinese student, and I've been here for quite a few years! Welcome!" All of a sudden I felt some pressure on my shoulders, thinking I better not mess up for the sake of representing other Chinese students.

Drama class was fun. We acted in plays, did skits for school assemblies, learned to critique each other's acting and even learned to write plays. One day Miss Perkins assigned each of us to write a 15-minute dramatic play, and the five best ones would be performed and directed by each winner with the cast divided equally from our classmates into different groups.

My play was about a bank robbery, planning it, the shoot-out between the cops and robbers, the drama behind the scene and the conversation between the cops and robbers. I wrote about people shot and the agony that followed until the bad guys gave themselves up. For a play with a 15-minute scenario, things had to move fast. I turned in my play and a few days later

Miss Perkins called me to her desk and said, "Tom, I like your play! Did you copy some of it from somewhere?"

I replied, "Why should I do that? If I did, it wouldn't be mine!" She smiled, and sent me back to my desk. Well, mine ended up being one of the five plays that got selected.

After performing the plays judged by the fellow students, mine came in third best, which pleased me a great deal. It pleased Miss Perkins, too, because I was her first Chinese student. Besides being a fun class, it was perhaps one of the most rewarding for me. It certainly helped me in many ways to better understand people. After all, it was Shakespeare who wrote the line, "The world is a stage and we are all actors!"

During my gym class, I tried out for the track team. I wanted to emulate my older brother James who starred in track, running the low hurdles four years prior, where he set a school record that lasted for over five years.

Aside from the hurdles, I also ran the 100-yard dash. I was pretty fast, but never dominated because there was one person who was much faster, a fair-haired boy named Harry West. Although we were on the same team competing against other schools, it never failed that I would be looking at his back when we approached the finish line. Harry not only starred in track, but football as well. He was named city All-Star in both sports. I am happy to report that the San Diego School District named a new gymnasium after him. Good old Harry West, a good guy who taught me humility and that losing is part of life.

Going back to school full time did not relieve me of my first obligation, to continue to help out at the produce company. After all, it was a big load on James, running the company at age 21. My schedule was going to work at 5 a.m. and leaving for school at 7:30 a.m., returning after school from 3:30 p.m. to 6 p.m., then home for dinner and study.

On weekends, I worked some at the farm, and on Sundays I got to take part in the church's youth programs. Needless to say, fun was always factored in somewhere, like dating, dancing, and partying, along with my hobby of oil painting and watercolor.

Now that I am much older, that sounds like an overly heavy schedule, but thinking back, for a teenager at 17, it wasn't really that tough. That's an age when energy seems boundless, always on the move and wanting to do more. Naturally in time, everything overly done has its limitations. In time it would show.

IN HIGH SCHOOL, ONE OF my favorite classes was art taught by Miss Kuhn. Ever since I was a young child, even before attending school, I loved to draw, and my parents would keep some of my drawings to show visiting friends. But in the Chinese way, there is a fine line between showing something that you are proud of, and playing it down at the same time. My parents would say something like, "Here is a drawing by little Tom. It's not too good, and perhaps he can get better if he would work harder at it. It could have been better if he weren't so lazy!" All along knowing it was good. It's a cultural courtesy to neither brag nor boast about your children, because it may bring on a bad omen, or make them too conceited. I think most Chinese kids know this, especially if their parents are from the old country.

Nevertheless, I managed to thrive in the area of art because I loved it. It was normal for the teachers, from early school years through high school, to post drawings or paintings in a prominent place in the classroom as examples of good artwork. Mine, among others, would be there.

Miss Kuhn helped nurture me to become a better artist. She was impressed enough with my artistic talent that she helped me apply for a scholarship at one of the finest art schools in California, Chouinard in Los Angeles. Before graduation, I received a letter notifying me that I had been granted a scholarship. I was elated and felt it was a new door of opportunity opening up for me. In spite of this great opportunity, in a short time the harsh reality began to set in. The scholarship was for tuition, which amounted to quite a large sum, but living quarters and expenses were my own responsibility. That was no problem as far as I was concerned, as I could get a job to take care of my expenses. But after basking in the glory of having been granted the scholarship for a few days, I became mindful of Dad's parting words that last night time we saw him alive before he left for the hospital, when he said, "You older ones, I want you to always remember to take care of the younger ones!"

With nine siblings younger than me, some still in diapers, it didn't take long to decide that going away to school for the sake of my art was not the thing to do. So instead of looking upon art school as a route to become a professional art illustrator, I decided that art would be a hobby instead, which I have done so for over 65 years. No regrets!

CHAPTER 16

The End of World War II and the New Atomic Era

WITH ITALY DEFEATED, AND GERMANY FACING CERTAIN DEFEAT, ADOLF HITLER COMMITTED SUICIDE ON MAY 2, 1945. A FEW DAYS LATER, HITLER'S SUCCESSOR, ADMIRAL KARL DOENITZ, SURRENDERED UNCONDITIONALLY ON MAY 8TH. THIS DAY WAS DECLARED V-E DAY, VICTORY IN EUROPE. THROUGHOUT THE ALLIED NATIONS CELEBRATIONS WERE HELD, BUT WITH SOME RESTRAINT, FOR THE WAR IN THE PACIFIC REGION AGAINST JAPAN WAS STILL BEING FIERCELY FOUGHT.

TO END THE WAR WITH JAPAN, THE ALLIES WOULD HAVE TO either invade Japan with at least one million men or bomb it into submission. For the sake of saving lives, President Truman decided to end the war as quickly as possible by using the United States' newly invented atom bomb that had been in the making for the past several years.

On August 6, 1945, the first atom bomb, equivalent to 20,000 tons of TNT, was dropped on the city of Hiroshima, and the next day another atom bomb was dropped on Nagasaki. A few days later the Emperor of Japan surrendered unconditionally, finally ending World War II. Since Pearl Harbor the war had lasted three years and 250 days. The victory over Japan was declared V-J Day, and mass celebrations happened throughout the Allied world.

In San Diego, like everywhere else, people poured out of their homes and businesses and onto the streets to hug and dance. I'll never forget, I was 18 at the time and a group of my friends and I went around town popping firecrackers, throwing them out of our car as we drove around downtown. Getting ready for the next round, my friend Bob Sue lit a bundled package of 48 firecrackers to throw out the window, but instead it hit the top of the inside door and bounced back into the middle of the car. Immediately, the firecrackers started to explode and it created pandemonium. Before we were able to get out of the smoke-filled car, with burnt smoking holes in the upholstery, we all got some pretty bad burns that took some time to heal. Aside from that bad experience on a happy occasion, we also created a huge traffic jam. Good thing everybody around was in a jovial mood, otherwise the cops would have taken us in for creating a major nuisance.

VI. Back to Normalcy

AGES 19 TO 25

一只兔子崎岖的心路历程

"Hawaiian Grandfather," by Tom Hom (watercolor).

CHAPTER 17

A New Beginning

WITH WORLD WAR II ENDING, THINGS WERE BEGINNING to return to normal. But what is normal? For us kids, the past four years, perhaps our most impressionable years, seemed to be more normal than before the war years.

Yes, normal for those war years was gas rationing, with the A, B, and C stickers for the cars. If I recall, the A stickers were allowed 4 gallons a week, B sticker at 8 gallons and C, good for 10 gallons. The stickers were allocated according to how essential your work was relating to the war efforts.

Many other things were rationed as well, like meats, sugar, eggs, butter, and items that were essentially needed for our armed forces and our Allies overseas. To help alleviate the food shortage, many households grew their own vegetables, called Victory Gardens. There were no new cars manufactured for 5 years, as the factories were all converted to building war supplies like battle tanks, cannons, Jeeps, radar equipment, and everything that the government needed for the military.

To us kids, the norm was getting adjusted to a way of life that seemed to be so out of place for us; but in due time, like all young people, we adjusted pretty well. In its transition, the city began to see the large military camps, Callan and Elliot, which had trained hundreds of thousands of soldiers, close down. The 1,500-acre Balboa Park, located in the middle of the city and used during the war for the military, was returned to the city. Our waterfronts and beaches were demilitarized so citizens could start visiting them again. Aircraft plants were closing. Tens of thousands of men and women were coming home, and many were leaving San Diego now that their war work was done. What changes!

One of the major changes for our family was that the Japanese American population was now coming home from their relocation camps, and that included the Yamashita family who had turned their farm over to my dad. We returned the farm to them and helped them where we could to get started again, mostly in their farming business. The Japanese farmers, of which there were many, were sorely missed when they were taken away. The high quality of vegetables that they produced was also greatly missed. James and I were happy to give back the farm, as the produce company was beginning to grow and our first priority was to solidify our efforts there.

With the general American public still angry with the surprise attack on Pearl Harbor by Japan, many people here did not distinguish the difference between Japanese of Japan and the Japanese Americans, and still had grudges and resentment against them. I did not like that, but I did understand, for some of the people lost loved ones in the war and still had strong feelings. At that time the returning Japanese Americans were not too welcomed to rent a house, to eat in certain restaurants, to be given jobs, and even some barbers would not cut their hair. As loyal Americans, they were treated badly.

In my school days at Memorial Junior High, before the war, I had a number of Japanese American friends. They were good guys. Many of these kids belonged to the Japanese Congregational Church, located about a mile from my church, the Chinese Congregational Mission. In wanting to help heal some of this strong resentment against the Japanese Americans, I organized a youth program between our church's young people to meet with their church's young people, to play basketball and softball games, to folk dance, and such. Reverend Kikuchi of the Japanese church expressed appreciation for my doing this. Sadly, a few of the older folks of my church thought I was out of line, for some of them had families in China that were ravaged by the invading Japanese troops. However, happy to say, as time went on most of them thought I did the right thing.

To my surprise, one day I received two separate telephone calls from New York. One was from Gabriel Heater, a national radio news commentator, sort of the Walter Cronkite of those days. And the other, Elmer Davis, another famous national news commentator with a different station, who once was featured on the cover of *Time* magazine, may have been the Tom Brokaw of those days. Although the calls were separate, they both asked me about the same subject and questions regarding my efforts and work in helping assimilate the Japanese American youths that were coming back from the relocation camps into the mainstream. How were they doing in getting back into the American society? I told them both the same thing as to what was being done and the people who were involved. The interviews were not long, about five minutes. They told me their broadcast time, which was in the evenings, so I could tune in. I did listen, and later I found out that many other people heard it too.

The broadcasters talked about "this young American of Chinese descent who set up programs to welcome and help assimilate the Japanese American youths back into American society ... This is true Americanism and America can learn from this young man, Tom Hom, as to what America is all about...." Then it went on about another three minutes. Since I was a nobody, I was somewhat puzzled and amazed that this subject was so important and newsworthy as to catch the attention of two very prominent broadcasters. As time went on, I realized perhaps this was part of the natural evolution of healing a nation that had gone through some very traumatic times. It was also a learning curve for me.

For many years I had wondered how these two famous news commentators learned about the assimilation of the Japanese American kids in the first place. I had only one guesstimate.

About two years prior to this broadcasting event, I met a friendly Caucasian woman who was visiting our church. Her name was Margo Loring. She had a New England air about her, proper and refined, dressed conservatively, and wore her gray hair in an upswept manner; one could say she was an attractive middle-aged woman. Over time, she eventually got to know some of the young people and occasionally would join in our youth group activities and help fund them. She was kind and considerate, never pushy or outspoken, and acted as our advisor, offering suggestions to help us solve a problem. She was well traveled throughout Europe, South America, Asia, and other parts of the world, and often shared some of her travel adventures with us. And her 19-year-old son, a college freshman, would come to town during the summer and holidays to spend time with her, and sometimes with us as well.

Since I was one of the so-called leaders of the young people, she would often spend more time with me to help direct and plan youth programs.

At times she would come down to David Produce to visit, and she would give me books on poetry and philosophy to read. We had gone to lunch together a couple of times to one of the small restaurants owned by a Greek immigrant family in the produce markets. She showed me various magazine clippings about articles she had written regarding life in South America and elsewhere, and some poetry as well.

She had a hobby that fascinated us kids, palm reading. She said that she did not believe in palm reading to tell the future, but she did believe it could tell the characteristics of a person. The kids were always interested in having their palms read. She seemed to know what every little line represented, and she could spend up to a half-hour reading and discussing that one palm. When she read my palm, she told me that it was one of the most interesting and unusual palms she had ever seen. I sort of took that as a compliment. "Some parts of it were slightly negative," she said, "but mostly all very positive."

One day, about two years after she first arrived, she came down to David Produce to tell me that she was leaving San Diego and didn't know when she would be back. She said she would write and keep in contact with me. She gave me three books, one on poetry, the other on philosophy, and the third, about the changing times to come in the world.

That was the last time I saw Margo Loring, somewhat of an amazing woman, and somewhat of puzzlement as well, as to the way she appeared and left. I did receive two letters from her, telling me she was busy with her writing and travels. I wrote back once.

In the back of my mind, I always thought it was Margo Loring, through her travels and connections, who initiated the interest of the two major radio commentators regarding my involvement with the Japanese American youth. I doubt I will ever know.

CHAPTER 18

Moving Ahead

WITH THE ENDING OF THE WAR, MY BROTHER ALLEN CAME home from the army as a three-stripe sergeant. As a veteran, he decided to take advantage of the GI Bill and attended San Diego State University. Allen worked at the produce company early in the mornings before going to school. During summer vacations he worked fulltime, except for the few hours he spent taking summer classes for extra school credits.

After San Diego State he applied to get into the University of California San Francisco Dental School. Allen's application was turned down due to the reason that the so called "minority quota" had been filled, which was five percent of the class. Of course, Allen and the family were disappointed, and we were incensed with the quota policy. Here, Allen, a GI veteran honorably discharged, and with good grades, was turned down because of his race. With the help of several Caucasian business friends along with an elected official, Assemblywoman Kathryn Niehouse of the 79th District in San Diego, Allen was finally accepted. After graduation, he established his practice in Downey, California, and became quite successful as a dentist as well as in the investment field. He also gave back to the community by being active in civic affairs.

Allen was the first sibling to move out of the produce line of work. With his success, he contributed generously, along with the other older siblings, to financially support the younger ones so they could pursue higher education.

As the years passed on, I'm inclined to think that the experiences that we acquired in the produce business gave us exceptional insight as to how to deal with people: loosely, friendly, and in fairness. It was such a fast business that trust and your word meant a lot, for tomorrow you would be dealing again with these same people. Tons of truckloads of produce were bought and sold every day by verbal agreement and trust, and word moved quickly as to a person's business character.

With a family of twelve children and mother to support, we had to hustle a lot in maintaining and building up the business. Our hours were long, but it didn't seem that long because in the produce business we were always intermingling with other people, and time passed by quickly. Before we knew it, we'd worked 10 to 12 hours. Being young helped, too.

With the auto factories now back in production building cars and trucks for domestic use and not for war, we decided that we needed new trucks for our growing business. We looked at several makes, and decided on purchasing two red 10-ton Ford trucks with high side gates. Naturally, at that point, we were not in the position to pay cash for it, but needed a bank loan to finance the purchase. James and I went to the Bank of America branch at 5th and Market where we made our deposits. Up to this point we had never borrowed money and, therefore, never established any credit rating. We approached the manager, Mr. Joseph Zung, and described our business, the progress that we were making since we had taken over, and our need for a loan to buy the trucks. James did all the talking; he, being 23, had more credibility than me, a teenager. Fortunately, Mr. Zung knew Dad and that we had taken over the business, and said he heard nothing bad about us, but rather good things. After he asked a few questions, he then consented to make the loan. Bless our Dad! That was our first experience in big-time financing. Having a good reference can never hurt.

With our big new trucks we were able to expand the business, catering to larger customers and handling a greater variety of merchandise. With the younger siblings, like fourth and fifth brothers Wellman and Herbert, then in high school, we shared work by working after school and weekends. I cannot recall when we kids, after reaching an age where we could help, did not pitch in and work. It also gave us some spending money as well, not much, but enough to make us feel a bit of worthiness anyway. Our priority each week, however, was to give Ah Nuing a certain amount of money for household expenses. With thirteen in the family, of which seven were still under 12, it was pretty challenging to keep it up, and yet still retain enough capital to expand the growing business. It didn't take much to remind ourselves that Dad did it, and that we should be able to do it too. And we did do it, even as time went on when needs were even greater. It was a work of unity, led by the pecking order, oldest brother James.

SOMETIMES IN LIFE ONE MAKES MISTAKES. I've made my share. One I haven't forgotten, in spite of the fact it was not that big of a deal in the way of dollars, affected me in later life. We had a customer, Louis Barrak, who owned several boarding houses, where people would rent room and board. We serviced his produce needs. He complained a lot, such as the quality that we sent him, then would ask for credit towards it, and would also claim that he never got the merchandise that we billed him for. All not true. And he would at times steal items by putting them in his car when no one was watching. He was always several weeks behind in paying his bills and when he did pay, sometimes he would arbitrarily deduct 10 percent to 20 percent off the payment saying that our produce was overpriced. He was a very difficult customer. But he had his problems, too. Since the war ended and much of his clientele who were defense workers had left town, his business began to erode, and from there he went into deep debt, owing a lot to his suppliers in back bills.

When Barrak's bills to us amounted to about $900, we decided to cut him off as a customer. At the same time, I received a phone call from a Mr. Lawrance Holsman, director of the San Diego Credit Association, an organization that would call creditors together to work out a logical solution to pay off one's business debts. It was a well-respected organization, supported by the business community and the Chamber of Commerce. Mr. Holsman said, "Mr. Hom, I have here a file on a Mr. Louis Barrak, and it says that he owes your company a little over $900. He also owes a lot of other people in town, and he's thinking that he might file for bankruptcy. We don't want that to happen."

"But what can we do, sue him?" I replied.

"Not at this point," he said. "We may be able to work it out cooperatively with him so that none of the creditors would be hurt too badly. I've scheduled a meeting of all the creditors next Friday morning at 10 a.m. at my office and would like you to attend with others to discuss this matter. Will you be there?"

I said, "Yes!" And he gave me the address.

At the meeting there were about 25 men and women representing different creditors. Louis Barrak was there, too, dressed in his normally flashy manner. He was a rather imposing figure of a man, about 6'3", weighed about 250 pounds, and he sported a heavy mustache. I was by far the youngest one there and probably the most naive in solving business problems. The meeting lasted about two hours with a lot of questions asked and answers given. Finally, Mr. Holsman said, "Now that we know more about the bills and assets involved with Mr. Barrak, we'll have the office work out a recommendation for a settlement and we'll go from there. Let's see a show of hands if that is agreeable with you." Everyone raised their hand, including me. "Thank you for your unanimous vote," said Mr. Holsman.

After leaving the meeting, because I still did not have the confidence that Barrak would be cooperative in resolving the debt issue, I decided on Monday morning to go down to the Small Claims Court to file a suit for our $900. That afternoon, I got a call from Mr. Holsman, and he said, "Mr. Hom, I'm terribly disappointed in knowing that you filed a suit against Barrak when we all agreed unanimously that we would work together on this. Why did you do it?"

At that moment I was tongue-tied, embarrassed, and ashamed. Not knowing how to explain it to him, I just said, "We needed the money!" which we really did not, it was not that much. Since I voted for the settlement, I just couldn't say I didn't like or trust the guy.

He replied, "Mr. Hom, before calling you I made arrangements with the other creditors that we would pay you the $900 so you can withdraw the suit. I'll have the check in today's mail. I'm terribly disappointed that this happened!" Then he hung up.

I did get the check the next day. After talking with Mr. Holsman, I felt like a real heel, even a double crosser, to a good guy, a gentleman, who was trying to work out a fair solution for all on a tough problem. I had only thought of myself and to heck with the others, even after I gave my word. That was strictly a selfish act, getting revenge at the expense of others, simply because I didn't like Barrak.

That was one of the biggest regrets of my life. I often have thought of that occasion when I had a moral issue before me. It helped set a benchmark as how to better come to a decision when dealing with people. Seeking personal revenge has a way of rearing back at you and you in turn can end up to be the victim instead.

By the year 1948, David Produce Company had continued to grow, with the need for expansion. Our hours were long, but we didn't mind, we were young, and we were making progress. Fourth brother Wellman, right below me, graduated from San Diego High School and joined the company. That seemed the natural thing to do at that time, to pitch in and help with the company's growth and family needs. It was then, with the abundance of fresh produce coming in every day, that we decided to open a retail operation by leasing the produce concession in National City, just outside of San Diego city limits, in a new supermarket called Tang's. It was indeed a supermarket, being the largest in San Diego County. We hired a Mexican American fellow named Paul Tamayo as manager. He knew a lot about the retail produce business, having worked at it for over 25 years. Our knowledge in retail produce was limited, since we were in the wholesale end of it all our lives. We learned a lot from Paul.

Wellman worked there for about a year and then was drafted into the army, as the North Korean and South Korean conflict erupted into a major war. Communist China sided with North Korea against the Allies, consisting of the United Nations countries along with the United States, which supplied the major part of the armed forces there. Congress passed legislation to again institute a military draft. By that time, fifth brother Herbert had graduated from high school and was able to take over Wellman's place at the family business. I would work at Tang's part time and on weekends, mostly after I got through working at David Produce. I enjoyed working at Tang's and met a lot of nice people, but everything was at a slower pace. The wholesale business, on the other hand, was much faster paced and had less decorum, and I felt freer to express myself there.

About a year later, Herbert was also drafted. He was ordered to boot camp for six-week training, and then was immediately sent to the Korean frontline. He was in combat for about 18 months when he was wounded. Herb left the service after two years as a sergeant and was awarded a Purple Heart.

Wellman's experience was a little different. He served in combat, and, fortunately, was never wounded. His most hair-raising experience was when he was posted on the frontline to observe and report any enemy movements, when along came an Allied soldier, a Hungarian, who mistakenly took Wellman to be an enemy Red Chinese soldier. The soldier quickly drew his gun and pointed it at the back of Wellman's head and started shouting in Hungarian. Wellman, trying to calm the soldier down, didn't move and talked slowly in English, which the Hungarian did not understand. Luckily, within a few moments, a Hungarian officer ran up shouting that Wellman was an American soldier and for him to back off. The soldier, who thought he had caught a Communist spy, dropped back and profusely apologized. Wellman, one of the most kind and forgiving persons I know, accepted the apology and chalked it off to battle fatigue. Wellman received several medals for excellence, and returned home a corporal.

We kept the Tang's retail produce business for about three years and afterwards sold it to Jimmy Tang, the proprietor of the grocery and meat departments. It was a wonderful experience, but in that time we realized that the retail business was not what we were cut out to do. Selling fruit and vegetables by a few pounds at a time when we were used to selling it by the hundreds of pounds at a time, as well as tons at a time, did not fit into our future plans. Aside from that, our greater priority, the wholesale David Produce Company, was growing rapidly, and we were all needed there.

CHAPTER 19

Our Own House at Last

I N 1947, WITH THE DAVID PRODUCE COMPANY DOING WELL, AND especially with the younger siblings growing bigger, we thought it was time to have a bigger house. Up to this point we had always rented. We felt owning our own house would give us a better sense of security as well as more room to spread out, and we had been setting aside funds for this purpose for about two years. James asked a family friend, Mr. Alan Arlington, a real estate broker, to find a suitable house for us in a good school location for the kids.

After several weeks of trying to find the proper house and location, Mr. Arlington reported to us that he was having a hard time because what we wanted was in areas that had Racial Deed Restriction Covenants, which meant that only people of the Caucasian race were allowed to buy and own. We, being of Chinese descent, were prevented from buying in these areas. James and I were stunned. Here we were, having saved for the past two years to buy a house, and we were prevented from buying because of our racial heritage. When this racial restriction was revealed to us, I could not help but immediately think of Mr. Oakes, my junior high school principal, who lectured to us frequently at our school assemblies, saying that we were all Americans and that we all had the same rights as everyone else according to the U.S. Constitution.

I said to Mr. Arlington, "This isn't right. We have the money and are a responsible family, and yet we can't buy a house where we want to live. This just isn't right!"

He heartily agreed and said, "Let's not give up on this. Let me keep working and see what we can come up with!"

A couple of weeks later, Mr. Arlington came back and told us of his new finding. He said, "I found a three-story house in a nice area of North Park, on Redwood Street, not far from Balboa Park. It has been vacant for over a year, with overgrown weeds and needs painting on the outside. The inside is very nice with six bedrooms, a large living room with a separate dining room, a good-size kitchen, and a large yard. The neighbors are anxious to see the property sold so it can be brought back up to what it used to be!" He went on to say, "I spoke to several of the neighbors on whether they would have any objection to a nice Chinese family, who has a thriving wholesale business, buying the house. No one objected, and only expressed that the family be a good neighbor and keep up the property!"

Mr. Arlington took Ah Nuing and James to see the house. They loved the house and decided to put in an offer to accept the asking price of $12,000 with $5,000 down. During the interim of escrow, Ah Nuing was determined not to have anything stand in the way of purchasing the house, so she went from neighbor to neighbor, with our four-year-old brother Paul, hand in hand, introducing herself and Paul, by saying in her broken English, "I am Mrs. Hom. I am buying the big house on Redwood Street for my family. The children are all good and have never been in trouble. We are a good family and want to be a good neighbor. Maybe later, when you have time, please come to my home for tea!" Needless to say, Ah Nuing was effective, because no one complained or took any initiative to enforce the racial deed restriction covenants.

Our family lived there for over 40 years and made many friends in the neighborhood. Incidentally, the U.S. Supreme Court struck out the racial deed restrictions covenants as being unconstitutional in 1954, seven years later. It was at this stage, once again, I had thoughts that one day I might want to get involved in politics and run for public office.

IN SPITE OF MY HEAVY SCHEDULE at work, like most young men, we had the tendency to burn the candle at both ends, like spending any spare time one might have in socializing and recreation. Much of my recreational time was spent at the church. A lot of the fun events were when we shared activities with other Chinese Protestant churches, like Summer Camp Conferences at Big Bear Lake and Lake Tahoe. That's when we were able to meet other kids and sometimes even fall in love. Thank goodness summer romances are generally short lived.

At times, after work on Friday, several of us would pile in our cars and make a beeline to Los Angles to pick up our dates and go to a dance, followed by a midnight snack, then we'd take the girls home, getting us to our hotel room about 2 a.m. Next day there might be a sports event, like basketball, against one of the L.A. churches, then eating out, socializing, and then back to the hotel. After attending Sunday morning church service, again we'd eat, call on friends, mostly girls, maybe go to a picnic or movie and have dinner, then leave for San Diego by midnight. That would get me to San Diego by 4 a.m. and I would go directly to work at David Produce.

We would look forward to repeating the same routine about once every couple of months during the next year or two.

CHAPTER 20

A Crisis

B Y 1949, AT AGE 22, I BECAME A LITTLE MORE SETTLED, WANTING to improve my knowledge in business. Everything I had learned up to this point was through the college of hard knocks. I wanted to learn more about accounting, finance, and management so I enrolled at San Diego City College for these evening courses, going four nights a week. I had a lady friend who wanted to take a course in Mandarin, and I decided to do that too. With these courses, I crammed pretty hard and found great satisfaction in realizing that there was an abundance of opportunities out there for David Produce to grow economically. At this stage, I was also beginning to grow fond of this particular girl. That was probably part of the reason for my becoming more settled in life. But as time went on, we drifted apart and nothing became of it.

At this stage I was no longer a minor and tried to think of myself as an adult. I even thought I might be sophisticated enough to smoke cigarettes, which, after six smokes, I hated. Then later I tried a pipe, as that seemed be the fashion of many of the leading men in the movies. But after a month of inhaling a pipe and trying to appear debonair, I hated that, too. After that, I said to myself, "Hey, I'm still acting like a kid, trying to be something that I'm not. Time to shift gears and grow up!" Well, everything has a learning curve.

One day while I was delivering produce to a restaurant downtown on Fifth Avenue, I saw a large trailer parked across the street with a sign that said GET A FREE X-RAY, SAN DIEGO COUNTY HEALTH DEPARTMENT. I thought why not, so I went in and got my free X-ray.

Two weeks later I got a letter from the San Diego County Health Department to come down and take another X-ray, as the first one showed some complications. So I did, without concern, for I was healthy, strong, and full of body strength.

A week later, a nurse called me to come to the health office to meet with a Doctor Gardner, as he wanted to talk to me about my recent X-ray. I met with the doctor and he told me something that would change the direction of my life. He said, "Tom, your X-rays show that you have a case of tuberculosis in your upper right lung." He showed me the X-ray films, which I did not understand, but I listened to the doctor's explanation. He told me, "It is still in the early stage and has not yet affected your overall health. But if it is neglected, it can progressively get worse!" I almost fell out of my chair. My immediate thought was that Dad died from tuberculosis and there was no medical treatment that could cure it. The doctor went on to say, "Tom, my strong advice to you is that you go into a sanitarium and not stay home, as it may possibly get worse and then it can infect the rest of your family. If you go into a sanitarium, you will have good care and a good chance of recovering, since your case is at a very early stage!"

It's funny how quickly the mind can think and go through so many things within seconds. In a flash I thought of the family of kids at home, my responsibilities at the produce company, my friends, and how I would tell everyone I got TB and would be going into a sanitarium. Within a moment, I decided that going into the sanitarium was something I must and should do now. Everything else, in time, would take care of itself.

Although my doctor said at this early stage TB was not transmittable, I doubt the average person knew that. It would be difficult to live with the knowledge that there was no medicine to cure TB, other than to rest and eat healthy food. I made up my mind to fight it with whatever it took.

The doctor summoned the nurse to make the necessary arrangements for my entry into the Vauclain Tuberculosis Sanitarium, located at the edge of the Hillcrest area overlooking the farmlands of Mission Valley. I had never been a patient in a hospital before, so going to Vauclain Sanitarium would be a new experience and created some apprehension. That feeling of apprehension was only momentary, because I knew it was necessary and that I was going to beat it. I felt that way because I had absolutely no feeling of illness at all.

My first inclination after leaving the doctor's office was to go down to the produce company and tell James about the situation. He was shocked and upset by the news. After some discussion, he wholeheartedly agreed that going to the sanitarium was the best thing for me, and to not worry about the business, that I needed to take care of my health first. Next, I went home to tell Ah Nuing and the rest of the family. Ah Nuing was quite taken aback by the news, as Dad, only a few years prior, had died from tuberculosis.

WHEN I ENTERED THE SANITARIUM, I brought a suitcase packed with some casual clothing, pajamas, art supplies, and sundries. I even brought along my tennis racquet, and baseball glove and ball, just in case we had leisure sport time. Needless to say, that was not included, so the nurse confiscated these items and stored them away. Seeing my disappointment, she said, "Tom, when you get well, soon enough we hope you can have them back!" Nurse Hamilton was a tough talking cookie, but later I found her to be a very caring person. I liked and respected her.

I was assigned to Ward C, a barrack-like setting with about 20 patients, of course all men from all walks of life, some elderly and some as young as their late teens. The nurse said, "The first order of business today is to unpack your suitcase and get into these hospital PJs and have a physical examination. Afterwards, you will be confined to your bed for the next 30 days, not leaving even to go to the bathroom, for you will be using bedpans for all your toilet needs!" I immediately thought of what Doctor Gardner said earlier, that to cure TB you need complete rest and not overwork your lungs. I never thought, for the life of me, that getting out of bed to go to the toilet was exhausting. The nurse went on to say that the only time I would be leaving the bed was to have X-rays taken, and that a wheeled stretcher would transport me. Since science had not yet discovered any medicine to cure TB, I accepted that bed rest must be the best bet there was.

The first week in bed, trying to do my toiletry needs was extremely difficult, especially since when we kids were very young, we were taught not to pee in bed, let alone do a number two in bed. Now using a bedpan for the first time in my life, and for the next few times, it took me about half an hour before I could let any pee go. For my number two, it took about an hour. That was tough. Wiping was equally tough too, lying on my back, under a cover, with a room full of people. And this not to mention the embarrassing odor it caused, as well.

Amazingly, after two weeks of struggling with the bedpan challenge, I began to ease into using it without too much difficulty. But there were other challenges and these were bedsores, aches, and pains. I never knew people could get those things just lying in bed. To give some relief, the nurses gave me body rubdowns. Those were my first rubdowns and, boy, they felt good!

With all the other men in the ward there for the same purpose, it didn't take long to make friends, especially since none of us were going anywhere. At least for a while. There was an old saying among the patients, and that was, "There are only two ways you will get out of here, either walk out or get carried out!" Carried out meant you were being carried to the mortuary. That didn't sound too encouraging, but to me—I expected to walk out. I couldn't help feeling that way because I never felt sick or lost any weight, which was one of the symptoms of TB. I guess it was partly my youthfulness, too, believing I was invincible and "I can do anything!"

After 30 days of being bedridden, I was granted the privilege to go to the bathroom once each day. After that I had to use the bedpan for the rest of the day. A male attendant came by and said, "Tom, this is the day to use the bathroom. Let me help you!" I immediately thought to myself, "Help me? This is crazy, I can do it myself!" I slid out of bed, planted my feet in a pair of slippers and, lo and behold, I almost collapsed onto the floor. Luckily, the attendant was holding me up by one of my arms. I was that weak.

The attendant said, "After 30 days confined to the bed without any physical activity, your body has the tendency to weaken, but you'll get your strength back. But all this time, with your body at rest, your lungs are fighting against the TB germs!" With his assistance, I slowly and wobbly walked to the bathroom which was about 100 feet away. It seemed more like a mile.

While slowly struggling across the ward, some of my newfound friends would shout encouraging words like, "Tom, do it slowly, you'll make it!" and "Don't lift your feet, shuffle!" I did my business and shuffled back to my bed. I did this, of course, with the aid of the attendant. The bed never felt so comfortable.

After the once-a-day bathroom month, the next month I was put on a three-a-day program which worked out pretty well. By this time, I had gained some of my leg strength back and walked regularly, but slowly, to the bathroom. On a few occasions I would mischievously break the rule and visit some of the other men's wards. Women's wards were out of bounds.

After three months I was getting used to the pace of the schedule and the sanitarium environment, and with no pressure or deadlines and responsibilities, it was an easy life. Mainly, at 7 a.m. I ate breakfast, 12 p.m. lunch, and 5 p.m. dinner, all this served in bed by the nurses and attendants. Wednesdays, Saturdays, and Sundays, at certain hours, were Visitor's Days. Everyone looked forward to that. I had my share of visitors; family alone contributed quite a few, plus my friends from church and work. Some of my friends bought me a very nice RCA radio along with earphones, on which I listened to some of my favorite programs, like Jack Benny, Red Skelton, *The Hit Parade* and others, often late into the night. Once a week, a lady from the public library rolled a cart of books through the ward. We could choose a book from the cart, and if we wanted a certain title, she would have it for us the next time around.

Although visiting hours were a happy period of the day for most of us, for some it was not. Next to my bed was another patient, an elderly Jewish gentleman by the name of Abe Horowitz. He and I had become good friends. He would often relate to me that the Jewish people and the Chinese had a lot in common, that we were an ancient people and had similar cultural values, like family, hard work and tolerance. His wife had passed away several years earlier and his only living relative was his son, a rather prominent attorney in town. The anxious moments for him were when the buzzer rang signaling the beginning of visiting hours. He watched the doorway to see who entered, and it was an obvious let down when whoever entered wasn't his son. Abe's face said it all. At the end of the visiting hours, Abe would curse his son out loud for not coming, telling us that he had a lousy son and was going to disown him. Abe would be miserable for the rest of the evening.

During my first three months I saw his son only once. I felt sorry for Abe, as many others did, too. One evening after his cursing tirade, I quietly asked the nurse if she could get me the address of his son. She gave it to me and I dropped the son a short note about the depressed situation of his dad from not seeing him more often and how much he loved him. Within a week the son visited and did so at least once every other week, often bringing some of his father's favorite foods, or a gift of chocolates for Abe to share with the rest of us. In a short time Abe was praising his son and marveling how he was even able to find time to visit when he was so busy and successful in his work, and that he was so lucky to have such a good son. To this day I don't really know whether my letter helped or the son just finally found time to visit. Of course, the importance of it all is that the son did come regularly thereafter.

By the fourth month, I was able to visit the bathroom anytime I wanted, around the clock. But instead of going in the semi-darkness after nine o'clock when the lights were lowered, I generally preferred to use the bedpan. Imagine that! I'm not sure whether I was getting spoiled or just being plain lazy—probably both.

During the following month, I was granted an hour to walk around visiting the other wards as well as walking around the outside grounds of the sanitarium, which was quite scenic with many kinds of flowers and trees. After an hour of walking and visiting I found my strength coming back and wasn't tired at all. It was at that time when I brought out my art supplies and started to draw and paint again. I did this in bed with the food table over my upper legs to support my drawing board. I enjoyed doing art. At times I would draw caricatures of some of my roommates, and other times I'd do some of the nurses, as well. Caricatures were hilarious and always brought a lot of laughs.

One day the middle-aged head nurse of our ward asked me to paint her a scene of a lighthouse with the waves splashing against the rocks. I painted the scene she wanted in oil, and I added seagulls and a cloudy sky with the sun breaking through to give it a little drama. She loved it and asked how much she owed me. Because she was such a nice and caring person, I said, "It's free, my compliments. It's my pleasure to do it!"

She pressed her lips, and said, "Let me pay you at least $15!"

I paused, thought for a moment, and replied, "No, just the cost of materials is okay, five dollars."

She then quickly came back and said, "Then how about $12?" By this point several of the patients were listening in on our bartering.

I replied, "Hey, we seem to be negotiating backwards. Why don't we settle for six dollars?" She smiled, pinched my cheek, left for a couple of minutes and came back and stuffed a $10 dollar bill in the breast pocket of my pajamas. As she gleefully left with the painting I cautioned her to be careful and not touch the paint, as it was not quite dried yet. Apparently she really liked the painting, for she went around the sanitarium showing it to everyone.

I got another request for a painting by one of the other nurses. She had a 10-year-old son who was very interested in animals and music. She asked me to paint him an ensemble of four animals, each playing a musical instrument. Instead of the ensemble of four, I painted a symphony orchestra of 80 animals playing different types of instruments, in an animated style. I depicted an owl as the conductor, a lion as the pianist, cats at the violins, wolves at basses, dogs at trumpets, pigs at clarinets, donkeys at cellos, anteaters at harps, and so on. I did it in watercolor and thought it came out pretty well. It took a little longer than I anticipated, but the challenge was worth it. I had great satisfaction!

From then on I took no more requests, but I did continue to paint and draw whatever and whenever I felt like it. When I had painted at someone's request, there was some degree of pressure and that was contrary to the doctor's orders to rest. I'm sure the people requesting to have a painting made did not think that painting would cause me to feel pressured; they probably thought that doing art was a relaxing activity. To me, there was a big difference between painting for others and painting for myself.

SINCE SCIENCE HAD NOT YET come up with a medicine that was effective in curing TB, there was a treatment that was called Artificial Pneumothorax that helped. They would do this by semi-collapsing the lungs to partially inactivate the breathing, to rest the lungs, so that the body's immune system could fight the TB germs. That's not a scientific way of explaining it, but in essence that's how it was explained to me.

To do the treatment, the doctors would insert a hollowed needle into my diaphragm, which looked like the kind of needle used to blow up a football or basketball, connected to a tube that was attached to an enclosed empty glass container, and next to it was another glass container partially filled with colored liquid. Both of these containers had measurements marked on them. They would pump the container with the liquid into the empty container, and doing so, the air from the empty container would be forced to go through the tube into my diaphragm, and then the bloated diaphragm would push upward to force my lungs to semi-collapse to about one-fourth of its capacity.

It sounds gruesome and the twice-a-week treatment was painful, especially at the beginning. But in time, I got used to it … somewhat. The tough part about it was at the early stages of treatment I would spend most of the time in bed, for the limited breathing capacity restricted my activity in walking and movement. In about two to three weeks I could walk fairly well again, but not too rapidly, for the shaking of the air in my diaphragm caused strong pain in that whole region.

On the lighter side, this treatment not only bloated up the diaphragm, it also bloated up the stomach, which is right below the diaphragm, making the stomach pop out as if the patient was pregnant and due in a few short months. The women could get away with it, but the men were constantly teased about it.

In time this Artificial Pneumothorax treatment proved to be effective for people like me whose case of TB was at the early stage and had not yet affected my overall health. With this treatment, good rest, and a healthy diet, my X-rays progressively showed that my TB germs were slowly but surely being arrested. Instead of calling the treatment by its long medical term, which sounded too ominous, we patients simply called it the Air Treatment. That was better, especially for those newcomers to the sanitarium.

As my X-rays continuingly showed improvement, I was given the privilege of leaving my bed, as long as I did not tire myself and I took naps in-between. I often would wander around the various wards making new friends. In spite of what we all had in common, TB, we all had a story to tell that was new and unique. I think it was at this point in life that I really learned more than ever to take people as individuals and try not to prejudge before knowing them.

In wandering around, a couple of times I noticed that a barber would come in once a week to give haircuts for 75 cents to whomever wanted one. One day it was announced that the barber would no longer be coming because he had moved out of town. It was "Aw shucks!" with some of the men, because a lot of them always wanted to look their best, with hair trimmed, combed, and face clean shaven for when visitors came. They wanted to reassure their loved ones that they were not going downhill or about to expire.

Being from a family of nine boys, I learned to cut hair when I was about 14. My dad brought home a haircut kit with a clipper and attachments so I could cut my brothers' hair. Up to that point, most of our haircuts were performed by Ah Nuing, which would turn out to be bowl-like, or at the barber college on Market Street, which cost 25 cents. It was at the barber college where I observed how to cut hair, along with a lot of practicing on my brothers. In a short while, after a few nicks and cuts, I became pretty good at it, where I was able to do a trim, a regular or crew cut, or whatever. And if someone showed me a picture of a style they wanted, I could do that, too.

Because there was no barber, I volunteered to cut hair until one could be found. At first, some of the guys were dubious of my ability to do a decent haircut, but in time they saw I was doing a pretty good job. Soon I had more requests than I could handle. Because my first priority was not to overstrain and tire myself and to take the necessary daily naps, I limited myself to four haircuts a day and none on Saturdays or Sundays, as those were special Visitor's Days. I charged 50 cents, or whatever a guy could afford. It worked out pretty well, with most paying the 50 cents.

I did not charge terminal patients for haircuts. They were isolated in a private room where their demise would be within a short time. Generally, the doctors would be able to determine when that would be, so as that date came near, the nurse would ask me to give a "last haircut" so that patient would look at least half-decent when the loved ones would come to visit for the last time. In these cases when I did the haircut the patient would normally be only half-conscious. I needed them to be half-sitting, propped up in bed, held up by an attendant, so I could do the cutting. Each time I gave a haircut like this, it was sad, for I couldn't help but think of my dad who also died from TB just a few years earlier.

After a few weeks a new barber was found, and I decided to phase out my haircutting. In spite of my quitting, some of the patients still wanted me to cut their hair. I'm not sure if it was because I was cheaper at 50 cents or whatever they wanted to pay, or because of my good styling. I surmised it must have been that I'm cheaper. After all, the new barber was a professional, properly trained, and did cut very well. I even had him cut my hair—and I was pretty fussy back then.

By this time I was in my seventh month at the sanitarium and my treatment of Artificial Pneumothorax was producing good results, thereby giving me more free time to move around. With that free time, the office administration asked me whether I would like to take on the job of being the editor of the monthly newsletter of the Vauclain Sanitarium as the last editor, Jim Madison, a friend, was well enough to go home. I asked what being the editor entailed. They said that each ward had its own reporter who gathered news, like events, personalities, how some patients were doing, birthdays, and other note-worthy items. I, as editor, with helpers, would gather the reports and put them all together in a readable format. The office would run the newsletter off on their mimeograph-printing machine.

I took the job on and had fun doing it. I had lots of volunteer help and I kept the job until I left the sanitarium. It was really an easy job. I had an assistant editor, Molly, who was really a trouper and did most of the work. I got the credit for putting the paper out, but I knew it was she who got it done properly. Molly just never wanted to be the editor, because she thought it had too many responsibilities that went with it. I think I learned then that it was always good to have people working for you who were smarter than you, because they would always make you look good. Yet after each issue, Molly would congratulate me for a job well done. Imagine that!

By the ninth month of my rehabilitation, the doctors said that my recovery was coming along fine, and if it continued like that, I could be released to go home the following month. It was with the understanding, however, that I would continue the Artificial Pneumothorax treatment for about a year to be sure that I would not have a reoccurrence of TB. An outside doctor would do this treatment.

That month passed quickly. Soon it was time to gather all my personal belongings and pack up. It was an emotional last two days for I had spent so much of that time saying goodbye to the many nurses and doctors who had treated me so well, as well as to the patient friends that I had made in ten months, all of us striving for a common cause in fighting TB. The hardest part of saying goodbye was to those whose illness was at the advanced and terminal stages. That episode of my life in the sanitarium really made me grow up quickly. I learned a lot about people and it also taught me not to take life for granted.

In leaving, I wasn't sure what the future of my life would be like. The doctor advised me not go back to working in the produce business as I had done before, with those long hours and heavy lifting. In spite of not knowing what the future would be, I never felt discouraged, for I knew that I would manage to make my way back somehow. Perhaps that thinking stemmed partly from an older friend, who worked in the produce market and once said to me, "Tom, the main thing in life is not security, it is courage!" Come to think about it, how true ... with courage you find security along with everything else.

FOR THE FIRST COUPLE OF WEEKS at home I stayed around the house pretty much. I managed to call a few of my friends to tell them I was now home and to learn what was going on in the community. During this time I was mostly relaxing, as doctors had advised me to do, which included two naps a day for a month and afterwards once a day. Some of my friends would come over to the house to visit, but some did not, for their parents had told them that TB was contagious and they did not want the chance of catching any infection from me. In the sanitarium we all knew that as former patients we would be confronting this infection issue upon re-entering society, so I didn't take too much offense to this viewpoint. I did initially tell people that my particular case was so much in the early stage that it was never at that point where the TB germs could be passed on to another person. But I also knew that the more I defended this fact, the more pronounced the issue became, so later I never mentioned it unless I was asked about the situation.

With time on my hands, I mostly relaxed, read, and painted. I decided to look into the possibility of using my art ability to seek a new career. Since a child I had always enjoyed comic strips in the newspapers, like *Flash Gordon*, *Jungle Jim*, *Orphan Annie*, *Popeye the Sailor* and a number of others. Comic books like *Superman*, *Captain Marvel*, *Batman* and *Spiderman* were favorites too. Now that I was older, I had become more intrigued with the artistry and economics of comics, such as who were the creators and the artists and what kind of money they made. I was also interested in how one would get started in creating a comic strip and how to get it accepted in the marketplace.

Since I occasionally read *The Saturday Evening Post* and other magazines as well, I noticed that many of them had humorous panel cartoons on various pages. I was interested in knowing more about that as a business. In order to learn more, I spent time at the library checking out books pertaining to all this. I found out that a successful comic strip like *Flash Gordon*, and others of that popularity, brought a huge income and fame for the artists and creators. The humorous panel cartoons in magazines also paid well.

After all the research, I became excited and decided to set up shop in my room, which was located on the third floor, a penthouse at our family home. It had a lot of room and storage space and good natural light. I first started on the panel cartoons, as they were easier to create, for the situation humor was about everyday life. I would dash off five to ten of them a day in a sketch form, and then mail them out to the magazines that would be interested in the cartoon of that type, such as a sports cartoon to sports magazines, and so on. If they wanted the cartoon they would send the sketch form back to me to do a finished drawing. Then, subject to their final approval, they would send me a check for the going rate. Smaller, less well-known magazines would pay between $10 to $25; the big ones, like *The Saturday Evening Post, Colliers, Liberty* and *The New Yorker* would pay $75. The famous name cartoonists got paid more.

In a short time, I realized that this was a very competitive business. I was told the chances of getting something accepted by the big magazines were about 500 to 1; and the smaller ones, about 100 to 1. Needless to say, I didn't do too well with the large ones, but I did get one in *The Saturday Evening Post*. I did fairly well with the small ones, though. That gave me just about enough money to cover my art supplies. The amount earned wasn't that important, but getting it accepted brought me great sense of accomplishment.

While I was working on panel cartooning, in between I created a comic strip titled *Kit Venture*. It was an adventure story with the main character sort of like a James Bond guy: sophisticated, debonair, and a woman killer. I drew up the sketches and outlined the story of the strip and mailed it to several comic syndicates. I got rejections from all, with some commenting that there were too many like it already, or that it was not original enough. I did get one that said, "We like the art work but not the plot."

I spent about six months intensively doing my art. Aside from my comics, I did some commission work such as designing food product labels, logos, and portrait paintings. But in time, I realized that making a living in art was really not for me.

I always liked associating with people, whether through business or socially. So slowly, I gravitated to working at the produce company where there was more action, doing bookkeeping. Bookkeeping confined me to a small area, which I didn't especially like. Being young and energetic, I just wanted to do something that was more people oriented and more challenging as well.

CHAPTER 21

A New Direction

ONE DAY AFTER WORK I WAS LEAFING THROUGH THE NEWS-paper, and I came across an ad by the Kelsey Jennings Business College. The ad described their program to become a licensed real estate agent/broker. The introductory class was free, so since the college was downtown, not too far from my work, I attended that evening to find out more about it.

After three hours of classroom introduction to real estate's financial potential and how to acquire licensing to work in that field, I became very intrigued with the business of selling real estate. I saw great potential in this new field, and I was excited about it. The next day I shared my thoughts with James. He encouraged me to pursue it, as it could help diversify the family's income in the future. The next day I enrolled in the class. That was the beginning of my real estate career, which would span over the next 50 years.

After about a year of studying at Kelsey Jennings Business College I finally came to the point where I was ready to take the test for my license as a real estate sales agent. To be a broker required that one first needed to be an active licensed sales agent for at least two years in the field. Since I had only limited knowledge of real estate, I readily accepted that. I had a lot to learn.

I passed the test with a 96 percent score. Being a beginner in this field, I felt elated with that score. Next, I needed to be hired by a licensed broker, so I turned to my family friend, Mr. Arlington, who had sold us our house, to mentor me. He said he would be happy to take me on, as he had always worked alone and to have a salesman would be helpful to him. As it turned out, it was extremely helpful to me, for he had me do a lot of the grunt work for him, like checking titles, getting sales comps, and lots of other things that were entirely new to me. I learned and he earned, but he was generous too. Whenever he made a sale on the properties that I worked on for him, he would give me a small portion of his commission. That was great for me, for I valued my education in this area more than the money. The money, although not much, was still a windfall.

Within a year I was getting calls from some of my family friends and other minority ethnic groups. In the early 1950s, racial deed restrictions were still in existence, meaning that many of the properties, especially those in the nicer areas of town, could only be purchased by Caucasians. This probably covered about 80 percent of the properties in the city at that time. With that type of barrier in dealing in real estate, many of the Caucasian real estate firms did not make the effort to deal with the racial minority groups. For that reason, I started to get many requests from minorities to find a house for them. In no time, I had a list of clients who kept me very busy. Obviously, getting clients was not a problem; it was getting listings to sell to them. Many of the brokers did not cooperate in sharing their listings with me due to the deed restrictions. Some agents, with access to listings in the less desirable areas without the restrictions, would often send clients to me, because many of them did not want to work in those kind of neighborhoods. Even though I did good business in these undesirable areas, many of my clients wanted houses in better neighborhoods, with good schools and a safer environment.

In order to solve that problem, I would drive my minority client around in the neighborhood where he wanted to buy. He would point out the houses that he would like to see and possibly buy. I would then follow through the next few days and research the names of the owners. Then I would knock on their doors and ask if they were interested in selling, explaining that I was an agent and my client was interested in buying a house in the neighborhood. In most cases, people were always courteous, and some would invite me in to discuss the possibility and ask me questions. Interestingly, most people didn't even know there was such a thing as racial deed restrictions. In this case, I would normally tell them about the house we bought for my mother in North Park with deed restrictions, and that no neighbors bothered enforcing it, which would have to be done through the courts, if necessary. In most cases, there would not be a problem. I would round it out saying, "My client has the cash and can afford to buy in the neighborhood and is a very responsible family!" That helped a lot. I quickly learned that cash talked ... a whole lot!

Cold calling was a hard way of getting listings, but it worked, and I made many sales through this method. Aside from that, social mores were rapidly changing. People of all backgrounds working together in the war effort had removed many of the social barriers that existed in earlier times. Later on in the 1960s the California State Legislature passed the Rumford Act, nullifying racial discrimination in real estate. The U.S. Supreme Court also ruled that racial deed restrictions were unconstitutional.

CHAPTER 22

Aloha Oe

T HE YEAR 1950 WAS A VERY SIGNIFICANT ONE FOR ME AS WELL. That was the year I entered and came out of the tuberculosis sanitarium, and, to a large degree, was just starting out all over again. The biggest impact in my life occurred during late spring at church where I first met an 18-year-old girl whose family had just moved over from Hawaii. She had recently graduated from Roosevelt High School in Honolulu and was spending the summer in San Diego before attending the University of California Berkeley on a scholarship. Her name was Dorothy LaVerne Akana, a super attractive girl with lots of charm and friendliness, and I was immediately taken by her good looks and bright bubbly personality.

When I was introduced to her by the church minister's wife, Kay Fung, who had brought her to church, I was fascinated by how outwardly friendly and talkative she was, without being boring or offensive or critical of anything. I just said a few words like, "I hope you'll like San Diego!" and she took off from there, telling me how much San Diego was like Honolulu and described the beaches of both areas and the types of foods, and went on for at least 10 minutes without stopping. I stood in amazement, not so much listening as to what she was saying, but watching her lively way of expressing and describing things and events. After we parted I thought she was one of the most fascinating persons I'd ever met.

Two weeks later, I saw Dorothy again at a dance put on by the House of Pacific Relations Association in Balboa Park, of which I was a member. It was an annual event, and when I saw her on the floor dancing the foxtrot with one of my friends, I decided to cut in. During the dance she again began talking, and she asked me whether I was a student or what kind of work I did. With a bit of hesitation, I said, "I'm really not doing much of anything, maybe trying to be an artist and doing part-time bookkeeping in the family business. I'm just trying to start over again!" I hesitated for another moment, and then said, "I just got out of a sanitarian a few months ago where I was being treated for TB!" I said that knowing that people in general were still leery and hesitant in associating with people who have or had TB.

When I told her this, she stopped in the middle of the dance floor and looked at me straight in the face and said, with twinkling eyes and a smile, "Why, Tom, I can't believe it! You look so healthy and robust! One of my uncles had tuberculosis and was quite sick, but you look like a picture of health!" That did it! She was different from any girls I had known. And she went on to say, "And you have such rosy cheeks!" The music started again and she said, "If you don't mind, Tom, can we dance some more?" We did, and she talked throughout the next three dances until I was cut in by one of my buddies. I didn't dance with her anymore that evening. Being attractive and having a good personality, in addition to being a new girl in town, made Dorothy pretty popular.

I thought she must have found me fairly interesting, having asked me to dance some more, and yet I hadn't hardly said a word. Going home that night I was determined to see her again, hopefully, the next morning at church. I wanted to know her better.

The next day, Sunday, I took a little extra care in brushing my hair and dressed a little better than I normally would, wearing a coat and tie. That was unusual for me. When I arrived, I saw Dorothy in front of the church with several people, among them was her girlfriend Carolyn, a childhood friend who came down from Chapman College, just south of Los Angeles, to visit her. I didn't stop, but went directly into the church, for I had a regular assignment to do, which was to make sure all the chairs were arranged properly in a row and the floor clean before the start of church service. We didn't have pews, so the folding chairs constantly needed arranging.

During service I sat two rows behind Dorothy. I noticed she wore a Hawaiian muumuu dress, the kind that is quite loose and covers the whole body, down from the neck to almost the floor. She looked typically Hawaiian: tropical, casual, and somewhat romantic. During the singing of the hymns, even from two rows back, I could detect that her voice seemed to have a slight flow reminiscent of Hawaiian singing. I might have imagined it, but in any case I thought it was beautiful.

Often after services a number of young people would get together and go to a Chinese restaurant for lunch, eating mostly chow mein, won ton soup, and such. They invited Dorothy and her friend Carolyn to join them. In a short time, everyone started to pile into their cars to leave for the restaurant, but I had a bit of a dilemma as I couldn't just leave since I had the responsibility to straighten the chairs and sweep the floor in order to get it ready for an evening service that day. I decided I had to stay, for Rev. Bob Fung depended on me to take care of these matters. Meanwhile, one of my best friends kept honking his horn, saying, "Come on, Tom, let's go! Don't be the goat!"

After doing my job, an hour later I arrived at the restaurant to join my friends. A few of them had left by then and I found myself sitting next to Dorothy. She offered to share some of her food with me since she only ate about half of her chow mein. I gladly accepted as I was hungry, and I appreciated her thoughtfulness. As time lingered on with everyone chatting and laughing, I managed to talk with Dorothy a bit about her life in Hawaii and her future plans.

She told me she was born and raised in Honolulu, loved the outdoors, especially spending lots of time at Waikiki Beach, that reading was a favorite hobby, that during the previous summers she worked at the Dole Pineapple Cannery, that she did volunteer work at the community hospital, and that she had a boyfriend in Honolulu with whom she corresponded with regularly. Her ambition was to be a doctor specializing in working with children, a pediatrician. One day when she married, she hoped to have a large family like her grandmother who had eight children, but she would be satisfied with five or six. She loved her parents, but she loved her grandmother just as much. Because both her parents worked, she spent a lot of time at her grandmother's house. Her grandmother taught her how best to be a lady, how to cook, and she taught her the traditional customs and culture of the Chinese.

After relating all this to me, one thing struck me rather sensitively, which was that she already had a boyfriend. I quickly rationalized that since she was not married or even engaged, there was no reason why we should not continue to get to know each other better. With that purpose in mind, I asked if I could take her and her friend Carolyn home following lunch. She responded by saying, "Tom, if it's not too far out of the way, yes, we'd love to have you take us home! On the mainland here, everything is so far apart. Are you sure it's okay?"

With a smile, I replied, somewhat kiddingly, "Dorothy, it's no problem. I can either take you home through the long way or the short way, it's up to you, but I will get you home safe and sound!"

She responded with a grin and said to me, "I was told that you mainland boys were bold and forward. Can that be true?"

I answered, "Well, on the way home is it too bold to ask if we could stop off at a nice place and have an ice cream soda?"

With a pause and then a smile, she replied, "Not at all!" I decided later that I shouldn't be too aggressive in my ways, for it could scare her off.

I did get Dorothy and her friend Carolyn home in about two hours. During ice cream soda time, we talked about all the things to do and see in San Diego, and later we ended up in Coronado, visiting the Hotel Del Coronado. She wanted to see it, for earlier I told her it was an icon among hotels, and it was the Chinese laborers who built it in the 1880s. They had a museum there showing the construction of it. I also told her a lot about San Diego Chinese history, its Chinatown and its culture, and how my dad came over from China.

In turn, Dorothy shared her experience growing up in Hawaii. She told me what it was like growing up in a diversified society, and how the Chinese first came and the progress that they had made. She was what in Hawaii is referred to as Hapa Haole: part Asian, in this case Chinese on her father's side, and part Caucasian, that was the Irish on her mother's side. She went on to relate that through her grandmother, Ah Po, she learned a lot about Chinese customs, etiquette, the protocol of filial piety and so on. It surprised me. I sensed that she was very proud of her Chinese heritage in a very Americanized way by blending the two cultures.

Upon arriving at Dorothy's home, I met her dad and mom. Her mother greeted me very cordially and her dad had that "who is this guy?" look when I extended my hand to him. He took my hand and shook it, didn't say a word, and grunted "Humpt!" At the moment I thought he was just reacting as a protective father, reserving judgment, but that was not so. Later I found that he was simply not sociable, but still a rather nice person. When I got to know him better, I would bring him some of his favorite foods from different restaurants, and he would just grunt his "Humpt!" upon receiving it. All the years I had known him, I can only remember him thanking me only once, when I gave him a gift for his birthday. He said thank you in a very, very soft tone after he said his "Humpt!" He was an excellent mechanic as that was his line of work with the U.S. government shipyard across the bay in Coronado. Often he would tune up my car and do whatever was necessary to keep it running well, all for free, even paying for the parts himself. We got along fine. I always thanked him for the kind things he did for me and as usual he replied with his "Humpt!"

After a few visits, Dorothy's parents made a point to let me know that I was welcome to visit any time. I became aware that there were other boys calling Dorothy for a date or just coming over to visit, which I was not happy about. She went out a few times with others but from what Dorothy's younger sister Rosie told me, not with the same guy twice. Her dating others eventually stopped when I stopped coming over and started dating other girls. Shortly afterwards, at one of the social events at church, she said to me, "Tom, I haven't seen much of you lately. I kind of miss our talks together and sharing your knowledge and, of course, your jokes and humor!" Naturally, I was flattered to hear her say that, but I also had been thinking that I really hadn't gotten out of the TB sanitarium that long ago, about a year, and was still under the doctor's care, and I shouldn't take any girls seriously at this point. With that in mind, I felt secure enough to ask if I could take her out for dinner and home after the event. She answered with a bright smile and said, "Yes, if you promise that we'll keep in touch from here on!"

We had dinner in a little Italian restaurant that was located in the Italian district of town, near the waterfront. It was a quaint place with a trellis in the ceiling intertwined with artificial grape vines that looked so real, with hanging wine bottles. Each table had a large lighted candle, and music was provided by a strolling accordion player singing songs like "Solo Mio" and "Come Back to Sorrento." I ordered lasagna and she, meatballs and spaghetti. It was one of those evenings where eating and talking just lingered on and on. We spent over two hours just picking our food and talking, mostly sharing our dreams and where we saw our lives going in the next few years. Obviously, we were falling in love, but didn't want to admit it to each other. The night passed all too quickly and when I took Dorothy home, we kissed goodnight, our first kiss since meeting about a month earlier. That kiss sealed my love for her.

All night I wondered how I was going to handle her going away to college. The next morning, after a restless night, I called her to take her to lunch, and maybe to apologize for my boldness the night before. She answered the phone with her normally pleasant voice and I told her I'd like to take her to have lunch in a typical Mexican restaurant in Logan Heights where they made good homemade tamales and *carne asada* tacos. With enthusiasm, she asked me to explain what they were and how they were made as she was very fond of different types of ethnic foods, and since there were no Mexican restaurants that she knew of in Hawaii, she had never eaten Mexican food before.

I learned quickly that Dorothy was not a fussy eater. She immediately liked the tamales and tacos that she ate and wanted to try everything, including a fresh jalapeño chile. When she asked what it was and how it tasted, with a slight grin, I said, "It's a Mexican strawberry and it has a kind of a sweet and sour taste. It's one of the favorite fruit of the Mexican people. Try it!" I sat back trying to look innocent.

She took one big bite, chewed a couple of times and then gasped, choked, and spit it into her napkin. She quickly drank some water and with her eyes tearing, said, "Tom, you rascal, you tricked me! Now you owe me one. How can I make you pay? Yes, you've got to come over to my house sometime so I can cook you a dinner, and you must eat every bit of it!"

"How about tomorrow?" I said.

She cooked that dinner, consisting of Chinese and Japanese dishes that she learned from her grandmother, Ah Po. It turned out Dorothy was an excellent cook. And our playful joking created greater intimacy between us. Many times during our 48 years of marriage, Dorothy laughingly would refer to that incident as the Mexican strawberry joke.

It had been about four months since we met. And during that time, except at the beginning, we saw each other practically daily, spending time going places, sharing thoughts and ideas, and of course, eating out a lot. I would normally pick her up in late morning and bring her home before midnight.

In the middle of August, while I was mentioning that she would be leaving soon to go to UC Berkeley, she interrupted me and shocked me by saying, "Tom, I decided that I won't accept that scholarship and I will attend San Diego State instead! Besides, that scholarship is for tuition only, and does not cover any living expenses and I don't want to burden my parents with those expenses. I've been studying the catalog for San Diego State and they have all the preliminary courses I need for my work toward becoming a pediatrician!" After a long pause, she went on to say, "If I went away, we wouldn't be seeing each other anymore, except maybe on rare occasions. Aside from that, people tell me that San Diego State is an excellent school!"

I tried to read between the lines of what she said. I was pleasantly surprised, happy, and confused. Mostly happy and pleasantly surprised.

Dorothy enrolled at San Diego State and attended for a year. We saw each other just about every day. I would pick her up after school and many times we'd go to the main library for Dorothy to do research for her studies, then go out to dinner and spend time visiting friends and family. During this time, we got serious enough to where we shared each other's views and opinions on how to raise kids.

I told her, "I want to have at least five, and maybe even seven!"

She replied, with a bit of teasing, "Oh, your poor wife, how can she handle so many? Poor thing!"

I quickly responded, "Please, 'no poor thing,' these kids can very well be yours too!"

Dorothy gasped, covered her mouth with both hands, closed her eyes, held that position for a moment, then threw her arms around me and said, "I've always loved children. That's why I wanted to be a pediatrician. If I can have so many of my own, I don't need to be one!" I suddenly realized that I indirectly proposed and I didn't mean to at this time. I'd always thought I'd propose in a more pleasant and romantic setting, like with the sun setting, at a fancy restaurant on a terrace overlooking the San Diego Bay with soft background music playing.

Grandfather Hom Fung, arrived in America from China in 1884.

In re
Hom Chong,
Minor son resident Chinese merchant.

--oOo--

State of California, }
                     } SS.
County of San Diego. }

We, the undersigned, being first duly and severally sworn upon oath, each for himself and not one for the other, do depose and say:-

That we are acquainted with Hom Fung, who makes the foregoing affidavit, and whose photograph is attached hereto. That the said Hom Fung is a merchant lawfully domiciled and resident in the City of San Diego, State of California, and engaged in business therein as a member of the firm of Hong Far & Co., which said firm is engaged in buying and selling and dealing in merchandise at a fixed place of business, towit:- No. 1135 "J" Street, in the said City of San Diego.

That the said Hom Fung has been a merchant and a member of the said firm for more than one year last past, and during the said time has engaged in the performance of no manual labor except such as was necessary in the conduct of his business as such merchant.

And we do fu[...]
the said Hom Fung for t[...]
good.

Signature.

Subscribed and sworn t[...]
this 11 day of January[...]

My father, Hom Chong (David Hom), arrived in America from China at age 15, in 1909.

In re
Hom Chong,
Minor son of Resident Chinese merchant.

--oOo--

State of California, }
                     } SS.
County of San Diego. }

Hom Fung, being first duly sworn upon oath, doth depose and say:-

That affiant is a merchant lawfully domiciled and resident in the City of San Diego, State of California, and engaged in business therein as a member of the firm of Hong Far & Co., which said firm is engaged in buying and selling and dealing in merchandise at a fixed place of business, towit:- No. 1135 "J" Street, in the said City of San Diego.

That affiant has been a merchant and a member of the said firm for more than one year last past, and during the said time has engaged in the performance of no manual labor except such as was necessary in the conduct of his business as such merchant.

That affiant makes this affidavit in order to identify Hom Chong, as his son. That the said Hom Chong is the lawful son of affiant, and is a minor. That the said Hom Chong is now in China, but that he is lawfully entitled to admission into the United States, and that he is now about to come to the United States to take up his residence therein with affiant.

譚傳

Subscribed and sworn to before me,
this 23 day of January, A. 1909.

A Blochman
Notary Public,
In and for the County of San Diego,
State of California.

1

My father, Hom Chong (David Hom).

Mother and me, age 2.

Church picnic, 1932, after Mother passed away. L to R: Allen, Wellman, Father holding Herb, me, and James.

My father and second mother Ah Nuing with my six siblings. L to R: Allen, Herb, Helen, James, Albert, Wellman, and me.

Me at 17, ready to make a delivery for the David Produce Company.

Brothers in front of David Produce Company, 1959. L to R: Me, Herb, James, and Albert.

Annual David Produce Company picnic 1966, employees and their families; I'm on the far right holding cowboy hat.

In front of our 6-bedroom house in North Park. L to R: siblings Beatrice, Paul, John; second row, Margaret, George, Wellman; third row, Albert, Helen, me.

Quarantined at Vauclain Tuberculosis Sanitarium when I had TB. Here I am looking over Mission `Valley, 1950.

My Sunday School 2nd graders at the Chinese Community Church. I think at times they knew more than I did, 1947.

Dorothy, age 5, in Honolulu, Hawaii —
always vivacious with her aloha spirit.

Three generations: Dorothy,
her grandmother, Apo, and
our oldest daughter, Nora.

Dorothy and me on one of our
first dates to Balboa Park.

Wedding Day and a new beginning —
Dorothy and me.

On an honorary cruise aboard the world's oldest sailing ship, Star of India, to memorialize Dorothy. L to R: Jennifer, Nora, Winthrop, Cindy, Gayle, me, and Phyllis.

Family at 2013 San Diego County Women's Hall of Fame event posthumously honoring Dorothy.

Co-founder and Manager of the Southeast Little League with Assistant Carlos Hinojosa. I am standing in the back row, far right.

Winthrop, our fourth child, born at a clinic in Culiacan, Mexico, 1958. The complete medical bill including doctor and nurse came to only $48 U.S. dollars.

Our first crop of eggplant ready to harvest at the 1,100 acre farm in Culiacan, Mexico.

Members of the Hom Family Association San Diego meeting to raise funds for the Chinese school (back row, second from the left — my father, David Hom), 1928.

East West Optimist Club, Co-founder and Charter President, 1960. I'm seated third from left.

Campaigning with my brothers for San Diego City Council. L to R: Albert, John, George, Wellman, James, me, Paul, Herb, and Allen.

With some of my dedicated campaign volunteers who helped get me elected to the San Diego City Council.

Sworn in as the first minority Councilmember in the City of San Diego, 1963.

A young politician with his family. L to R: me, Winthrop, Dorothy, Cindy, Phyllis, dog Tippy, Gayle, Jennifer, Nora.

Task Force Chairman to build the San Diego Stadium, called the Qualcomm Stadium today.

I shared the podium with Martin Luther King, Jr. at the Bethel Baptist Church in San Diego, 1964.

Being entertained by the Children's Choir of Hong Kong at San Diego City Hall when I was Deputy Mayor.

Among my greatest honors was receiving an invitation to be Commencement Speaker at Grambling College, Louisiana, 1967.

Speaking with Grambling College students after delivering commencement speech.

First day as California State Assemblyman.

Honorary Speaker of the Day in the California State Assembly.

Discussing local and State issues with Richard Nixon.

With President Richard Nixon, who offered me a position in the White House.

Governor Ronald Reagan signing my "Compensatory Education Bill" — largest of its kind in the country.

Co-chairing a fundraiser for Mayor Pete Wilson's run for the U.S. Senate (L to R: daughter Phyllis, me, Mayor Pete Wilson, and daughter Cindy).

The Gaslamp District. Photo courtesy of
San Diego History Center.

Dorothy and me being honored by the
Centre City Development Corporation
(CCDC) for our contribution in the
development of the Gaslamp Quarter
and the Asian Pacific Thematic
Historic District.

The General Plan for the Gaslamp Quarter.

Of course, before any formal announcement of our engagement, I met with Dorothy's parents. When I asked for their daughter's hand, the first thing her father said was, "You mean she's not going to finish school? Humpt!"

That caught me off guard, and the only thing I could think of saying was, "Ahhh ... when we settle down she might go back!"

In spite of that awkward moment, I felt that he was happy for us; he just didn't know how to express it. The mother was elated and congratulated me and gave me a big hug.

We made the formal announcement a couple of weeks later. For the engagement and wedding rings, I bought them at Kay's Jewelers for $110 with $15 down, and monthly payments of $7.50. For Dorothy's wedding dress, she preferred to make it herself, a high collar Chinese-style *cheong-saum* in white with silver floral designs. It turned out beautifully.

Dorothy was 19 and I was 24 as we planned for our future married life together.

CHAPTER 23

The Honeymoon

AFTER 20 YEARS OF DEMOCRATIC PRESIDENTS, A REPUBLICAN WAS ELECTED TO THE WHITE HOUSE IN 1952. WAR HERO GENERAL DWIGHT D. EISENHOWER WAS ELECTED PRESIDENT OF THE UNITED STATES AND SENATOR RICHARD NIXON, VICE PRESIDENT.

IT WAS THE YEAR DOROTHY AND I WERE MARRIED. OUR WEDDING took place on May 20th and was held at the Mission Hills Congregational Church with about 200 attending. Relatives and friends helped prepare food for the reception at the church. Dorothy and I decided that we would pay for the wedding ourselves, and with the help of siblings and friends, it cost less than $200.

The wedding went off quite well. We had a little problem earlier though. A month prior to the wedding we had decided to go to Mexico City for the honeymoon. Dorothy was very excited about that, as she had never been there and had heard so much about it. When I made the reservation for the airfare and hotel I was told that Mexico City didn't have any available hotel rooms because the International Rotary Convention was being held there at the same time as our planned honeymoon trip. When I told Dorothy that, she teared up, for she really had her heart set on going there. I felt so badly for her that I outright said, chivalrously, "Dorothy, we are going to Mexico City regardless, even if we have to seek a room in a private home or sleep on a park bench. Life has lots of flexibilities!"

The San Diego Airport did not have a flight to Mexico City then. The nearest one was through the Tijuana Airport in Mexico about 20 miles away, and the other was the Los Angeles Airport. Mexicana Airlines flew out of both, but flying out of Tijuana was about one-third cheaper than

Dorothy and my Wedding Day. Dorothy sewed her own dress, a Chinese Cheongsam, for ten dollars. L to R: Dorothy's parents, Sam and Leona Akana, me, Ah Nuing and brother James.

flying out of L.A. So, after the wedding, a caravan of cars drove us down to the Tijuana Airport for our 10 p.m. flight. As we arrived at the airport, a fog started to roll in. Soon it was announced that the plane would not take off until the fog lifted. Of course, we waited and waited, and eventually our caravan of friends had to leave for home, and left us alone on the airport bench. We waited until about 7 a.m. before the fog lifted and then we took off.

When I think of the many stories about the romantic period of the wedding night, I think of how we spent our first night together on the airport bench. I had, however, twice suggested to Dorothy, that we get a room at a nearby motel and get a little sleep, and have the clerk call us when the fog lifted. She'd say, "No, Tom, the fog will lift soon enough. Probably very soon!" In later years, I would tease her of her first night wedding jitters.

During the flight we got acquainted with a couple of Mexican businessmen from Ensenada, a port city south of Tijuana, and told them about our dilemma in not being able to book a hotel room because of the large International Rotary Convention. They suggested that we should stay where they're staying, called the Hotel Avenida, a small excellent business hotel.

When we landed after about 12 hours, with four stops, our newly found business friends called the hotel and made arrangements for us, a penthouse, for only $2 a day, at the price of a regular room. The penthouse was first-class nice, and the businessmen went out of their way to help us get settled, and, on top of that, the hotel people knew we were honeymooners and treated us royally. Romantic Mexico!

A few days later the Rotary convention was over and first-class hotel rooms were then available at $4 to $5 per day. But we weren't interested for we couldn't have had it any better than what we already had. That was serendipity!

The honeymoon was great and adventurous. We returned home from Mexico City after 14 days to settle at our Hom family home, occupying the third floor penthouse where I stayed. It wasn't as nice and fancy as the one at the Hotel Avenida in Mexico City, but we didn't care, for at that age and stage in life, we felt we could adjust to anything and could confront any problems that would occur. And besides, the rent was free and my family all loved Dorothy and she loved them as well.

Since Dorothy's college education was deferred to a later date, she decided to get a job with the Pacific Telephone Company as a company representative. After several interviews, she was put into a department where normally more experienced and mature people would be placed. She trained for four weeks and adjusted very well into it, making many new friends along the way. That's Dorothy, a hard worker with an affectionate personality.

As for me, I had to settle down and start concentrating my efforts in the real estate business. I felt that was my future. I did that in the daytime. And in the evenings, I would work at David Produce to help take orders from customers and also work with the receiving farmers bringing in their produce for the next day's business. With both of us working, our goal was to save enough, hopefully within two years, to buy our own home. My further goal was to have a family and eventually open my own real estate office.

VII. Entrepreneurship

AGES 25 TO 30

My first real estate office in Logan Heights, San Diego, with wife Dorothy and daughter Nora.

CHAPTER 24

A Partnership

L IVING AT HOME AFTER OUR MARRIAGE HAD A NUMBER OF advantages, like having the privacy of our own penthouse on the third floor all to ourselves, and, with no rent, the opportunity to start our savings for a place of our own. The penthouse wasn't fancy, but comfortable and spacious, and with a view that covered much of the 1,500 acres of Balboa Park and the downtown skyline. Since Dorothy got along very well with my mother Ah Nuing before our marriage, they became even better friends after our marriage.

I think a lot had to do with Dorothy's understanding of broken English, as that was the way Ah Nuing spoke. Many Chinese immigrants spoke English that way. Dorothy, being from Hawaii, understood it quite well and could return that broken English talk, called Pidgin, very easily. The two of them sometimes would have lengthy talks that way. It was quite amusing to me that Dorothy could turn to broken English so well, especially knowing that she had attended a special English Standard high school in Hawaii and spoke proper English. Later I learned that her grandmother spoke Pidgin, and that's why Dorothy could switch over so easily. And besides, Pidgin English was when people combined two languages and it was not uncommon among the islanders, Dorothy explained to me.

My mother Ah Nuing was always a busy person; she was seldom ever idle. She always had a large garden of flowers and vegetables to tend, cooking for a large family, and at the same time she would help a friend who had a laundry down the street from us, working four days a week, six hours a day. It was a fun place for her, too, as many of the workers there were also from the same village back home in China, which created a lot of camaraderie. They would enjoy playing Chinese opera music while they worked.

After a little over a year of our marriage, Ah Nuing excitedly came to Dorothy and told her that she had just heard that a small family grocery store was up for sale and she wanted to see it. If she bought it, she wanted Dorothy to be her partner. For a moment Dorothy was dumbfounded. Ah Nuing said, "Dolatee, you no put any money in, I buy it! You help me and you my partner!" Dorothy later that night told me that Ah Nuing was so excited about the store that she did not have the heart to tell her that she was thankful for her generosity, but she was not interested in working in a grocery store. She also felt that once Ah Nuing's enthusiasm in buying the store would slacken, she would most likely change her mind.

The next day, Saturday, I was recruited to drive Ah Nuing, who was all excited, and Dorothy to see the store. The store was located at the corner of 32nd and Market Street, a low income, racially mixed neighborhood, with no major grocery stores within two miles. When we arrived, I found out that it was owned by Herb and Anne Lowe, friends from church. The store was named Lowe's Market and was busy as a beehive. Aside from the grocery section, it had a little butcher shop, produce section, freezer, etc. The floor space was about three-fourths the size of a 7-Eleven store, plus it had a storage room, and a very nice two-bedroom apartment in the back of the store, with a huge fenced backyard.

Anne Lowe was good enough to show us around, in spite of how busy they were. As she pointed out the store operation, the volume of sales and what one can make of it. I could tell my mother was beginning to become more and more interested in becoming a grocery store tycoon. "Oh no," I said to myself, "I think she is getting serious about buying the store." I literally crossed my fingers that she wouldn't do it.

After about an hour of looking and asking questions, Dorothy asked Anne if she could see the sales records and the profit and loss statements. Anne took us to the back apartment and brought out her business records. After quickly reviewing them, Dorothy asked Anne why they were selling the business, since it seemed to be doing so well. Anne said, "Herb and I had been in the clothing business for over 20 years, with the San Diego Toggery store in downtown, and we miss that kind of work. We recently came across a nice clothing store that was for sale, a well-established business by an elderly couple that had it for over 20 years and wanted to retire. We have already negotiated a price, but cannot buy it until we sell this store! If you're interested in this store, we will sell it to you for the low price of $2,500 plus the cost of the inventory." My mother, with a straight face, paused, bit her lip, and said, "Let me think about it!" We thanked Anne and left.

On the way home, Ah Nuing again reiterated that she would put up the money and Dorothy would be her partner, splitting the profits between them. She went on to say, almost pleadingly, "Dolatee, at the store I can learn more English, but I cannot read it. I need you to help!"

Dorothy, who felt close to Ah Nuing, responded, "Don't worry, Ah Nuing, if you want the store we'll see what we can work out!" With those remarks, I realized that my life was about to take another change. Can't say for better or worse, but a big change.

That evening, in the privacy of our modest penthouse, we discussed the day's events. After sorting out the pros and cons of buying the store, Dorothy did say something that influenced me towards the purchase. She said, "Tom, you know, we've been married for about a year and a half now, and we always talked about starting a family early enough to have five or six kids, and even maybe seven. With that apartment in the back of the store, it'll give us a good start. Besides, splitting the profits with Ah Nuing would give me about twice what I am making at the telephone company. We can save quickly enough for you to open your own real estate office when you become a broker, which will be in about a year!" Then she went on to add, with deep concern, "Besides, Tom, Ah Nuing has been good to me, letting us live here for over a year at no cost. I do want to help now that she needs me!" I always knew Dorothy was a practical and caring person, and this told it all in a nutshell.

A few days later after more discussion between Dorothy and Ah Nuing, they decided to make an offer to Herb and Anne Lowe for the store business, of $2,000 plus the cost of the inventory. The offer was accepted, and escrow was opened. During the process of getting the paperwork done, I took Dorothy and Ah Nuing each morning to the store to learn from Herb and Anne how to operate it. They were taught how to order goods from the wholesalers, how to price the different items, and the different cuts of meats. They were introduced to the regular customers, and learned other ins and outs about running a Ma and Pa grocery store. They were both excited about going into this new business venture and went into this with much anticipation, realizing it would take long hours of hard work seven days a week, from 8 a.m. to 8 p.m.

Dorothy and Ah Nuing made a good team. With Dorothy helping, Ah Nuing quickly picked up her English. She began speaking with less Pidgin accent and could hold short conversations with customers. They both would go around the store, with Dorothy pointing and naming each item and having Ah Nuing repeat it several times. Within a short time, with her strong desire to learn, she came to know each product by name. There were some items she had trouble pronouncing, like watermelon and cauliflower, items with four syllables.

Running the store became a family affair. In the beginning, they had me cutting the meats in the mornings before leaving to work in the real estate business. In the evenings I would work at David Produce taking orders from customers. It was a three job schedule, but I didn't mind because it was part of building for the future. My sister Helen, who was then going to San Diego State, would help out on weekends. During Christmas holidays, my two younger brothers, George, 15, and Johnny, 14, would set up Christmas trees to sell in front of the store.

Since we had such a big backyard, I bought a German Shepherd puppy, something I always wanted, and named him Bruno. Also, I found a new hobby in raising parakeets, so I built two large cages that held about 100 of these love birds. Soon I had so many demands from people who wanted to buy a pair that I decided to turn this hobby into a small business. Parakeets at that time were quite the rage.

After about a year of being in the grocery business, and everything going quite well, Ah Nuing, decided to change her schedule from five days a week to two days a week at the store and two days a week at the laundry where she used to work. She said she missed her friends there, the Chinese lunches, and the Chinese operas that they played from records all day long while they worked. She also missed working in her garden at home. With that in mind, she suggested that Dorothy give her only one-fourth of the profits and that would be sufficient. It wasn't long, about two months later, she decided to turn the store over to Dorothy altogether and go back to her original four days a week at the laundry. Dorothy understood, for friends and cultural ties were important to Ah Nuing.

Dorothy suggested to Ah Nuing that when I got my real estate broker's license and established my own business and was doing well enough, we might be selling the store. And in so doing she would pay Ah Nuing back for all the money she had invested, and split half the profits from the sale. Ah Nuing was more than delighted to hear that, and exclaimed, "Dolatee, you are a nice partner and nice Chinese girl!" Dorothy, being part Chinese and Irish, always felt much closer to being Chinese, so being referred to as a Chinese girl was a great compliment to Dorothy. Sometimes, though, when Dorothy got mad about something, she would defer to her Irish side, eyes blazing, temper in check, saying, "Boy, that really gets my Irish up!"

Prior to Ah Nuing's decision to leave the store, Dorothy and I began talking about starting a family. With our intent to eventually have a large family of at least five or more children, Dorothy, for all practical purposes, would become a full-time mother and, in due time, would have to leave the store. It would be up to Dorothy to decide when that sale should be. We did not set a timetable.

With Ah Nuing now gone from the store, I got more regularly involved. I really didn't mind, but it did cut into my efforts in the real estate business, an area that I was determined to make succeed. I also continued to help in the evenings at David Produce. Long hours and lots of work sound a bit overwhelming, but when one is young and ambitious to carve out a life of success, it's not too big of a task, and besides, working 8 a.m. to 5 p.m. has never quite agreed with me. One thing about being in our own business, we always managed to find a little free time here and there to relax and joke around with others during the workday.

To replace Ah Nuing, Dorothy hired additional help, a loyal customer, Lola Baca. She was a good worker, but occasionally we would have trouble with her husband, Enrique, when he drank a little too much beer. Sometimes he would become boisterous around the store and act like he was part owner. Aside from that, sometimes at home he would beat up Lola, leaving her with bruises, and once, a black eye. There were times when she was afraid to go home, so Dorothy had her stay overnight with her two small children at our apartment. The next day, when Enrique was sober, he would come over and beg Lola to come home and offered apologies to us for the problems he had caused. Enrique was really not such a bad guy when he was sober, which was only half the time. In due time, we had to let Lola go. But we still kept her family on the "Okay to give credit to" list. Enrique always paid his grocery bills by bringing in his weekly check for us to cash. We never lost a dime on him.

To replace Lola, we hired another customer, a widowed lady named Mrs. Hubbard. She was a friendly, motherly type, very outgoing, who stayed with us until we sold the store about two years later. With Mrs. Hubbard living only a block away, she was always willing to work extra time if we needed her. We also had a teenage boy, Roberto, working part time stacking up canned goods and moving things around. Aside from that, most of my siblings were always willing to help whenever needed, so labor-wise we were pretty well set. Dorothy, in her competent way, did all the supply ordering and administrating, along with taking care of the customers.

At this point I was anxious to move on and focus more on the real estate business. My two years of apprenticeship working as a real estate salesman were fulfilled, so I studied to take the California Real Estate Broker's License exam. As soon as I could, I took the exam and about four weeks later I was notified that I had passed. Dorothy and I were elated and that evening we went out for dinner at one of our favorite restaurants, Anthony's Seafood, down by the bay overlooking the harbor. Most of our talk that evening was about the coming baby and the establishing of my own real estate office.

With what savings we'd been making, mostly from my real estate sales as an agent and the profits that Dorothy shared in the grocery store, we were able to start looking around for a good location to set up the real estate office. From my viewpoint, I was going into business to make a living and to provide a future for my family, and at the same time try to right some of the wrongs regarding the discriminatory issues in our society. Due to the racial deed restrictions and discrimination in general, having an office in a higher-end neighborhood would not be practical. I knew in time these issues would change for the better, for there were too many good people of all races working for equal rights. But at this point, my priority was to establish myself in business to support Dorothy and a coming child.

After scouting around town for several weeks, I finally zeroed into an area in the newer section of southeast San Diego, with communities named Southcrest, Valencia Park, Encanto, Citrus Heights, and parts of National City. These areas in 1954 consisted of average income wage earners, and were about 90 percent Caucasian and 10 percent minorities. The building address was 1246 South 43rd Street, with some very nice areas for offices in the front of the building and in the back was a two-bedroom apartment, almost similar to the grocery store, but nicer. It also had a large backyard for Bruno and additional space in the front for parking and advertising signs. It was ideal for us. With limited funds and just starting out, we would have to pinch on our personal needs in order to get the office ready. That would include a new paint job for the building, inside and out, furnishing, equipment, and a free-standing steel pole supporting a rather large electric sign out front, with Thomas Hom Realty in big letters.

The owners of the building, a nice elderly couple, were eager for me to succeed, and kind enough to give me two months free rent in order for me to get the offices ready. On the lease, they offered to charge me only $55 per month for the first six months, and thereafter $75 per month. I thought that was a real bargain, especially since that included the two-bedroom apartment. We signed a five-year lease, paying the first and last months' rent in advance. With that accomplished, I felt good. That was part of phase two of my real estate plan. The first phase had been to get my real estate broker license. Now it was time to start planning and working on improving the property. I figured it would be about a two to three month job. It was about then we started thinking of selling the grocery store.

Alas! A couple of weeks later, things began happening much quicker than I had expected. We got an inquiry that someone might be interested in buying our grocery store. It was from a friend to whom I had sold a house about a year earlier, Mr. Foo Wong. He telephoned and said, "Tom, I have a friend who recently moved in from Phoenix, Arizona, with his family and is looking for a small business to buy, like a small grocery store!" And he went on to say, "My friend used to live in New York City, where he said the schools were not very good for his children, and winters were too cold, so he moved to Phoenix, where the schools were good, but the weather in the summers were too scorching hot, so he moved to San Diego where the schools are good and the weather near perfect!" That seemed to make sense.

Then I asked my friend Foo Wong how he heard about the store being for sale and he said he had a friend in the laundry business who had told him, which he heard from another friend in another laundry business. I would say it probably originated from my mother Ah Nuing, mentioning it during her work at her friend's laundry. There must have been at least 75 Chinese laundries in town and they had their own grapevine of circulating news. I once heard someone say that to get news out to the Chinese community, "Don't telegram … don't telephone … just tell a Chinese!" It was cheaper than advertising in the newspaper, and faster.

Foo Wong inquired about the price and when his friend could see the store. All this caught me by surprise, so I had to think quickly, as I didn't want to quote a price that I would regret later. Aside from that, I needed to coordinate this with Dorothy, as she was the one who needed to be satisfied with the price as well as the timing of the sale. Besides, I hadn't even gotten half of the things in order to get my office ready for business. With Dorothy being pregnant, we also had to get the apartment in the back of the new office completed and ready to move into.

With a moment of hesitation, I replied, "Ahhhh, Foo, my wife Dorothy is in charge and I will need to check with her on the price and when we can sell it! I'll let you know!" I'm not sure whether he believed me or not since he was from the old country, where Chinese men didn't like to admit that the wife was in charge. But in a way, Dorothy was absolutely in charge. Since she was pregnant, it was absolutely up to her to decide the best time to sell and move, along with other matters, like keeping me calm. Our first baby was due in about three months, in August, and it felt so soon.

That evening Dorothy and I discussed the selling of the store. We realized that if we had a buyer ready to make a deal, we would need to move faster to get my office ready, and especially the back apartment ready to move into. Knowing that a sale would take about 60 days to close escrow, we'd have to move quickly. The next day I called Foo Wong and told him that we could show his friend the store to see if he was really interested. I gave the price and some of the particulars. He said he knew the location, as he had already driven his friend around the area when he heard it was for sale. We made an appointment for the following week on a Friday morning.

The following week came quickly, and on Friday morning Foo Wong brought his friend and his wife, Mr. and Mrs. Jung Wah Thin. I was there with Dorothy to greet them. We exchanged pleasantries about our families and offered tea and coffee before we discussed business. That seemed to be the formality one would go through in a Chinese business transaction. Since these potential buyers were from China, I thought it wouldn't hurt to be a little traditional. I had seen my father do this a number of times, especially with first time meetings.

One thing Dorothy and I were quite surprised about was that the prospective buyers, Mr. and Mrs. Jung, hardly spoke English, and of course, nor could they read or write it. My first thought was how could they run a store when all the customers spoke only English, or perhaps Spanish? But that didn't seem to bother them. In that split moment, I fleetingly thought of my dad and the many other Chinese who had come to this country, as well as to other parts of the world, and who had done well in business without first knowing the local language. I guess one can call that adaptability! So I just let that concern pass.

We gave Mr. and Mrs. Jung a tour of the store, told them what was included with the sale, showed the financial reports, what the rent was, and answered many questions that they asked. After about an hour, they went outside and conferred among themselves. Finally we came to the price. I told them $5,000 plus the inventory, the same as had I told Foo Wong earlier. Then they asked that if they should buy the store, would we be willing to stay in the back apartment at no cost to us, for 30 to 60 days after the close of escrow. They wanted us to help train them to run the store. That was fine with us, since the office and apartment would not be ready before the close of escrow. Following that, Mr. Jung asked in his broken English if we would accept an offer of $4,000 plus the cost of the inventory. I mentally calculated that it still gave us an additional profit of $2,000 from what we paid. That seemed reasonable, because we had built up the business since we bought it.

Like I had learned in the produce business where a lot of negotiating took place, I hemmed and hawed, bit my lip, and said, "Mr. Jung, we haven't had the chance to show the store to anyone else yet, let my wife and me think about it!"

There was a pause, then Mr. Jung's wife cried out in Pidgin English, "We likee. We payee $4,500!" A pause.

Then Dorothy popped up and said in a firm voice, "That's fine, we'll take it!" I looked at Mr. Jung, and he looked at me. We both smiled, and nodded our heads. It was funny how we men had started the negotiation and the women finalized it, just like that.

At that point, we adjourned to the back apartment and outlined a Memorandum of Understanding so we could take it to escrow to process the sale. The following Monday, together we went to the escrow company to set up the terms of the sale, and also started the process of making the necessary license applications and transfer of permits. About two weeks later we had the Jungs come in daily to learn, hands on, the operation of the store. This was all new to them, so it took some patience, with their limited English and all, but it was enjoyable working with them. They had a teenage daughter, Joanie, who also came along to learn. She was a typical Chinese American youngster, bright and full of enthusiasm. The Jungs were quick learners, and in no time they were working like seasoned grocers. Their four children, very Americanized, were a great help. It was a typical immigrant family all gung-ho pulling together.

During the escrow period while we were helping at the store, at the store, our first child was born. Doctor Viola Erlanger delivered Nora Faye Hom, a bouncing baby girl of 6 pounds 9 ounces, on August 20, 1953, at Mercy Hospital. This indeed was a new beginning for us in more than one way. Not only was this the arrival of our first child, but the first business of my own, and also we were moving into a new home. I felt challenged by this new phase of our lives.

Shortly after the close of escrow, Dorothy and I continued to help with the details of running the market as we had agreed to do, but since the Jungs had caught on so quickly, we were free to move on sooner to our new real estate office and apartment. It had been a good deal for both families. The Jungs, with their four children helping, kept the grocery store for about 15 years and did quite well, retiring and living comfortably on their investments in real estate. Their success once again reminded me of the business adaptability of Chinese immigrants in a new environment.

With the sale of the grocery store, we returned all the money that Ah Nuing initially invested, plus the profits from the sale. She was happy with that, but shared with Dorothy that she felt badly to have left the store so early and leaving Dorothy with the responsibility of running it. Dorothy responded, "Ah Nuing, don't feel badly about it. While running the store I learned a lot about business and people, and we also were able to earn and save some money so that Tom can now open his real estate business! I want to thank you for having me as your partner!" With that said, Ah Nuing gave Dorothy a big hug.

CHAPTER 25

A New Opening

I N 1945, WHEN JAMES AND I WERE FULLTIME AT DAVID PRODUCE, we had to formalize the company as to its partnership for government permits, reports, and licenses. Our partnership was structured so that James held 60 percent and I held 40 percent. In 1954, when I was no longer actively involved in David Produce, except for policy meetings and such, I decided to give 30 percent of my 40 percent to my two younger brothers who were working in the business full-time. Herbert received 15 percent, Albert received 15 percent, and I retained 10 percent.

I wasn't being noble. I was being realistic, because they were full-time and I wasn't, and I could now focus on my new priorities, being a good family man and starting my own real estate business.

I think one of the high points in a young couple's life is working together on a new venture. For Dorothy, this meant being a full-time mother to Nora, and to another in about a year, and another until we had our five or six as we dreamingly planned when we first married. This was especially dear to her heart as she loved children so much. And as for me, I was excited that at last I had my own business, and I was looking forward to the challenges that came with it. We quickly started to do our planning.

With most of our savings having gone into preparing ourselves for this new beginning to get the office and apartment ready, like buying furniture for the apartment as we left our old furniture with the sale of the store, we had to economize wherever we could. One thing that saved us money was a $10 used stove that was offered to us from one of our new neighbors, who had bought a new one. For added furnishings for the apartment and office, I built shelves and bookcases, and installed new light fixtures, along with putting up some clothes lines for drying clothes and diapers. A clothes dryer was too expensive for us back then, but it was on top of Dorothy's wish list. We did, however, have a washing machine. All and all, I estimated that we had enough funds saved to keep us going for about six to seven months without relying on any income from the real estate business. But deep down, I felt confident that we would be generating income within three to four months, as I was already getting a number of people who wanted to buy a home or invest in real estate. Dorothy was always helpful, making time to create a beautiful flower garden on a strip of land in front of the office, which gave it a nice homey look.

Along with the priorities of getting the office equipped, I splurged in buying a hand cranking mimeograph-printing machine. As a guy who believed in advertising, an essential part of my business plan was to target my specific areas instead of advertising in a general circulation newspaper, which would have been expensive. Within a month of leaving the store, we were ready to open my office. At last! High hopes! But even at that young age, I knew nothing would come easily, that there would be pitfalls along the way, but because I was young, I felt I could always recover. What's that old saying? "We fall to rise!"

To announce my office opening, I sent out notices to friends and relatives, and posted them in churches and neighborhood grocery stores. I also made sure that the notices were sent to Asian American communities and organizations, for many of them now were in the financial position to buy houses and to invest in real estate. At that time, there were only two persons of Asian descent in the real estate business: myself and a Filipino American friend named Chris Cantos, a retired U.S. Naval Chief Petty Officer with 30 years of Navy service. He worked alone, had a small office on Market Street, and said that he just needed a place to hang his hat and to take care of some of his own apartment units. Nice guy!

Lo and behold, within one month of my announcement of the office opening I was deluged with calls and potential customers. Shortly after, I had to hire additional sales persons, and within three months, I had four on the staff, plus a part-time secretary. Up to that point, I depended upon Dorothy to do the bookkeeping, but with our baby Nora so active, she practically had to give it up. She did some of it in the evenings when Nora was asleep, but with my business booming she couldn't keep up with it.

As a first time mother, Dorothy had to learn a lot about child raising and caring, which she did through the Dr. Spock baby book. I pitched in too, having put into practice what I learned from helping to raise some of my younger siblings when they were quite small, like diaper changing, feeding, and bathing. These were exciting times.

I credit a lot of this early success to offering my clients the opportunity to buy homes in the newer and better areas of town, which had not been openly available to people of minority background, and mine was the first aggressive effort made to provide this service. The minorities consisted of a large mix of Asians, Pacific Islanders, Latinos, and African-Americans. We also had a few Caucasian clients as well. As time went on, with more minorities moving into the region, some real estate agents were accusing me of "block busting," breaking up a good neighborhood with so called "lower class elements," meaning minorities.

My intention, of course, was to find housing for whoever wanted it, and at the same time, to make a living. Aside from that, I knew the people who were purchasing the houses were good, responsible people. In order for a person of minority background to buy a house and obtain financing, the banks generally required more down payment than normal and also charged a higher interest rate as well. They justified the more stringent terms of borrowing by claiming minority borrowers put them at higher risk. In the 1950s, many banks were simply not interested in making loans to minorities, especially to African-Americans. One banker, with whom I had worked on several loans, told me in a very gentlemanly manner, "Tom, we appreciate your business, but can you not bring in anymore of your nigger clients for a loan? We are not in that type of business!" I was appalled and grossly disappointed by those remarks. Especially since the African-American clients I brought in to him were financially well-qualified people who had provided large down payments and were well established and responsible people in the community.

I responded, "In that case I guess we can't do anymore business together. After all, their money is as green as anybody else's!"

In driving back to the office, I couldn't help but wonder if a Caucasian real estate broker brought in a large number of Chinese applying for loans, would the banker have said the same thing, except saying "Chink" instead of "Nigger!"

With the real estate office doing well and Dorothy pregnant with our second child, we decided to buy a house for our expanding family, since more were to come. We decided to space the pregnancies about one-and-a-half years apart, giving us some relaxing time in between. It really didn't work out that way, for later on Dorothy was saddled down with as many as three in diapers at one time. That, along with cooking, bathing, washing, housekeeping, other chores and doing her church work, was a handful. I suggested several times that we should get some help for her, and she would say, "No, I love what I'm doing. Don't mess it up!" She seemed to thrive on that. The goal of having a large family, five to six kids, seemed to be achievable. The house we bought was just down the street from the office, a very nicely kept, fairly large two bedroom with a spacious backyard with avocado, peach, and apricot trees and several grapevines. We knew we would need a larger place in due time, but because the seller gave us such a good deal, we decided to take it and expand to a larger house later. Or, later add on to it. I really wanted a larger home, but Dorothy nixed that and said, "First things first! As a newer mother, I will be more efficient in a smaller house. We can get a bigger house later!"

IT WASN'T ALWAYS ALL WORK and no play, for within a year of opening the office I got together with several of the neighboring groups to discuss the possibility of starting a Little League for playing baseball. After several meetings, we created a league. I always loved baseball and had played shortstop at San Diego High School. It gave me a chance to give back. Aside from that, it would be good for the young kids to be involved in something, and it would help keep them off the streets. The baseball league was named Southeastern Little League, composed of four teams, with each team having a sponsor to provide uniforms and equipment for the players. I was one of the sponsors; the team I sponsored was named the Tigers.

After the successful formation of the baseball league, I was asked to serve as one of the team managers for the Tigers. I had a couple of assistants, who were a great help in teaching the kids the art of pitching, fielding, strategy, and other aspects of baseball. It was great fun working out with the kids. But a few of the dads with sons on the team ... that's something else! Occasionally we had a dad who would demand that the coach play

CHAPTER 26

Politics, the Art of the Impossible

A FTER BEING IN BUSINESS FOR MYSELF FOR ABOUT FIVE YEARS, and things were going well, I managed to take time off to get involved in more civic matters, such as politics. In this case I got to working with Democratic candidates running for public office, either for City Council, State Assembly, or for Congress. The area where we lived was heavily registered Democrat and I was registered as one too.

One day after being involved for about three years and meeting a lot of the people and learning a lot, I happened to mention to the Democratic Party chairman that one day I would like to run for State Assembly.

The chairman responded with a caring and serious tone, laid his two hands on my shoulders and looked at me and said, "Tom, I think one day you'd make an excellent candidate for an office. But the time isn't now. People are not used to having a minority elected to public office. Perhaps in 10 years things will change. I hope so! But it isn't now!"

I was disappointed to hear him say that, as I wanted some encouragement in my decision to run for office. At that moment I thought of my junior high school principal, Mr. Oakes, who often lectured to us kids, especially the ones from immigrant families, that we were all Americans, we had all the rights like everyone else and that we should go after them. And then I fleetingly thought about my business, real estate, where the restrictions of racial covenants prevented minorities from legally buying until recently. I liked the chairman, and I knew he was well meaning, but I felt let down by his comments and that he was behind the times. I also partly understood his reasoning, as a minority had never before won an election to a public office in San Diego, which had an 85 percent Caucasian population. But that part did not faze me.

Several weeks later at a real estate seminar I met an old friend attending the same class. He used to be in the U.S. Navy, working as an oversight buyer for the Navy Commissaries and now a retired Commander. He had gone into the real estate business too. We had lunch together, talking real estate and everything else, including politics. I related to him my recent disappointing conversation with the Democratic Party chairman about my interest in running for public office one day. He listened and afterwards said, "Tom, I have a friend that you should meet. Don't ask me who he is and what he does, but just trust me. You've got to meet him!"

I said, "Okay," and he set up an appointment two days later.

We went together to a downtown high rise, the Home Federal Tower, and there I met retired Rear Admiral Les Gehres, a nationally known World War II hero who fought many sea battles in the Pacific as the captain of an aircraft carrier. I was not only aware of Admiral Les Gehres' status as a national war hero, but also as a figure in the San Diego County Republican Party, as well. I quickly thought to myself, "Why am I here?"

Before I could think any further, Gehres extended his hand for a handshake and said, "Tom!" in a booming voice, which went with his 6′3″ height and bulldog build., "Ken here told me about your encounter with the Democratic chairman and about your interest in running for public office, and that the chairman said it wasn't time for a minority to do it. It's hog wash! That's what's wrong with the Goddamned Democrats, they put people into categories: Mexicans, Blacks, Chinese, Japanese, Koreans, and Whites too, like Greeks and Italians, and pass judgment as to who can best fit in where and how!" I never thought of that. Then he went on and said, "As far as I'm concerned, the Republican Party don't give a damn who or what you are, as long as you have the guts and character and the will to run. YOU run! Young man, if you're looking to get into politics, this is the party you belong in. If you're willing to work hard and come across in meeting and treating people right, you CAN win!"

I was somewhat taken aback by his frank and colorful description about people and Democrats. As a matter of fact, I kind of enjoyed that, because many of the people I grew up and worked with in the produce business were generally frank and honest and with an in-your-face type of talk. He went on giving me further advice in politics and how one could get started. We were getting ready to leave after spending about an hour of Gehres answering my questions, when he said, "By the way, Tom, call on me any time, here is my card. We want more young people like you!" He reminded me a lot of Principal Oakes, except Oakes was more gentlemanly and used less colorful words.

As we were approaching the door, Admiral Gehres said, "Tom, if you are really interested in one day running for public office, this is a good place to start. I want you to meet some of the good people involved and learn how to get people elected. You will be good for the party and the party will be good for you!" He went on to say, "Nothing is worse than when good people do nothing!" Again, that sounded like Principal Oakes. Gehres was rather gruff, but I liked him, mostly for his frankness and sincerity.

Later I learned that Gehres was an enlisted man in the Navy who worked his way up in the ranks to become a Rear Admiral. Then I understood his rough and tough approach to dealing with people, unlike the more polished and diplomatic ways of most Naval Academy graduates. A short time after, I changed my voter registration to become a Republican.

Meanwhile I did take up his offer to meet with some of the notables in the party, especially candidates for public office and elected Republicans. I eventually ended up working for candidates and learning the hard knocks of running for office. I did most of this during the spare time I could find from my business, as my business was my livelihood and that had to come first. The experience did give me the determination that one day I really did want to run for public office. It was a few years later that I decided to do that.

CHAPTER 27

No Business like Good Business

THE REAL ESTATE BUSINESS HAD NOW BEEN ESTABLISHED FOR several years and was doing well. I decided to do some expansion into small real estate investments, mostly buying older houses, fixer-uppers, which were rundown and needed repairs. I bid out the repair work to a number of friends I had made during my involvement with the Little League, as a lot of them were carpenters, plumbers, cement layers, electricians, and everything else. We started out with one house and later we had up to three to four houses being fixed up at once. I took care not to overextend myself, for I knew the perils of that, as I had seen it happen time and again with business friends. Buying these fixer-uppers was the forerunner of my later years when I bought much larger properties, mostly commercial buildings, partnered with my brothers, and eventually managing to buy up city blocks of properties at a time. All this came much later when I had more experience and capital.

It was the year of 1957 when the Soviet Union shocked the world by sending the first satellite into orbit, circling the globe at 18,000 mph. That year Dorothy and I took on a new challenge in life.

In spite of how busy I was in the real estate business, and doing other things, I always managed to find some time to visit my brothers at the David Produce Company, along with meeting old friends at the different markets. I guess this was one of those things, "You can take the boy out of the produce markets, but you can't take the produce markets out of the boy!"

Well, during this one occasion, it so happened that Charley Iguchi, who managed our company's farming operation of 1,100 acres in Culiacan, Mexico, about 1,200 miles south of the U.S. border, was meeting with my brother James. I sat in with them. Charley reported the problems he had with the operation that year and why it didn't make any money. He explained that the farm still had great potential for big returns. The next farming season would start in September, which was still about three months away. Charley said what he needed was some managerial help, as he was really a farmer working the fields, and not an executive coordinating the entire operation. I listened and was intrigued with the whole discussion.

On the way home I thought about the meeting. When I got home, I shared the problems of the Mexican farm project with Dorothy, along with other things I did that day. Sharing my activities with Dorothy, and she sharing hers with me, was what we did on a regular basis. As the days went by I kept thinking about the Mexico farming operation, and whether I could help. But the only conclusion I could come up with was "What can I do? I can't go down there. I've got my real estate business, Dorothy is pregnant with our fourth child, and my Spanish is limited. How could I really help?" After several days of mulling this over, I mentioned it to Dorothy in passing. "What would you think if I went to Mexico on the farming project, coming home about every two weeks, stay a few days, and then go back again, until the season is over, which is about eight months? And the real estate business could be handled by my office manager, Carlos Hinojosa."

She looked at me and said. "Tom, I know you've been thinking about this Mexico deal for several days now, but I wouldn't for a moment consider that you go down there alone without me! We've never parted, even for a day, since we've been married!" That surprised me. That meant that she too wanted to go if I went.

"But," I replied, "what about the three kids ... and you're pregnant? How can that work?"

Dorothy, with her arms crossed, eyes narrowed, answered, "Tom, Mexican women have children too, lots of them, and they also have babies, you know, all the time! If you go, we go!"

Personally, I was stunned for a moment that she would actually pull up stakes and go into the unknown without knowing what it all involved. In a way though, I admired her gutsiness. I always felt she was a very clear thinking person, and I trusted her decisions. With that, the matter was settled—rather she settled it. The family was going. I think that was one of the fastest major decisions I had ever encountered.

So the next day I went down to David Produce to talk to James about going to Mexico to oversee the farm project. He readily accepted my offer to go, but, at first, he had apprehensions about my taking the family with me. Knowing Dorothy, it didn't take James long to accept the fact that she was capable and could very well handle the new challenge of living in Mexico. The next two hours we worked out a business plan for the farm operation.

Now, all I had to do was work out everything, like getting the real estate office business settled, deciding to see what to take with us, getting the visas, and tying up a lot of personal loose ends. With three children between the ages of four and one, and another due in about six months, it took some anxious planning. By the time we decided what to take with us, which was a whole lot, I had to buy a utility trailer to hook up to my new Mercury sedan. Dorothy was the type that packed everything to meet just about every conceivable circumstance. As time went on, I must admit, she was right in most cases.

In the interim, my friend Carlos Hinojosa became ill and also got a divorce notice from his wife, which devastated him. He told me that he could not take over the management of the office under the present situation. I felt so sorry for Carlos, as he was not only a good friend and business-man, but also a fine individual. Even with the several salespersons I had, I didn't think any of them could handle the business the way I would want it to be managed. So in discussing this unforeseen problem with Dorothy, since we had already committed to going, and were even looking forward to the adventure of working in a new culture, we decided to put the real estate business up for sale. I did that the next day by running an ad in the newspaper to appear over the weekend. To my surprise, I received over 20 calls. Within a few days I sold the business to a nice, middle-aged Caucasian couple, Walter and Betty Lutes, who had formerly been in the real estate business and had just recently moved to San Diego from Los Angeles.

After the sale was completed, I knew that was the right thing to do, for it wiped out a lot of concerns and anxieties for me, especially worrying about the business that I would leave behind. As for our house, we rented it to the new minister of our church and his family, with furniture and all. This gave the minister and his wife a place to settle while they did their own house hunting, and this gave us the peace of mind that the house and many personal items were in good hands—and they were.

WE PREPARED FOR OVER TWO MONTHS and now it was time to go. The night before leaving was spent with family and friends, getting addresses, saying that we'd write and keep in contact. It was a unanimous opinion by everyone that pregnant Dorothy was a brave girl and she got a lot of advice as to how to conduct her life in the new surroundings. I had all the confidence in Dorothy to handle any situation that would come up, in spite of the fact she spoke very little Spanish, learning only a bit from the grocery store. As for me, my Spanish was adequate, as I had learned it from working in the produce markets.

We left for Mexico on the morning of September 15, 1957, the kids all excited, with the new car pulling the utility trailer, loaded with two baby cribs, beddings, clothes, Chinese food stuff (we didn't know those things were available there), gift items for friends that we would be making, and items I thought were not necessary, but later proved to be very handy to have.

Not knowing the road conditions in Mexico, after talking to our manager, Charley, and studying maps, I figured it would take about four days to travel the 1,200 miles, averaging 300 miles a day. Our first stop would be in El Centro, California next to the border crossing into Mexicali, Mexico. To my surprise, when we crossed the next day, I found out it was Mexico's Independence Day, their Fourth of July, and all the government buildings were closed. As I had to get my car and trailer registered before proceeding into the interior of Mexico, it delayed us a whole day. We took advantage of the delay and spent the day visiting and mingling with the crowd at the plaza. It was a great experience for Dorothy and the kids, a preview of what was to come in a new country and different culture.

The next morning, I was first in line to get my vehicles registered, but to my dismay, I was told that the person that does the registering would not be in until an hour later. I thought for a moment that the clerk was implying that if I paid an extra fee, I could get it done there and now. I didn't do anything to say that I would pay extra for the service, as I didn't want to take the chance of getting in trouble with the authorities. I waited an hour, and sure enough, the proper person, who was very cordial, came in and registered the vehicles in no time. Before leaving, I asked the clerk why it was necessary to register the vehicles before entering the interior of Mexico. She politely said, "Señor Hom, Mexico has a problem with car smugglers, people bringing cars across, acting as tourists, and then selling them in the interior, therefore avoiding the duties and taxes for imported cars. When you leave Mexico, you will be required to show that you still have the same vehicles you just registered!" That made sense.

When I got back to the hotel, Dorothy and the kids were all ready to take off. Within 15 minutes we were on our way. At last! The initial landscape of the area we drove through was mostly arid and hot, typical of the northern part of Mexico, mostly all desert. Along the way we saw many small towns and villages, and stopped at some to rest and eat, as well as to practice our Spanish with the people. The locals were nice and courteous, knowing that we were visitors, and went out of the way to please us. They were especially attentive to the children, as the culture was so very family orientated. We enjoyed that.

As we traveled further into the south, the terrain became much greener and lusher with a tropical climate. After three days, we finally arrived at Culiacan, Sinaloa, a quaint city of about 50,000, founded by the early Spaniards in the 1600s. It was raining in tropical heat. That was my first experience in a climate of such extreme humidity. It was very uncomfortable for the kids and me, but for Dorothy, it was like being in Hawaii and not a problem. I could already see that Dorothy would be adjusting very well.

The first order of business was to check into a hotel to get the kids and Dorothy settled, and then to contact our farm manager, Charley Iguchi. I did that immediately, and that evening we went out to dinner in a small Mexican restaurant where Charley, Dorothy, and I laid out our priorities for the next few days. Of course, number one was to rent an apartment for my family, and also to see the farm and catch up where we were in its operation and to meet with the rest of the management team.

In a short while after setting our planning priorities, a group of mariachis with their guitars and trumpets came in and started entertaining us with their rich ranchero type of singing. This unforeseen event was real special for Dorothy, because the first time she experienced this type of music was when I hired a mariachi band, rather than a regular band, to play at our wedding, and she loved it ever since. That capped off a nice evening for us, the first day on our new venture for the next several months.

The next day Luis Beltran, the man from whom we were leasing the 1,100 acres of farmland, took us around to find an apartment. We looked at several and finally rented one on the main street in a new four-story building. We spent the rest of the day buying furniture and supplies. The prices of items were much cheaper than stateside, so the money went much further. We enjoyed that. Within two days of arriving, we moved in, which was much faster than I had expected. Getting settled was important for Dorothy and the kids. Within three days our kids were out playing with other kids in the neighborhood, ours not knowing Spanish and they, any English. But they still managed to become friends and have their own world of fun. Since Culiacan was not a tourist town, but an agricultural one, we stood out more readily there doing business, especially being of Chinese extraction from the United States. We were treated very nicely and were catered to with fast and courteous service wherever we went.

Chinese were not always treated so well in Mexico. During the revolution in 1910, the army led by Francisco "Pancho" Villa killed a number of Chinese who owned businesses to seize their supplies and money. Later in 1934, when Lazaro Cardenas was elected President of Mexico, he nationalized the major foreign businesses in Mexico, including the likes of Standard Oil and Shell Oil, along with confiscating the Chinese businesses, of which many were rather good-sized companies. During that period he also deported the Chinese, of whom many were Mexican citizens, to China, claiming that they were a menace to society. Those that were married to Mexicans were excluded, but because of the harsh anti-Chinese movement created by the new regime, many of the mixed couples with families elected to leave for China. Included in the nationalization of the many businesses owned by foreigners, President Cardenas also made a number of major reforms, including the land reform movement, to help benefit the peasant class. He was considered by the masses of Mexico as a great president for his time.

In 1957 when we were in Culiacan, there were only four Chinese families, two with Mexican wives and two with Chinese wives. Interestingly, the two with Mexican wives were in the grocery business and the two with Chinese wives were in the restaurant business. They were all doing very well and all had several children each, attending the best private schools all the way through college. They became professionals in such fields as accounting, engineering, medicine, or they joined the family businesses.

The ethnic mixture of Mexican and Chinese seemed to blend quite well together, not only physically, but mentally and socially as well. Whenever a Chinese family saw me, they would go out of their way to talk, asking where my parents were from in China, the township, village, dialect, our business in the United States, life in the states, and so on. On a number of occasions, when we ate at their restaurants, they would insist on not charging us. It's funny how Chinese are so curious about each other, especially whenever there are only a few in the area. It was like this wherever I went.

In spite of the hard times the Chinese had in Mexico at a certain period, credit must be given to the late President Lopez Mateos, who in 1964 had the parliament pass a bill to restore Mexican citizenship to all the Chinese and their descendents who were forced to leave during the 1930s and welcomed them back to Mexico. They were also partially compensated for their earlier losses as well. That was a good gesture. There were several chartered planeloads of these former exiles brought back from China.

After a couple of days of getting Dorothy and the kids settled, I worked with farm manager Charley Iguchi on the planting and harvesting schedule. The produce would be shipped during the off growing season in the states, November through March, going through the U.S. entry port at Nogales, Arizona, where we would have one of our employees work with a brokerage firm to sell the produce. From there, based on the produce market prices of the different regions, it would be shipped to that area by refrigerated semi-trucks. Eastern cities like New York, Chicago, and Baltimore were good markets, as that was their harsh wintertime with no fresh produce being grown, and therefore would bring the best prices.

The farm was located about 15 miles from the little town where we lived. I was impressed with the farm area of Culiacan. It was quite expansive, with many other farms, some as large as 10,000 acres. With the latest farming technology available, which many of the farmers learned from attending the University of California Davis, known for its agricultural department, the Culiacan valley bloomed with healthy produce fields as far as one could see.

One of the first orders of business was to start the planting of the seed-beds for transplanting later on. Twenty-five acres were devoted to this. Our main crops would be tomatoes, bell peppers, varieties of chilies, cucumbers, squash, and eggplant. We also planted smaller crops for the more specialized markets, such as Chinese and Asian vegetables for the markets with a large Asian population, mainly located on the west and east coasts.

With the good weather and rich soil, the seedlings were ready in a short time for transplanting. At the beginning we started with about 50 farm workers, migrants from another area, who would come into the valley during the season. By harvest time, and with additional plantings, we had about 300 on the payroll. This included a large number of women to work in the packing shed. The women seemed to be better, faster, and neater than the men when it came to packing.

To keep and house the workers for the duration of the season, the workers and their family lived in the many tar-papered bungalows that were on the farm premises. During the daytime, most everyone worked, including some of the kids, who had the job of firing off rocket firecrackers at the flocks of crows and birds to keep them from eating the young plants. In the evenings, after their meal, there would be several bonfires where workers would sing and share refreshments, tequila, beer, or soda pop. I occasionally joined some of the bonfire groups, sharing drinks and singing along. The workers had a name for me, El Patron, the big boss. Most of the songs were the ranchero type, about sweethearts, broken romances, love of a mother, and the dream of one day owning a ranch. All was very folksy and homey. I loved those songs.

Each morning I turned on the radio to get the weather report for our region as well as the weather in southern Florida, where winter produce was also grown to compete with our winter crops from Culiacan. Naturally, if Florida's crop should be wiped out with bad weather, our crops would bring a better price, and vice-a-versa. Farming was such a gamble, especially when it came to things that we could not control, like hurricanes. But the rewards could be great if all should fit into place: good crop, good weather, and good prices.

Dorothy and the three daughters adjusted very well and very quickly. Since labor was cheap, compared to stateside, at two dollars a day with meals, we were able to afford three maids to help Dorothy and to take care of the girls. The maids would show Dorothy how to cook some of the more popular Mexican dishes, do housework, take the children to the park to visit their friends and teach them Spanish. Phyllis, our youngest, conversed more in Spanish than she did in English. Very soon Dorothy was speaking fluent Spanish and, in turn, the maids learned English as well.

In our new apartment building with 12 units, we were the only non-Mexican family. I think because we were like guests, we were treated very cordially by everyone, bringing us local types of foods, and inviting us to parties and special events, like weddings and anniversaries. They were very warm people. This was especially meaningful to Dorothy, to be included in a new culture like this.

At the beginning, perhaps the hardest part in living and working in Mexico was making appointments and to abide by its date and time. Several times I had meetings scheduled at a certain time and the other party would show up an hour or so late, if at all. Later, I learned to roll with it and not feel offended. In turn, I probably irritated some of them by expecting exactness, not leaving enough leeway for adjustments. I did learn one thing, though, the Mexican culture was very relaxed and less pressured than I was used to. I enjoyed that pace. It's full of music, family, flowers, friends, and parties. But when they work, they work hard and seriously, as they did on the farm.

With the weather coming along very well, as we had hoped it would, the crops were growing vigorously and free of disease, thanks to the proper dusting of the crops early on. It was in December when we started to hire more workers, getting ready for the harvesting in early January. The packing shed was being prepared; lumber was brought in to make thousands of containers in which to pack the produce.

It was like a busy beehive, with a hundred things to be done in preparation for the harvesting and packing that would eventually fill about 40 or more refrigerated semi-truckloads of produce, each load averaging 22 tons. It would take the loaded trucks two to three days, depending on the road conditions and weather, to travel the 800 miles to the border city of Nogales. For fresh produce, time was of the essence.

CHAPTER 28

One Never Stops Learning

ONE DAY IN LATE DECEMBER, CHARLEY IGUCHI CAME TO tell me that he needed to buy some old large tires to fight off the coming frost that the weather bureau had forecasted for the coming weekend. I went with him to the used tire yard which was next to the railroad terminal to buy 40 large old tires that we would spread throughout the fields, putting oil in them and then setting them on fire, whereupon an old propeller bi-plane would fly over the burning tires in order to create a turbulence of warm air that would eliminate the frost that could damage the crops. Ingenious! That was a new approach for me.

Charley bought the 40 tires. As we were leaving, I asked him, "How are you going to get the huge tires to the farm?"

He said, "Oh, I'll send Enrique and Pancho to pick them up today around 3 o'clock."

He dropped me off at home. During lunch, I got to thinking about Enrique and Pancho who were little guys, neither one of them weighing over 125 pounds. How in the world were they going to lift and load 40 huge tires, mostly weighing between 100 to 150 pounds each, onto the truck? I didn't see any forklifts in the tire yard or any workers, just the lady clerk who sold the tires.

I thought about giving those poor little guys a hand. I knew the age old tradition that the patron, that's me, did not normally do this type of common labor work, but I didn't care about that. So I went to the tire yard at 3 o'clock and waited half an hour before they showed up with the truck. I offered to help, but they politely insisted that that was not necessary. So I accepted their refusal and stood by to watch how these 125 pound guys were going to do it.

What they did was back up their truck to a large boulder imbedded in the ground, which had a slant of about 30 degrees. Then they both went to the pile of tires and rolled a tire to a mound that was set back about 20 yards from the slanted boulder. Next, they lined up the tire, aiming for the slanted boulder, and then Enrique would hop on the back of the truck bed and signal to Pancho to start the tire rolling. By the time the tire got to the imbedded boulder it was moving at a good speed. When it hit the slanted boulder, it popped up and flew several feet upward, and little Enrique would get under it, flipping it over to a designated spot where he wanted it to land. I was impressed. They did this 40 times—and I was then really impressed. They never missed once. "Wow!" I thought. "What would I have done in the states to load these tires? I probably would have hired four big strong guys or rented a forklift to do it." These things, and others to follow, taught me that one can always be more innovative and that there *are* many different ways to skin a cat.

As we got closer to harvesting, James thought I should have more help in coordinating the operation. He decided to send our brother Herb to assist. He was a big help as it freed me from some of the details that bogged me down. It was extremely important to meet the payroll for the workers on time. The Mexican federal government was particularly stringent in enforcing the law that prevented an employer from cheating or miss paying the employees; they could be closed down and fined very quickly.

For that reason, I personally assigned myself the responsibility of bringing the cash in from the bank each week for the payroll. I did this for several weeks, until one day a Greek immigrant farmer with a large 5,000 acre farm, whom I had befriended, was robbed of his payroll and killed by having his throat cut. I was shocked! Robbed and then killed. I asked a friend, "Why in the world would they have to kill the guy, when they could just rob him for the money, and then maybe beat him up and take off?"

The friend explained, "Señor Hom, you have to realize in Mexico we do not have the death penalty. Since we do not have it, the robber reasoned that if he should be caught robbing, he'd be thrown in prison and will probably rot there. So for protection, by killing the victim, he gets rid of the witness and he stays out of prison." After that, I decided to have Charley bring the payroll funds in each week instead.

We lived in Culiacan, Mexico, where maids were too reasonable, going for two American dollars a day. We had four. L to R: Daughters Phyllis, Nora, and Gayle.

The next day Herb and I decided that we should carry a gun since just about all the businessmen carried one. It was suggested that we go to the largest department store in town, Sears, which had a large selection. We went to the gun counter and told the clerk we that we wanted to buy a couple of automatic hand guns. He asked what caliber.

I said, "A couple of 22s."

He asked, "Are these for protection or target practice? If it's for target practice, that is okay, but for protection, it won't do. When someone comes to attack you, a 22 caliber may not stop him, unless you hit him between the eyes. What you want to do is stop the man, like with a 45, or at least a 38 caliber."

"It's for protection," I said, "but I don't want to kill the guy, just stop him, like shooting him in the leg." The clerk chuckled, and we went back and forth as to the caliber we should buy. I finally settled for a 32 caliber automatic and Herb bought a 22 caliber automatic as he originally wanted. During all the months in Culiacan we always carried the guns in our inside belt holsters and they did give us a secure feeling. We never had to use them for protection, but we did do a lot of target practicing, just in case.

At the beginning of January 1958, various crops were about ready for harvesting. The first one, Charley decided, was eggplant. The following day it was tomato. By the third day we had enough packed and ready to load our first semi-trailer load of 22 tons to the states. Herb and Charley monitored the quality of the items that were being packed, for when the produce got to the border, the U.S. Customs and inspectors from the U.S. Department of Agriculture made sure the produce was rated U.S. No.1 Grade, otherwise the whole load would be rejected. If rejected, we would have to hire a crew at the border to repack each box of produce and discard the non-passable ones. It was tedious and costly to do this. So monitoring the initial packing was very important.

In spite of carefully monitoring the packing quality, we did have two loads that did not pass the U.S. Department of Agriculture inspection. Out of about 65 loads that we sent out, that's not a bad average. Some of the other outfits had as high as 10 percent of their loads rejected. The interesting thing about the quality of packing was that we found that on Mondays we had to be extra diligent in monitoring the quality control. Charley said that was due to the hangovers from parties over the weekend. Other than that, I found the packers and farm workers, as poor as they were, to be very good workers. I enjoyed their seemingly natural relationship to Mother Earth. It was not uncommon for them to sing, often at the top of their lungs, while they worked, especially while they were out in the field picking the harvest. They were good, humble people.

On various occasions, after the day's work, I would visit some of the worker's tar-papered bungalows and share some of their food, which mostly consisted of produce from the farm, a small amount of meat, beans, and freshly made tortillas. The sauces were something special. The meals were not fancy or elaborate, but they were healthfully balanced. Since most of the workers had never tasted Chinese food, I made it a point to cook up large batches of chow mein, squash with black bean sauce, sweet and sour pork, and share it with them. They really liked it. Soon word got around that I was cooking and giving out Chinese food. After a while I couldn't keep up with so much cooking, so I had to quit doing it.

Later on, though, a small group of ladies with a couple of men, on their day off, came and asked me to teach them how to cook Chinese food, which I did. They caught on fast and did very well. Cooking seemed to come naturally to them. In a short time they were sharing some of their cooking with others and the only debate they had among themselves was what wine went the best with Chinese food. I partly settled it by saying, "A light white wine with a bouquet fragrance is the best, because that's what the ancient emperors in China took with their food!" I'm not sure that was true or not, but that's the way I liked it, so I said it, with the emperors backing me up.

Apparently, what I said did have some impact on white wine sales, evidenced from the spike of sales at the little store on the farm that mainly serviced the farm workers. But as time went on, the national drink of tequila and beer became the best combination for them. To each his own, I always said.

As the weeks went by we continued to increase the work momentum in harvesting and packing and getting the shipments off. The pickers started early in the mornings and the packers would start at nine in the morning when new pickings arrived from the fields. They worked into the evenings until about seven, breaking for lunch and dinner. The refrigerated semi-trucks would be loaded by late afternoon for the 800-mile trip to Nogales. After the border inspection and paperwork, our broker then coordinated with our David Produce Company in San Diego, and together they would decide where the produce would be shipped.

My brother Herb was a big help, taking much of the workload off of me, monitoring the quality of the packing and getting the shipments off in a timely manner. Our manager and farm technician, Charley Iguchi, kept close watch over the maturity of each field section of crops as to when harvesting should start, as well as when the second and third pickings should take place.

I found working a farm on this level—1,100 acres with 300 workers—compared to what I worked on with my dad in San Diego, with one worker and three brothers farming 25 acres, was hardly any comparison at all. Our farming in San Diego was only on a mom and pop scale and did not really prepare us for agri-business. This Mexican operation was big business. The difference in culture, working environment, and language made it more challenging, but the stakes were much higher for a much greater return on our investment. We, being young and optimistic, willingly took this on.

As the operation continued to accelerate to a higher volume, our brother James decided to come down from San Diego to see how we were progressing. He flew down with our Nogales broker, Al Harrison, who had his own single engine Piper Cub plane. Al was a big, tall, swashbuckling-looking type of a guy with an eye patch over his right eye; he wore cowboy boots and walked in a swaggering manner. His appearance gave the impression of being carefree, but he was not. He was just the opposite: honest, hard working, and sincere in his dealings.

They landed the plane on one of the dirt roads in our field. It was great to see James again, since most of our communications had been through either telegraph or mail, and periodically through telephone, as the phone system was not always reliable. The best time for phone usage was about midnight, when the system was being the least used. And even then, if we did get through, we'd often get cut off within a few minutes. Many nights Herb and I would stay up late playing chess to kill the time, while we kept trying to get through, or hopefully, San Diego could get through to us. In time we learned to roll with it, and adjusted as well as we could. Herb and I did get something out of this ... our chess game got a heck of a lot better.

Afterwards a team of us showed James and Al Harrison around the farm operation and brought them up to date on everything, including walking the fields, examining the different crops, and learning when they would be scheduled to be harvested. James was impressed with the operation and the vastness of the farm, and complimented us on what we had done.

Later in the day I took them into town to our apartment. Upon entering, James, his arms loaded with gifts, said, "Hi, Dorothy, I finally made it, and you look great! Here are some gifts for the kids!"

Dorothy ran up to James and hugged him and said, "James, it sure is good to see you. Welcome to our modest hacienda. *Mi casa es su casa*, my home is your home!" That's a famous Mexican greeting. Then she quickly followed by saying a typical Chinese greeting, "Have you eaten? Let me get you something to eat!" In preparation for this visit, Dorothy already had the maids make tamales, enchiladas, rice, and beans. In a couple of moments, my three little kids were all over their Uncle James and his presents.

After two days of business talk, visiting the town of Culiacan, and meeting some of the business friends I had made, James and Al left to fly back to San Diego. Before leaving they took many dirt samples from different sections of the farm for soil analysis for future planning of the different crops to be grown. They took so many samplings, and with dirt weighing so much, I became very apprehensive when they were taking off because it took so long for them to finally get off the ground into the air. It must have taken at least twice the distance than it usually took, and they were heading straight for the packing shed. It was such a close shave that James and I, over fifty years later, still talk about it.

A few days later, our 22-year-old brother Albert came to visit for a couple of weeks. After visiting the farm, he got acquainted with some of the *señoritas* around town, and had a good time of it. He spoke fluent Spanish, which helped a lot.

During the peak of the farm season, our home life was also reaching a peak as well. Dorothy was getting ready to give birth. During the pre-natal care, our Mexican doctor made house calls and then arranged for the delivery at the town's best health facility, the Culiacan Clinic, a modest center, all painted in white with touches of light blue and pink here and there.

In those days, there was no way of knowing which gender the new baby would be, so with three girls already, we were rooting for a boy. After giving birth naturally, which Dorothy always did, she was elated when the doctor shouted, *"Es un hombre!* It's a boy!"* Dorothy said a silent prayer of thank you and went to sleep. After the baby was cleaned up, he was then given to Dorothy to breast feed. From then on the baby was always with Dorothy, night and day. Kind of the opposite how they did it in the states with our previous three kids. According to the Mexican doctor, he said the early bonding of mother and child was very important. Dorothy agreed, as having a first son made the desire to bond even greater, and besides, that's sort of Chinese thinking too. After all they've been having babies for thousands of years.

It was common practice for patients in the clinic to bring in their own help as we did with one of our housemaids, Rafaela, a capable eighteen year old. She came from a family of eight siblings, was the second child, and knew more about caring for a birthing mother and new babies than most, certainly more than Dorothy. The clinic provided a cot for her to sleep in Dorothy's room, where she would be with Dorothy 24 hours a day during her three-day stay in bed before going home. The food for Dorothy was provided by Rafaela, who brought in each of her meals. Dorothy liked that, having the chance to try the wide variety of Mexican foods.

Dorothy's stay at the clinic was very pleasant. The staff was extremely accommodating and excited and fussed continuously over their first Chinese baby. The big surprise at the end of the three days, when we were ready to leave for home, was the clinic's bill. It was only for $48, including the doctor's service! I first thought it was a mistake, but it wasn't. Compared to back home, with our earlier three births averaging $300 each, this was a real bargain. To show appreciation for the kind care they gave Dorothy, I had several boxes of fresh produce from the farm sent over to the clinic the next day.

Before leaving the clinic, Dorothy had to fill out a birth certificate for the government's recording office. Filling out the form was no problem until we came to the name of the baby. Weeks before we kicked around a number of names if it should be a boy, coming up with names like Thomas, Jr., Wolfgang, Jonathon, Richard, and many others, but none appealed, except for one ... Winthrop. The only one with that name that we knew of was Winthrop Rockefeller, part of the financial tycoon family of John D. Rockefeller, who was then the governor of Arkansas. I guess I foolishly surmised that to be associated with the Rockefellers by name would give him the incentive to become financially rich in later life, but it ended up to be the opposite.

As an adult all Winthrop ever needed, as far as money was concerned, was just enough to make ends meet. In his early 20s, Winthrop explored Europe and the Middle East backpacking with a couple of friends. He shared his travel experiences with me, particularly his visit to Egypt. He, like me, has a profound interest and appreciation of other cultures and ancient history.

He got his Bachelor's Degree in Business Finance at San Diego State University, and afterwards started his own business as a building contractor. He built houses and apartments, later downsizing to do smaller jobs like repairs, where it was less demanding with fewer headaches. Winthrop is the father of three lovely children. He's always had a lot of friends and a good knack for working with mechanical things. Although his lifestyle is different from mine, he's happy with it. You can't argue with happiness.

In the following months of March, April and May, we continued to peak our farm production, with it starting to wind down in the latter part of May, ending the season for fresh produce. Many of the farms in the valley would be shifting into growing rice, corn, wheat, maize, and other crops, but we were not going to do that.

During the months of operation I learned a lot. On one occasion, practically all the workers from the valley left the farms to rally for higher wages and better working conditions at a location about five miles away. I was told that the rally was sponsored by the Communist Party of Mexico. This left much of the scheduled cultivating, irrigating, harvesting, and packing undone. Things were going as scheduled, but this, especially not knowing how long the boycott would be, had me worried. I was also concerned there would be an outbreak of violence as well.

Shortly after the rally call, to prevent a potential outbreak of violence, the federal government brought in military troops and had them stationed on farms throughout the valley. We had about 50 soldiers on our farm, fully equipped with machine guns, radio equipment, combat vehicles with a gun turret on top, and camping facilities. Our foreman, Luis Beltran, told me, "This type of protest event occurs almost every year, and after about two weeks, the workers at the rally get tired of speeches, partying, and they run out of food. They'll be coming back to work!" To me, all this happening was pretty traumatic, and I didn't know how much to believe.

Well, sure enough, in about two weeks, as Luis Beltran had predicted, the workers started to straggle back, little by little, and within three days everyone had returned and the operation was back to normal. I have to admit, I didn't sleep much during those two weeks, but I sure learned a lot. I also learned that the Mexican workers were very resilient people who, even when defeated, could still maintain a sense of dignity and humor. And I also learned that the farmers, who were also the civic leaders of Culiacan, had the firm support of the federal government. Since Mexico was still a relatively poor country and the whole region depended so heavily upon the agricultural economy, the government was not going to allow anything to happen to jeopardize that base.

One time over lunch with several of my farmer friends, I happened to mention, rather causally, that, "I've been thinking in order to get better production from the farm workers, I might consider increasing their wages by 10 percent. Their wages are quite low as it is!"

"Tom, don't do that!" urged Gil Ochoa. "If you did, without the consensus and understanding of the other growers, you'd have a lot of problems. I can't say what, but there would be a lot of problems, and it could be very costly to you. Please don't even consider it!" Coming from a good friend, I left it at that. Someone changed the subject. *Status quo.*

Around the middle of May, when we were starting to wind down the operation, Dorothy started packing up our personal items to take back with us in our little trailer. The rest of the furniture we stored in a friend's warehouse. After nine months in Culiacan, we had made a number of friends, both in business and socially. We received many gifts, and several parties were thrown for us, with plenty of food and mariachi bands. It was a bit sad to leave our friends and the comfortable and casual lifestyle of the Mexican culture, but we were also anxious to get home to San Diego.

It took us seven days to arrive in San Diego, with a couple of overnight stops at quaint little seashore villages along the coast of the Sea of Cortez. When we got to the U.S./Mexico border at Nogales, the first thing Dorothy did was register the birth of Winthrop with the U.S. authorities, to make sure that it was properly recorded that he was our American child born in Mexico. Hence, Winthrop has dual citizenship, both American and Mexican.

In spite of the fact that we were still about 400 miles from San Diego, we felt that we were at home already. That day we stayed overnight in Tucson, Arizona and started early for San Diego next morning.

Our new church minister from Hawaii, Rev. Harold Jow, who was renting our furnished house until he could find permanent housing for his family, wrote us and said they had found a home and had moved out a week earlier; everything was ready for us to move back in. It was a relief for Dorothy, as she liked things to be in place, wherever it might be. We pulled in that evening, found the house in good order, unpacked, and went out to dinner at a McDonald's for the all-American hamburgers, French fries, and milk shakes. It was great to be home, in spite of the wonderful time and experience we had in Mexico.

The next few days I worked with our bookkeepers at David Produce to see how we made out financially on our Mexico project. After several days of working on the figures, we found that we had made money, but not as much as we had hoped. In spite of the prices of produce that year, strong competition from the Florida growers, and the high produce volume from other growers from other parts of Mexico, we came out fairly well. Farming was a gamble, but in our case the last two years in Mexico had been, I would say, okay. Not a bonanza, but worthwhile.

VIII. New Challenges

AGES 30 TO 35

一只兔子崎岖的心路历程

Campaigning hard for California State Assembly — can't take anything for granted.

CHAPTER 29

Back In the Saddle

FTER ARRIVING HOME FROM OUR ADVENTUROUS AND REA-
sonably profitable farming investment in Mexico, I knew what I
wanted to do. Go back into the real estate business. So first thing
after getting the family situated, I began to set up a new real estate office.
Dorothy had her hands full with four kids, with Winthrop only three
months old. Luckily, she had help. After planning ahead, one of our former
Mexican housemaids, Rafaela, came by bus from Culiacan, crossing the
border on a visitor's visa to work with us. She was a gift from heaven, such
a natural in caring for children.

Rafaela was one of the many young persons who were fascinated with
the image of America through the Hollywood magazines they read. She
was a good worker, honest, with a cheerful personality, and the kids loved
her. So she stayed and worked for us for four months and then went on
to Los Angeles to see Hollywood. Three years later we got a letter from
Rafaela, telling us that she was back in Culiacan and happily married to her
old boyfriend and now had a baby girl, and that Hollywood wasn't what
she thought it would be. She enclosed a lovely photo of her family. Good
for Rafaela, she was such a nice and innocent person, big city L.A. and fast
Hollywood wouldn't have been good for her.

It didn't take too long to get back into the swing of things. After a few
"welcome home" parties from family and friends, we were anxious to get back
to the practical side of living. And that meant being active in the church,
getting the business back on track to make a living, repairing the deferred
maintenance of the house, dog training our newly acquired German Shepherd, and registering for some special business courses in the evenings at
San Diego City College, along with helping Dorothy with the kids.

In opening my new real estate office, I looked up my old friend, Carlos Hinojosa, a very valuable and smart associate in my former office, to ask him to join up with me again. I called his home, but the phone was disconnected. So I called his sister Esther and she told me, "Tom, didn't you know? Carlos passed away five months ago. We're so sad and we are all broken up over this! He was so young. He wasn't the same since he broke up with his wife Barbara!" I was shocked, I just couldn't believe it. Carlos, one of my best friends since childhood, died so young. Then I recalled that before we left for Mexico, I had offered Carlos to be the general manager of my real estate business until I returned and he said he had to turn me down as he had just been served divorce papers from his wife and wasn't up to the responsibility of running my business. He was sad and completely dejected when we left for Mexico.

Later I shared the unexpected news with Dorothy and we surmised that Carlos died of a broken heart and major depression after his divorce. He might have even committed suicide, but no one said so. I never knew one way or another, but from that experience it taught me not to take life for granted.

With my new office I started recruiting a sales staff. Some of my former ones were still with the Lutes to whom I sold my old office when I left for Mexico. The Lutes were good people and I wouldn't even consider recruiting my old staff. Besides, the Lutes treated them very well and they would have no reason for leaving them.

I did hire several new salespersons. One was a Chinese fellow, John Wong, who I knew from church. Although he was little rough around the edges, he was honest and a hard worker. Another was a gentlemanly Puerto Rican, Luis Hustana, a cultured man who played the flute with the San Diego Symphony during the symphony season and in the evenings. Hustana's wife, Gertrude Peterson, played the harp in the symphony. Gertrude had married Hustana against the wishes of her father, a prominent general contractor in town, she being his only child. After the marriage, the father-in-law gave Hustana a job with the company doing mostly labor work, the pick and shovel kind. In a short time he quit, sensing that the father-in-law wanted to demean his character by doing that kind of work. That was probably true, for Hustana was a well educated person, a college graduate who spoke several different languages, namely Spanish, French, Italian and, of course, English. His manners were rather European, where he would click his heels when he was introduced to a person and bow slightly, extending his hand for the handshake. I liked him. He was a pretty good salesman.

Betty Riley, the third salesperson, was another matter. Betty was a rather attractive middle-aged Caucasian lady who lived in the neighborhood; her husband ran a little restaurant down the street. She was an experienced real estate salesperson and had a very outgoing personality. Betty always had a lot of phone calls from different men. She would talk for a long time and, invariably, she would end up meeting them for lunch or whatever else. One day, after a long phone conversation, I boldly asked, "Betty, does your husband Bob know about all these calls you get and about some of your outside activities?"

She replied, "Oh Bob? He's busy at the restaurant. We've been married for 20 years and what he doesn't know won't hurt him!" I was confused by that reply, until I found out that Bob had a girlfriend on the side. Thereafter, I never thought much of Betty's long phone calls and extended luncheons. I must say, though, she was a good saleswoman, both with herself and in real estate.

IN A SHORT TIME I STARTED to get involved in the church and other activities again, like helping in Little League, going to the YMCA, and spending some time painting, both in oil and watercolor.

I also started to think about real estate investments. By this time my siblings and I were beginning to accumulate a modest amount of surplus funds from some outside investments. And that was after giving more financial support each month to our mother, Ah Nuing, to meet the growing needs of our younger siblings at home. Aside from that, we also felt another priority; we needed to expand our businesses, which we declared was our "bread machine."

In spite of our limited extra funds, I felt we could start small and maybe deal in commercial properties that were cheap and in need of repairs and fixing up. They might not be in the best locations, but they would have the potential of being in a turnaround area in the not-too-distant future. These kinds of properties would be cheaper, with less buyer competition, and they didn't require much cash down. The owners, which could be banks that had foreclosed properties, were eager to get rid of them.

It didn't take me long to find several properties that met my criteria in the older section of the Logan Heights area. We managed to buy them for a low down payment with financing from local banks. Even though we were paying a higher interest rate, the process was efficient and fast, which gave us the opportunity to work on two to three projects at once. The people I hired to do the repairs were skilled workers who wanted part-time work after their regular jobs, and were willing to work on weekends. They were electricians, carpenters, cement layers, and so on. It worked out great, as they generally worked on the per job basis, rather than per hour. This way I was able to budget better. It was amazing how fast work could get done on the per job basis.

After completion of the repairs and remodeling, and the buildings were looking nice and clean, I listed them through the real estate office, giving my salespeople a chance to make selling commissions. This motivated them to also be on the lookout for other properties that fit my criteria, so they could earn another commission when we bought them.

Most of these remodeled buildings were sold to first-time buyers or more recent immigrants who had limited funds, so in many cases we would carry the second trust deed loan on it so they could afford to buy it. The loan we carried back earned a reasonable interest along with the monthly payments. That gave us some steady income and a comfort zone. I don't recall ever losing any money on these loans.

Meanwhile, while running the business, finding time to spend with the growing family, and other activities, I still had the bug for politics. I always managed to spend some time to work with candidates for public office, both in my believing in them and also wanting to learn more about political campaigning.

Being involved in politics was strongly supported by my wife. This was very typical of Dorothy, to support me in just about all my endeavors. I said just about all my endeavors, because there were some things she did not approve of, and that was my owning a motorcycle and playing tackle football, which I really loved. I was fast and a good scatback then. But as for politics, she took to it like fish in water. She had the gift of talking and getting along famously with people. Wherever we would go, she'd strike up conversations with people like they were long-time friends, and people responded favorably to her. With her bubbly personality she was a wonderful wife, especially for a rather young, eager guy like me with ambitions to get ahead. I always felt Dorothy was smarter than me, but she would never let me know it. She had a way of putting good ideas and solutions to problems in my head so subtlety that when I thought about it, and would later share my thoughts with her, she would praise me for being so brilliant in coming up with the idea or solution.

In my earlier involvement in politics, I was mostly assigned to passing out campaign literature and car bumper stickers, tacking up posters, and placing signs. Later, I walked with the candidates knocking on doors, attending meetings, and even representing and making speeches at meetings which the candidate could not make. Following that, I was invited to sit in meetings helping to strategize the campaign, in addition to working on the issues and how to handle them. All this was exciting work for me. It was new and challenging. I also learned a lot about a candidate, above all, their intelligence and their sincerity in working for the good of the people and for better government. Some I came to admire, and a few had been disillusioning. With those I did not respect, I managed to ease off gradually and worked with someone that I felt good about. It really didn't take long after working with them to find out about the character of a candidate. I know I'm no perfect specimen, either, but I always felt better and inspired by working for the good guys.

CHAPTER 30

New Pastor

W HILE WE WERE IN MEXICO, OUR CHINESE COMMUNITY
Church hired a new minister from Honolulu, Rev. Harold Jow,
a dynamic young man of 38, with his wife Lillian and their
two children. Since 1927, our small church facility was located at 645 First
Avenue, downtown San Diego, outside of Chinatown. It was situated on a
small lot of 5,000 square feet, with no off street parking. By 1958 we had
outgrown the church facilities so much that some of our Sunday classes
were held on the public sidewalk areas. The neighborhood surroundings
consisted of industrial buildings, rundown boarding houses, derelicts,
and across the street, an auto wrecking yard. Obviously, it was not a good
location for a family church, especially for some of the evening events.
Rev. Jow's church in Honolulu, the United Church of Christ on Judd Street,
was about four times larger than our church, both in facility size and in
congregation. He built that church, originally located in a problem area,
to its then present size and location. His motivation in coming to us was
to help us grow. This he did.

Upon our return from Mexico, Dorothy and I got back into the flow of
the church activities. In no time, I was involved with Rev. Jow as part of
his committee to build a new church to be located more centrally for our
families. The original Chinatown established in the 1860s had diminished
in size. Chinatown was located at the edge of a red-light district and brawly
saloons, known as the Stingaree District downtown, which gave many of
the people in Chinatown a good motivation to move.

Because of my background in real estate, Rev. Jow and I teamed up to
find a suitable location for the new church. The criteria were to have room
for future expansion, good road and public transportation access, and

something affordable. After looking at several locations that didn't meet our criteria, my friend Ed Hall, a real estate broker, showed us a seven-acre site for the price of $30,000 that was located at Federal Boulevard and 47th Street. It was more than we expected to pay, but Rev. Jow, with his faith in building for the Lord, said empathically, "This is it! We can do it!" So, with the congregation's approval, we bought the property. Next thing I knew, I was drafted to be the finance chairman to raise the funds to build the new church. Rev. Jow's enthusiasm for the Lord in accomplishing anything was catching, so I accepted the draft.

Upon acquiring the seven acres, we hired an architect to draft plans for the new church, with a high ceiling chapel, narthex, bridal room, classrooms, offices, social hall, kitchen, manse, playground, amphitheater, beautiful landscape, and plenty of off-street parking. The plans were impressive and the buildings would be a dream come true. But the harsh reality came quickly when the architect estimated the cost would be about $350,000. In those days that was a lot of money, especially for a rather small congregation. Rev. Jow quickly suggested that we do like many other churches did when building a new facility, build it in different phases, so we could be using it while planning for the next phase. No one disputed him since he had the Lord on his side, and experience, too.

My job then was to form a New Church Building Fund Committee, for which Rev. Jow did most of the recruiting. It was harder for people to refuse him than me. After that, we circulated promotional brochures about the new church and the need for building for the future, for our children, and the exciting things to come. After first approaching church families to raise funds, we then started a campaign to canvas all the Chinese-owned businesses outside of church, like laundries, restaurants, grocery stores and anywhere else where we might find them.

Next Rev. Jow and I set up an outreach program to contact the Chinese in Arizona: first in Yuma, which had only about three families, then to Tucson, Casa Grande, and Phoenix, hitting all the businesses and including a couple of large Chinese cotton-growing communities. Whenever we met with a donor, afterwards we would humbly ask if they could refer us to any of their family members or friends that might be interested in helping advance the work of God. I must say, the reception was good and that is how we were able to extend the Arizona campaign to six days. Arizonian Chinese were extremely helpful and were the friendliest, most hospitable people. We'd leave San Diego following Sunday's church service, drive straight to Yuma, and the following day onto the next city, and so on until Saturday when we drove home to San Diego.

Two weeks after the Arizona campaign, Rev. Jow and I used the same strategy in Los Angeles. We left on a weekday, early in the morning, and worked the L.A. community for two days and drove home. The fundraising was not as lucrative as Arizona because L.A. had about 12 Chinese churches, and for an outside church to come in and raise funds, where local needs must come first, made it more difficult. All in all, it was good enough.

Within a year of the fundraising campaign, we raised $71,000, exceeding our goal of $50,000. With the generous contributions made by many, and the funds we derived from selling our old church building for $30,000, we paid off the seven acres we purchased for the new church. We were then ready to proceed on the actual construction. The preliminary phase of construction would be the chapel, narthex, bridal lounge, offices, classrooms, paved parking, landscape, and land improvement for the future amphitheatre. The total cost of this first phase came on the low bid by the well established contracting firm of Riha Construction Company for $124,000. With a big turnout of happy parishioners, ground was broken in March 1960.

I received a number of congratulations for a financial campaign well done. Yes, I did work hard, but in reality, at age 30, I seriously questioned that it was me who deserved the credit. I was just part of the team and happened to be the chairman, a position no one else wanted. It took the leadership of Rev. Jow and other mature leaders to provide the confidence that was needed in order to raise the funds. And it was older people who made the larger financial contributions. Without our elders, we probably would not have succeeded.

FROM FIRST TO OUT, THEN third to first. I am not talking about a convoluted baseball umpire call, but rather, business. Unusual business. The year 1961 was a major turning point for our family's David Produce Company headed by our brother James, then 37, which experienced some unforeseen changes. Under his leadership and the help of younger brothers Herbert and Albert, they had built the business into a thriving entity. Herbert had been fulltime with the company since his return from the Korean War, and had declined to attend a college of his choice on the GI Bill to instead help support the growing needs of the younger siblings and mother. My admiration for him was most profound. I was not involved on the daily basis anymore; mostly I attended meetings to help form polices and plan for growth. At this point, with about 20 employees, the David Produce Company was probably the third largest wholesale produce firm in San Diego.

Because of the long hours my brothers would put in each day, and the work ethic they displayed in their relationship with the other produce houses, an unusual and unexpected bonanza fell upon the David Produce Company. This was in April 1961.

Across the street from David Produce was the largest wholesale produce firm in San Diego, named Growers Marketing Company, well established since the 1920s. The owners were two partners, older gentlemen, Art Glore, 79, and Fred Mercurio, 72. Art Glore was a rather slow talking gentle person who ran the accounting, strategy, and oversight of the business, and was also the president of the San Diego Produce Association. Fred Mercurio, who was gruff and had an in-your-face way of speaking, ran the day-to-day operation with 50 employees. He was tough, but a caring type of a person. They made a huge amount of money through the success of their business together.

One day after the morning's peak busy hour, my brother James got a phone call from Art Glore who said, "Jimmy, have you got time to come over here? Fred and I want to talk to you!"

James responded, "Sure, Art, I'll be right over!"

Before leaving to meet with Art and Fred, James thought to himself, "I wonder why they want to talk to me? Did we, in our marketing efforts, take away some of their prize customers? Or did we have some overdue bills with them that I overlooked?" With those thoughts and a bit puzzled, he walked over to meet them.

When James entered their office, he was asked to take a seat. Without any other preliminary remarks, Art said, "Jimmy, how would you like to take over the Growers Marketing Company?"

James was shocked and bewildered, and he stammered, "What? But, gentlemen, I don't have that kind of money!"

Fred responded emphatically, "Who the hell said anything about money?" James was really confused then.

Art, as the major partner and accountant for the company, went on to say, "Jimmy, Fred and I are reaching retirement age and we are not interested in making money anymore. We made plenty all these years and we don't need any more. I'm pushing up there in age and Fred is having some health problems and wants someone to take over the business. We are asking if you would do that!"

Still somewhat confused and skeptical, James said, "How can that work?"

As Art opened a tablet with notes on it, he said, "Jimmy, I knew your father David before you were born. He was a good, decent, and honorable man, and you kids have done a good job in building back up the company after he passed away. We know that you kids are hard working, we can see that from over here, and trustworthy like your father! We are willing to turn the whole company of Growers over to you without any money!"

James, still incredulous, asked, "How about the payments for all the trucks, equipment, and facilities? I'm not sure we could afford that!"

Art said in a reassuring voice, "Jimmy, listen to our proposal first, then we'll go from there. First, we'll turn all our trucks over to you, all 18 of them, including the big semi-trucks, with the pink slips, as well as all the equipment in the warehouse, along with all our customer base and business contacts, for absolutely no money. Our warehouse property and all the equipment are free and clear. We have no debts, other than the current bills on the rolling stock!"

Art continued, looking directly at James, "There are three requirements in this. One, that you pay rent on our building here at the going market rate; two, that at the beginning, you keep the same payroll of people we have now, which you will need anyway to service our many long-time customers; and thirdly, that I can come into this office anytime during working hours and sit at my desk here. I've been in the produce business so long, I'd miss the excitement and clamor if I had to stay away too long. That's it! Fred and I thought about this long and hard. We know this is sudden, Jimmy, so you and your brothers think about it and let us know."

With James still in shock, Art went on to say, "If it's okay, we can get the attorneys on it and get it done quickly. This is only something for you, Jimmy, and David Produce, and no one else! As I said, we knew your father for over 40 years and he was one of the most honest and hardest workers we've ever known. Fred and I, over here across the street, could see your father trained you David boys very well. We see that every day."

Of course, James was both stunned and elated. That offer was the biggest and most generous financial proposal he had ever heard of. Upon returning to his office, James called me and shared the unexpected event that just occurred between the owners of the largest produce firm in San Diego and him. It was hard for me to believe those giveaway terms and the unusual conditions. I immediately came down to meet with him and the other brothers, and we agreed that this was an opportunity that we could not pass up.

The next morning, James went across the street and shook hands with Art Glore and Fred Mercurio to accept that extraordinary offer. Within a month the agreement documents were completed and David Produce moved across the street into the large modern warehouse of the former Growers Marketing Company. David Produce Company became the largest wholesale produce firm in San Diego.

Much of the credit for this remarkable deal goes to James, who headed the company, and the supporting younger brothers, Herbert and Albert. But, behind it all, a deal like this could not have been conceived without the good name that our dad, David Hom, left behind. As I have gotten older, I've come to realize that the legacy the head of the family leaves behind can have great effects and consequences on how people deal with the offspring, which can be either good or bad. Thank heavens, Dad was one of the good guys.

CHAPTER 31

Hat in the Ring

WITH THE DAVID PRODUCE COMPANY IN GOOD SHAPE, MY desire to one day run for public office could finally be realized in the late fall of 1961, at age 34. Once again I decided to sell my real estate office in order to fully prepare for the run. Dorothy and I talked about this before making such an important decision. Dorothy always knew that one day I wanted to run for an elective office, even before we were married. Probably like all young couples, in the early stages of getting to know each other, we'd expressed many of our thoughts and ambitions, and she knew this was one of my dreams and top priorities. We agreed I should run while I was still young enough and not too set in our comfortable ways that could later possibly cause me to lose my drive.

With Dorothy's approval and full support, I next shared my decision with James and the rest of my brothers. They were excited about this and offered their full support, too. Although I had some savings to provide for my family while I took on this task, James suggested that I get on the payroll of David Produce Company, since I already had a 10% share in it and often took part in making major decisions, and to use my title as the vice president as my occupation. That was a practical idea, since at age 34 I couldn't very well list my occupation as "retired."

With the election for the California State Assembly 79th District coming up the next year, I decided to run for that position. That seat was occupied by a friend, Democrat Assemblyman James Mills. I would run as a Republican against him if I won the Republican primary nomination. As a courtesy to Jim Mills, I called to inform him of my intentions. He was a bit surprised and responded, courteously, "Tom, I think you'll find running for an elective office to be a very challenging and a wonderful experience!

It'll take a lot of hard work and it'll be exciting!" I appreciated those words, but he did not say, and I did not expect him to say, "Tom, I wish you luck!" I had the highest respect for James Mills, who in later years moved on to become the leader of the California State Senate as the Senate Pro Tem.

I had learned from attending some of the previous political campaign seminars it was important, at the earliest time after announcing my candidacy, to notify all the so-called important people that might be of help. Of course, among the top of my list would be the chairman of the Republican Party of San Diego, Les Gehres. He was happy to hear that I had decided to run, and said, "You'll be good for the Republican Party and you represent the new blood that is needed in order to stimulate growth for the party. We'll work together on this!"

A few days later he set up a luncheon for me to meet about 25 of the more influential men and women in San Diego, and for me to give a brief talk about who I was and what my basic philosophy was pertaining to social, business, and governmental issues. Apparently my talk, which included a question and answer session, went off well. I received an enthusiastic round of applause. Without wasting any time, Chairman Gehres had an assistant hand out addressed envelopes, urging them to send in campaign contributions. A week later, Chairman Gehres handed me a number of checks totaling $3,250, as a result of my first fundraiser. I was very surprised by the large amount that was contributed. Thanks to Chairman Gehres, this fundraiser was a huge success. Later, I found out that my future fundraising luncheons would not be quite as successful as this first one. But every bit helped.

One day before I left a meeting with Chairman Gehres, he laid his hands on my shoulder and said, "I want you to know something, Tom. In the history of San Diego there has never been a minority who was ever elected to a public office. I want you to be the first. You'll be good!" I thanked him for his confidence in me.

While driving to my campaign headquarters, I began to feel extra pressure that people may be thinking that I am running mainly to be the first minority elected. I never intended to run on that basis. I just wanted to run as an All-American boy who happened to be of Chinese descent. I decided long ago that the only way I could win was to run on the basis of representing everyone, including minorities, based on the issues and what I believed was right. I already knew there were discriminating laws on the books and real and *de facto* discrimination issues existed, and I would continue to work towards eliminating them. I also knew I had to look at the bigger picture, where there were many other important issues, such as health, safety, jobs, and much more.

The 79th Assembly District had a lopsided registration of 65 percent Democrat and only 32 percent Republican. As a Republican, I knew this going in and what the challenge involved, but like so many newcomers, we entered into a battle with full confidence and enthusiasm to beat the odds.

Soon a campaign committee was formed, headquarters were opened, and word got around pretty quickly of the need for volunteers. Through the network of the supporters, I got many volunteers of men and women from Republican organizations, as well as students from high schools and colleges. I also had a number of Democratic volunteers as well that made up about 20 percent of the volunteer work force. These were mostly friends and new people who came to support my stand on various issues. It was a good mix, especially for running in the 79th District, with a big plurality of Democrats and quite racially mixed.

I had two Republican opponents vying for the same nomination. We all knew each other, but in politics, the guy who gets the message across best will win. My campaign manager, Lillian Poltre, a tough taskmaster, said, "Tom, I want you to spend 75 percent of your time meeting people. Either through coffee meetings in neighborhoods, walking the streets and handshaking with people, and most of all, door knocking at homes." This I did. It was a little difficult at first, not knowing how the person opening the door would respond, but as I continued to do it, it got to be fun and easy. People were generally quite receptive and took the brochure I handed out, describing my platform and biography. I've even had people tell me, in a kindly manner, "Tom, I like you, but I don't think you can win!" Some of these were even friends I grew up with. Funny, when people tell me it can't be done, it only makes me more determined.

During door knocking I was often invited in for coffee or tea. Whenever I went canvassing for votes, I would have an aide walk with me, a fellow named Don Sullivan, a young man of 25. One of his main jobs, whenever

I got pigeonholed by people who wanted to keep talking, was to "remind" me that we had a schedule to meet and must leave.

Overall, after knocking on over several thousand doors, I don't recall that there were any outright belligerent receptions. There were a few cool ones, but that was to be expected, and then there was the occasional life-changing encounter. One day as I was going door to door, a well-built elderly gentleman invited me in to chat. He said he was 92 and told me walking was one of the best exercises we can do, and he added that balance is extremely important, too. He said he started his day by putting on his pants one leg at a time, standing, without leaning on anything. I took that as good advice and have been putting my pants on while standing, not leaning on anything, one leg at a time for the past 40 years. You never knew who you were going to meet on the campaign trail.

AFTER SEVERAL MONTHS OF CAMPAIGNING, fundraising, speech making, rallies, and seemingly doing a hundred other things, the 1962 June primary elections were upon us. With all the volunteers and working so hard, the feeling of victory was in the air. Indeed it was! When the ballots were counted, we won the Republican nomination by a good margin. I now had the major task of running against the Democratic incumbent, Jim Mills, with the outcome to be decided on the general election day, Tuesday, November 6, 1962.

Now it was another kind of campaign, to run against an incumbent from a different party, who had an enormous majority in party registration. Because of that, our strategy was to retain the vast majority of the Republican votes, like up to 90 percent, and at the same time get as many as we could of the independent thinking Democratic voters. These are what we called the swingables. In politics, we had a saying: "We need to fortify our stronghold and swing their swingables!" At the same time, it's the opposite for my opponent, where he would be fortifying his stronghold by keeping as many Democrats as he could, because with his huge plurality in Democratic voters, he wouldn't need to have many others. That is part of the strategy, but in spite of that, candidates always like to have a bipartisan look in their campaigns by having people from the opposite party working for them.

The campaign kicked off with a bang. My two opponents in the Republican primary election endorsed me, and I also had a number of the ministers from the Black churches endorse me. Much of the congregation of these churches were registered Democrats, so this was a big incentive for me to make a real effort to know the members better. Dorothy and I attended many of the church services and were always given an opportunity to say a few words about my candidacy. Aside from my campaign appearance, we really appreciated and enjoyed the spirituality of the church services. Very devotional!

Being a political candidate exposed me to many diversified cultural events. I got bundles of invitations to attend Hawaiian and Samoan luaus, where I learned to eat *poi* and raw fish *poki*. Since Dorothy was from Hawaii, she was right at home at these kinds of festivities. But, of course, Dorothy was such an outgoing person, she was always at home at any kind of event. She was my biggest booster without even trying. People always gravitated to her in open friendliness. I, on the other hand, felt right at home at Latino events, as I was raised in Logan Heights where there was a large Latino population. My schoolmates and many of the produce workers were Latinos. Besides I spoke some Spanish and was a great lover of the culture and Mexican food.

Many of my Caucasian supporters hosted coffee klatches for me in their private homes, inviting their friends and neighbors. Some were small gatherings; others had an overflow of people. All of them were important, as it gave me the chance to present my ideas of better representation in government and to answer questions. Aside from the political questions, I had been asked, "How was it growing up in old Chinatown? Are there still Tong wars?" I was even complimented by an elderly lady who I'm sure meant well when she said, "Mr. Hom, I'm so proud of you! You're so Americanized!" I smiled and thanked her. I knew I got her vote.

I learned early on that I should not come across like I had answers and solutions to everything. At times, not knowing the answer, I'd say, "I don't know, but I'll sure study it! Later, if you wish, give me your phone number and I'll call you back! " I didn't bluff it. I was sincere and didn't over extend my answers. After each event, I did feel confident that I picked up most of the votes that were present.

Going to all these events was fun and educational, and also challenging to my eating habits. At every event, I ended up eating and drinking much more than I normally would. Keeping my weight from taking off was always a concern. Luckily, I enjoyed walking at a fast pace, and door knocking gave me that opportunity. So I walked for a double purpose, to keep the weight down and to get votes, what I called "double whammy walking!" In the precincts that I did go door to door, I did very well, in spite of some of them being heavily registered Democrat.

Everyone was working hard on the campaign, including many of my siblings, putting up signs, telephone canvassing, raising funds, passing out literature, and everything else that was needed in political campaigning. One of the more difficult aspects of campaigns was raising funds. Incumbents, like my opponent, had the distinct advantage of raising funds because of his position and name recognition. As a newcomer, we had our challenges. We got a lot of donations, but in most cases in smaller amounts. In spite of that, those do count significantly because any contributions made by an individual meant they could become a multiple supporter by telling others about you, and that person would tell others as well. Word of mouth was one of the best forms of support.

Before we knew it, it was almost the first Tuesday in November, general election day. Panic started to develop, wondering whether all the ducks were in order, and what were some of the things that we should have done, but never got around to it. Yet, we were all excited about the coming results, especially because we'd been working so long and hard for over a year, and so many people told us that we stood a good chance of winning. The volunteers decorated the headquarters with balloons and tables were stocked with drinks and food for the big showdown celebration.

During the evening TV news, as the returns started to come in, we were then neck and neck until about 9 p.m. and thereafter my opponent started to slowly draw away into the lead. By 10 p.m. a trend had been established in favor of my opponent, and by 11 p.m. enough of the final returns came in to declare my opponent the winner. Of course, I felt badly, but mostly for my wife Dorothy, who was so disappointed, and for the many hardworking volunteers. Some broke down and cried and some just slowly drifted away to go home, or, like some of the younger guys, go to a bar. Some of the hardier ones stayed behind and expressed words of encouragement, like, "Tom, you still ran a great race. For a first timer, you did great!" ... "Don't give up, Tom, there will be other opportunities in the future!" Disappointed, but not discouraged, I knew that in life when one door closed, two more opened. In spite of that, I did not sleep well that night.

The following day, still wallowing in my disappointment, and trying to console Dorothy, I got a call in the late afternoon from the chairman of the Republican Party of San Diego, Les Gehres. It was Dorothy who answered the phone, and as I approached the phone, I fleetingly thought that the chairman was calling me to give his condolences for my loss. Instead, he started out by saying, in an exuberant tone, "Tom, congratulations on running such a great campaign! For a first timer, with such odds, you did enormously well! I have before me the print out of the election returns, and it shows you with 31,543 votes against 39,134 for your opponent. He won by only a little over 7,500 votes. According to my calculations, with the district 65 percent Democratic registration against 32 percent of Republicans, you did extremely well. You took a good percentage of his Democratic votes. You ran an excellent bi-partisan race, and with more money and more time, you could have shifted 3,800 of his votes over to you and you would've won!" He paused, then said, "Tom, take a week to settle down and also take some time to study the results from the different precinct voter returns and then let's get together for lunch. Let's talk some more about your political future!"

I took his advice and studied the returns, and then I met Chairman Gehres for lunch. He suggested that I look into the possibility of running for a city council seat that would probably be open the next year when the city councilman of the 5th District, Frank Curran, was expected to run for mayor, which would leave his council seat vacant.

Chairman Gehres continued, "The city council seat falls right into the part of California Assembly District 79, in which you just got through running. In studying the voter returns, you did very well in that area. Since local office elections are normally run on a nonpartisan basis, I think you'll do very well. There will be a number of other candidates, but your name now has some public recognition, so that will help. The important thing is to first win the nomination in the district's primary election. Then afterwards, the two front runners will run off on a citywide election. I think you can do it!"

Meanwhile, I got an unforeseen call from the chairman of the San Diego Unified School District, Dr. Frank Lowe, an active member of the Republican Central Committee. He asked if I would consider an appointment to fill out the balance of the term of school district board member Dick Grijalva's district seat, who had served two terms and wanted to retire. Here was an offer, without running for election, for me to sit on the important San Diego Unified School Board, which would give me an opportunity to serve in public office. But after thinking about it, I decided that what I really wanted was to serve in the capacity of making laws to meet the needs of the general public. As important as the School Board was, it really was not something I wanted to champion at that point. My priority was to focus on the feasibility of running for the San Diego City Council.

I spent several days thinking over what Chairman Gehres said. To win the primary election seemed within reason, since my name was already familiar in that part of the district. I contemplated the question as to whether I, as a racial minority, could win in a citywide election, as this had never been done before. The city of San Diego, like most large cities in the country, was not fully integrated. Most of the different ethnic groups were living in separate areas in town. Knowing this, it would pose quite a unique challenge in running for election on a citywide basis, where 85 percent of the registered voters were Caucasians.

I thought to myself, "Could I win in a citywide election?" Then I remembered my mother, Ah Nuing, who in 1947 went door to door in a racially restricted neighborhood to introduce herself, with my four-year-old brother Paul in her arms, before buying the house she wanted. This gave the neighbors a chance to get to know her and our family, reassuring them that we were responsible people and would be good neighbors. The results were that she was well received with friendliness. Following the sale there were no efforts by any property owners to enforce the racial deed restrictions on the property.

In further speculating, I also reminded myself that when I was campaigning from door to door, a few people commented that they liked me and would vote for me, but then said something like, "But I don't know whether my neighbors would vote for you, you know, because of this racial thing!" That prompted me to go meet the neighbors, and in most cases I came away with positive responses. Some even asked me to put an election sign on their front lawn. With these kinds of thoughts and reminders, I felt confident enough to know that I could present myself well and I felt I could win.

After I discussed my proposal to run for the coming vacant city council seat with Dorothy, along with my brothers, they were all very encouraging and expressed enthusiasm for the idea. I called Chairman Gehres to tell him of my decision to run. He was elated to hear that and offered some advice, including getting organized early and start raising funds.

At the end of filing the application to run for the vacant council seat, there were four other candidates. Two were Republicans and two Democrats, one a Black minister, a long time friend of mine, and a Caucasian businessman, Joe Stacy, who was popular with the downtown establishment, endorsed by the Democratic Party. We three Republicans were invited to appear before the Republican Central Committee to be evaluated as to who should be endorsed. After the preliminary voting, and the elimination of one of the candidates, two of us remained for the final vote. I got the endorsement by 26 to 3.

In California, all local office elections were supposed to be nonpartisan but, in actuality, behind the scene campaign activities were often quite partisan. However, because it's viewed as a nonpartisan office, crossover of volunteers and voters were not unusual and, in fact, quite common.

In the district's primary election of the five candidates, Joe Stacy, who got the endorsement of outgoing City Councilman Frank Curran, who was running for mayor, got the most votes, and I came in second, thereby qualifying us as the two candidates for the runoff in the citywide general election. The news media reported that I was the first person of minority background who had ever been in a runoff election in San Diego history. It was then I thought of my former Memorial Junior High principal, William J. Oakes, who would often preach to student assemblies, stating, "Regardless of your ethnic background, you are all Americans, and you can be anything you want to be, but you must work hard for it." I knew I had my work cut out for me!

I had four months before the general election to cover the whole citywide area of San Diego, so organization and fundraising were priorities. Along with hiring a good public relations firm, I asked a number of business leaders in town to either host a breakfast meeting or luncheon for me to meet their business associates and tell them about my campaign platform. These served as fundraisers as well. In addition, a great number of people who followed my campaign came forward to help. Some hosted coffee klatches in their homes to have the neighbors meet me and donate to the cause.

IN THE FALL OF 1963, 200,000 supporters of the civil rights movement gathered at the Lincoln Memorial in Washington, D.C. to hear Rev. Martin Luther King, Jr.'s speech, "I have a dream…."

Because I was a supporter of this movement, I made a special effort to meet with the ministers of the Black churches. Many of the ministers I already knew, but many I did not. I was encouraged to worship with them on Sundays, where I would be given a few minutes on the pulpit to speak about myself and what I stood for. This type of introduction was not unusual in Black churches, and I appreciated that. The people were always cordial and many wished me well.

The time went quickly as the campaign became more intense. When the polls showed us neck and neck, the opponent's camp started spreading bad rumors about me, saying I didn't have the experience or the wherewithal to serve on the city council because I wouldn't be able to represent all the people, implying that I couldn't because I was a minority. I thought that was a dumb thing to do. My personal relationship with opponent Joe Stacy was always good and friendly whenever we met and debated on issues at candidates' meetings. He never came across expressing those kinds of viewpoints. I think his staff was panicking and was reacting desperately, and in the end that really hurt him.

On Election Day, November 5, 1963, at the headquarters, we were all cautiously optimistic, being mindful of the last election where we thought foolishly we had it in the bag, and lost. After the polls closed at 7 p.m., the results started to come in, with my opponent leading the first hour, not by much, but enough to cause us some anxiety. Shortly after, by 9 p.m., we were neck and neck, and by 10 p.m. we pulled ahead and then further ahead, and around 11 p.m. the TV newscaster said the Registrar of Voters office had announced our victory.

The headquarters erupted in uproarious screams of joy for this long-awaited victory. Everyone had worked so hard. Some even broke down and cried, especially some of the older volunteers, who had come early and stayed late working on the phones and the mailings. They had a big part in changing the political climate of our city through my election.

Quickly following, the champagne was uncorked and poured. Within five minutes of the announcement of our victory, I got a call from a good friend, Tommy Sheng, who owned a large downtown Chinese restaurant, congratulating me and told me that he was sending some food over for my victory celebration. Within half an hour, we had enough Chinese food to feed a hundred. With champagne and all that food, it was a great evening. I later asked Tommy Sheng how in the world he was able to have the food prepared and delivered piping hot so quickly after the announcement. He said he knew I would win. Because many of the opinion makers in town and news journalists came to eat and drink at his restaurant, he would ask their opinion as to my chances. His informal survey convinced him that I would win. On that basis, he started cooking for one hundred people hours before the winner was announced. Amazing. That was a new way of political polling I wasn't familiar with, but it worked.

During the celebration, Dorothy and I, along with an entourage of volunteers, joined together to go to the Election Center where the TV, radio, and news media were stationed at the El Cortez Hotel Ballroom for the tabulation and display of the votes as they came in. There, candidates, both winners and losers, would be interviewed, and campaigns analyzed and speculated upon. The crowd was huge. As we entered the ballroom, there were a great number of people applauding me, as well as a few boos. The applause became louder as we progressed deeper into the ballroom. I knew there were more applause and congratulations than boos, because people normally liked an underdog winner. I was also well aware I had made history in San Diego politics, and it was important that I behave appropriately and not become cocky and turn people off. Be confident, stable, and humble, I said to myself. I got a lot of pats on the back and handshakes congratulating me on my victory. I even got a number of them from supporters of my opponent who said they voted for me. That's okay too, because that's part of the bandwagon effect.

Because I was somewhat of a novelty in this election, I was sought after rather intensely for interviews. Invariably, I would be asked something to the effect of, "How does it feel to be the first minority person to be elected to City Council?" I tried from the beginning to downplay that aspect of my election, because I didn't want people to look upon me as just a minority person on the City Council. I wanted to be regarded as a man out to do a good job who just happened to be of Chinese descent, much like Frank Curran, the newly elected mayor, who just happened to be Irish.

My reply was short. "I consider it to be an honor and a privilege to be elected, and being a minority is not nearly as important as for me to do a good job as a city councilman and for all the people of San Diego!" And from there I would go on and talk about my platform and the needs of the city.

It was a great night! I was not only happy for myself, but for Dorothy and the family and to my many volunteers. And I had a special appreciation for Les Gehres, who guided me through so much and had the utmost confidence in me that I could do it.

The next day I got a printout of the final election results from the San Diego County Registrar of Voters Office, and they were as follows: Tom Hom 89,871 and Joe Stacey 54,572. I was astonished by the margin of victory and thankful as well.

According to the polling records, I did quite well in the Black neighborhoods, too. The fact is that I was a minority, and that a minority had never been elected in San Diego before probably had a lot to do with my appeal. They believed by supporting me and having me elected would help open up the electability for other minorities as well. And, indeed, that did come true, for after I was elected, there have been minorities elected to City Council ever since.

IX. First Day

AGES 35 TO 40

一只兔子崎岖的心路历程

Sworn in as the first minority Councilmember in the City of San Diego, 1963.

CHAPTER 32

The Unbeknown Power

IN NOVEMBER 1963 PRESIDENT JOHN F. KENNEDY WAS ASSASSINAT-ED IN DALLAS. STUNNED, THE NATION MOURNED. VICE PRESIDENT LYNDON B. JOHNSON WAS SWORN IN AS THE 36TH PRESIDENT ON AIR FORCE ONE.

THAT SAME YEAR I WAS SWORN IN AS THE NEW CITY COUNCIL-man for the 5th District in San Diego before an audience of family members, friends, and interested citizens. I was 36 and felt enthu-siastic to meet the new challenges that would go with this position. I was mindful that as the first minority to be elected in San Diego for this high position, I needed to work hard and not foul up. I remembered what my dad told me when I was about 12, outside of City Hall, "Here in America, the kind of laws that come out of there depend on the kind of people the voters put in there!"

I did learn something that morning after the inauguration. As I was walking in the corridor of City Hall with my family, an 80-year-old friend named Don Campbell, a prominent architect who helped in my campaign, came up and put his arm around my shoulders while we walked, and advised me. "Tom," he said, "I know you worked awfully hard in winning this election, but I want you to remember, it'll be even harder yet to steady yourself now that you have been elected!" That was sound advice. My dad used to always preach to us something like that, saying, "Work hard and be humble, but confident! Always be a gentleman!"

My first official meeting as a new city councilman took place on a Tuesday, in the City Council Conference Room, along with the rest of the five other councilmen, of which one was also newly elected like me, Mayor

Frank Curran. Joining us was the city manager, and the heads of all the major departments under him and the city attorney. The main purpose of the meeting was to introduce ourselves to each other, and to have the city manager and his department heads bring us up to date about the important issues facing the city, along with time for questions and answers. As a new kid on the block, I mostly listened and made notes. After three hours, we adjourned. I remarked to one of the other council members, "I wonder how San Diego can boost employment with the recession that we're in ... and also reduce the high crime rate that has become so prevalent in certain areas." It wasn't a question for anyone to answer, but rather, some out-loud thinking to myself.

Lo and behold! The next morning when I entered my council office, to my surprise, on my desk were piles of paper, all cataloged in neat order, regarding employment matters and crime. The reports outlined what had been done in the past, what was being done presently, and what future planning may entail on those issues. There were back up studies and surveys included, along with an up-to-date cover letter. My! All this because I happened to share some casual thoughts with a colleague.

Later that afternoon, the city manager called me and said, "Councilman Hom, at yesterday's meeting one of my staff members overheard that you had some concerns and questions about various issues. They were important matters, so we took it upon ourselves to try to bring you up to date as to what has been done and what are some of the programs that are now pending to address those issues. We left studies and reports on your desk this morning for you to review. If you have any questions or suggestions on any of the issues, please call me. We'd be glad to meet with you!" After hanging up, I quickly realized how powerful and influential an elected official could be. It's a powerful influence that can be used either to be constructive or self-serving. I had no problem in being constructive, for I could hear my dad whispering in my ear, "Now that you're inside looking out, you better do some good!"

The first Council Public Hearing was exciting. Since I was a rookie at this, I did take the weekend before the meeting to read up as much as I could as to policies and procedure on the city council hearings. I didn't want to step on too many toes at my first meeting. I got my book on Roberts Rules of Order and read it twice before the meeting. Although I already knew the basics of parliamentary procedures, I wanted to refine myself in that area and not get caught looking ignorant. Overall, my first experience went very well, as the veteran council members were very helpful in acquainting me with its process.

The city council business hearings were held twice a week and open to the public. Resolutions and ordinances were discussed and acted upon, and the public got the opportunity to be heard on numerous issues. Meetings could last from three to ten hours depending on how controversial the issues were. On other days, we would have committee meetings and meet with individuals, public interest groups, and numerous other entities that wanted our help and support. That's what we were there for, to listen and make decisions.

Obviously, I couldn't satisfy all the needs requested, but I did what I thought was right from all the pro and con information and evidence presented to me. Sometimes people got mad at me regarding my stand on a certain issue, but later there would be other issues that I supported that they liked. I'd go from bad guy to good guy, and vice versa. In the end, hopefully I'd have gained some credibility as being fair and independent enough, earning some respect for my judgment.

ONE MORNING DOROTHY, WHO WAS nine months pregnant, said to me, "Tom, I think I'm going to have the baby today. I can feel the bag is about to break. So on your way to your office, why don't you drop me off at Mercy Hospital for the delivery? I can take it from there!"

What? My first impulse was I needed to be there, like I had been for all her other five deliveries. But I had a bit of a dilemma, as that same day the council had a very important public hearing regarding a new tax law for the city, with an overflow of people in the chamber ready to express their concerns about the pending issue. My vote, one of seven, would be sorely missed if I wasn't there. Besides, I had only been on the council six months and I could be accused of skipping out on a hot issue. Dorothy was aware of this, so she insisted that I was not needed at the hospital, that the council meeting was too important to miss, and that she could take care of herself.

"After all," she said, "this is my sixth one, and it'll be an easy natural birth like all the rest of them." Her confidence convinced me that I shouldn't worry, that I should just go to the meeting, so I did. But I didn't like the feeling that I was not doing my husbandly duty.

Five hours after leaving Dorothy off at the hospital, during the hotly debated public hearing, my secretary handed me a note that said, "Tom, you're now the father of our fifth daughter. Beautiful! All of 6 lbs. and 12 oz. Wait 'til you see her tonight. She's Cynthia Sue Hom, as we decided if it should be a girl. All is well. Hope your meeting is going well too! Love, Dot."

With a sense of pride and elation I slid the note over to the council colleague on my right to read. He surprised me by waving for the mayor's attention to be recognized, and when he was, he announced, now waving the note, "Your Honor, our new Councilman Tom Hom just became the father of a fifth daughter a few minutes ago and we want to congratulate him." The council members along with the audience broke out in applause. I was so embarrassed.

The mayor spoke up and said, "Tom, I hope you brought along enough cigars. There must be at least three hundred here." Everyone laughed. Then the hearing proceeded, but the tension and the finger pointing of this controversial tax issue lessened. It's funny how the joy of a newborn baby can calm things down, just like that.

After the meeting was over, the reporter from the *San Diego Union* came to me and asked if I was going to see Dorothy at the hospital from here. I told him I was, and he said that he would like to take a picture of Dorothy and me with the new baby and write a story. I thought that was okay, so he met us at the hospital with a cameraman. The article and photo were displayed on the front page the next day. Cynthia Sue, whom we called Cindy Sue, was often teased by her siblings about her seeking public recognition from day one. In later years Cindy Sue became a television journalist with NBC.

As the year progressed, I became more acclimated as to how government worked. Some days there would be hot controversial issues and the news media would press me for comments. Sometimes I could answer intelligently, and other times the issue might be so new that all I could say was that I'd study up on it and learn all the facts first because the matter was so important and I needed to make the right decision. There were always numerous meetings with neighborhood groups that sought better parks, police protection, repaving streets, stopping gang fights, and other concerns of everyday people. I thrived on this, as I felt I was making a difference. Hours were long, but at end of the day, I did have a lot to share with Dorothy, who was just as enthused with my work as I was. When I think back on this, I think being young and energetic had a lot to do with our enthusiasm. It had to be. At my age now, 86, I don't think I could handle it.

The first year on the council went by fast. The following year in early January 1965, the city council and mayor, as they do each year, voted amongst themselves to pick a deputy mayor. The deputy mayor's job would be to fill the mayor's role whenever he was out of town or when he was unable to perform a mayoral duty. Four council members were seeking that position, of which I was not one of them—not that I didn't want it—but I thought I was too new to be the deputy mayor. With seven members voting by secret ballot, each of the three got two votes each and one got one vote. It would take a vote of four to get the appointment. After three more rounds of votes, with no one getting the four votes, the mayor asked me if I would consider taking that position. It was a surprise to me, but I answered with an emphatic, "Yes!" Then a vote was taken, now with five running for the position. To my surprise I got five votes out of the seven. Of course, I was shocked and elated ... mostly shocked. I knew I was the compromise candidate, but so what? I did vote for myself, but it felt good to know that I still would have won with four votes even if I hadn't voted for myself. I learned a lot that day about the art of compromise.

It wasn't long until I was called upon as acting mayor to perform duties. That same year Mayor Frank Curran was elected by the League of California Cities to be its president. The league consisted of almost all the cities in California, which amounted to a few hundred. Because of the responsibilities of that position, he was absent from San Diego fairly often. Consequently, I was frequently called upon to preside over public hearings and meetings as well as perform ceremonies like ribbon cuttings and throwing the first baseball for the opening season of the Padres, plus many Little League games as well. In addition, I was also meeting many of the important guests that visited our city, where I would present the Key to the City to them. The schedule was hectic, but, all in all, I was enjoying it. Except there was a part that I didn't particularly like, and that was while performing my duties, I had to go to too many breakfasts, luncheons, dinners, and parties. I really gained weight that year.

One of the more challenging episodes for me as Deputy Mayor was during the civil rights turmoil that was taking place throughout the country in the summer of 1965. San Diego was not immune. Only 130 miles away the Los Angeles Watts riots were raging out of control with run-away violence, property destruction, fires, looting, and people getting killed. There were a number of business owners who felt the riots were so overwhelming and out of control that they organized themselves as a defense brigade to fight off the looters by firing their guns from the rooftops of their shops. It became so chaotic and destructive that 20,000 National Guard had to be called in order to help the 4,000 police and sheriff's officers quell the riots. To keep the riots from possibly spreading, Lt. Governor Glenn Anderson, the acting governor, as Governor Brown was then in Europe, declared a curfew of 35 square miles centered from the Watts area.

San Diego was deeply concerned that the effects of the riots would spread to our city, as the riots had done in a number of other cities in the country. At that time, Mayor Frank Curran was traveling in South America and I had to take over as the acting mayor. During that period, with some great concern, Stokely Carmichael came into town. Carmichael, a firebrand civil rights leader, was known to be able to create highly charged crowds wherever he spoke and demonstrated. Sometimes he caused such major disturbances that law enforcements would have to be brought in. He was famously known to end some of his arousing speeches by shouting, "Burn, baby, burn!"

The day following Carmichael's arrival in town, he requested a meeting with the Mayor of San Diego. Because the mayor was out of town, this request was referred to me by City Manager Tom Fletcher. Because I had a meetings scheduled all day, I instructed Tom Fletcher to inform Carmichael that I could not immediately meet with him, but would meet with him at our family produce business at 5 p.m. I proposed this because I wanted to talk to him more personally rather than having the news media hounding us.

He accepted. So it was set up. The city manager asked me if I wanted a bodyguard to be with me during the meeting. For a moment I thought he was kidding, but quickly realized that he was just being cautious. I said I had no problem being alone. So we met a little after 5 p.m. Carmichael had two other young men with him. After our introductions, I asked Carmichael what he had been doing all day. He said he had been busy, first picketing and demonstrating in front of the Bank of America Main Branch on Broadway for their unfair employment practices, later meeting with ministers of the Black churches and other Black leaders, and also meeting at length with Clarence Irving, owner and editor of *The Voice*, the major Black newspaper in town. Something struck me as he was telling me all this. He did not at all fit the image I had of him, or the way he was portrayed in the news media. He was calm and soft-spoken and not once came across as the rabble-rouser he was reported to be.

After he got through describing his activities of the day, and told me some of his viewpoints, he asked my opinion as to what progress had been made in San Diego regarding fair employment, and as the first minority elected to the City Council, what measures were being made for racial equality, and so on. I shared my thoughts with him on all these things, and after I did, I asked him this one question, which had bugged me from the beginning of our meeting. I asked, "Stokely, how is it now that we've been meeting for almost an hour, that you don't at all come across, one bit, like the image people have of you, nor the way we read about and see you on TV?" I added, "Instead, you seem like a regular everyday Joe, nothing radical or fanatical and arm waving, shouting 'Burn Baby Burn!'"

He grinned, and said, "Maybe I can best say it this way. I consider myself to be the cleaver that splits things apart and that it'll take people like Martin Luther King, Jr. and others to put it back together into better working order."

I thought about that for a few moments, and it seemed to make some degree of sense. This was a revolution, of civil rights long neglected, and it took radicals to make it heard, and it took the calmer and more sensible people to make it work.

Upon leaving, Carmichael said, "When I was at Clarence Irving's office, he showed me an editorial from *The Voice*. He wrote about you being the first minority elected to City Council. It said something like, 'Tom Hom appears to be doing a good job in helping the Black community. He has been responsive to our needs and returns phone calls. He will do, until someone darker comes along." We all laughed, shook hands, and they left to go to another city that evening. It was a long hot day, but I felt good about it.

It was during that same summer of 1965 when I got a call from my good friend Dr. Charles Hampton, a dynamic Black minister from Bethel Baptist Church, perhaps one of the largest Black churches in town with several thousand members.

"Deputy Mayor Tom Hom," said the pastor with enthusiasm "this coming week on Sunday afternoon, at 4 o'clock, Dr. Martin Luther King, Jr. is coming to town and will be speaking at my church. I know you have spoken highly of Dr. King in the past, and I would like you to say a few words as well, as the person representing our city government!"

Of course I was flattered to be invited to speak on such a platform, and without hesitation I responded and said that I would be happy to do so, not knowing whether I had any other engagements pending on that particular Sunday. Whatever I had could be adjusted, I was sure.

On the Sunday of the event, I decided to arrive earlier, as Dr. Hampton suggested, in order for some of the community leaders to personally meet with Dr. Martin Luther King, Jr. in a private reception in the church lounge. At the private reception there were about 25 people, of whom I was the only Asian American, two Caucasians, and the rest were African-Americans.

Towards the end of the reception, I had a chance to personally congratulate Dr. Martin Luther King, Jr. on being awarded the Nobel Peace Prize the year before.

Added to that, I said, "Dr. King, your leadership in this great crusade for civil rights is helping Asian Americans and Latinos, as well. And I want to thank you!"

With his normally serious look, Dr. King responded by saying, "Yes, thank you, Mr. Hom. However, in the bigger picture, what I am doing is really for all mankind!"

Later I thought about that. How true. Here I am, only thinking narrowly, and he was thinking globally. He was, indeed, a wise, worldly man.

CHAPTER 33

Chinese Food Syndrome

I N 1964 THE SAN DIEGO CITY CHARTER STATED THAT THE CITY Council, with a city manager form of government, in essence, was a part-time position. Although it was suppose to be part time, it was in reality at least a 48-hour a week commitment in order to attend the regular public hearings, committee and neighborhood meetings, studying the pending legislation before Council hearings, responding to complaints, etc.

As busy as my council duties kept me, I was able to squeeze enough time to get involved in establishing a business that was partly inspired by observing the operation of the new Jack-in-the-Box hamburger restaurants. We had built a Jack-in-the-Box building for them to rent on one of our properties. It was fast food, everything very efficient, with a limited menu, and was supplied by a commissary to assure its food was uniform. It was gaining fast popularity in its short time in business.

I thought to myself, if that can be done with hamburgers, why couldn't it be done with Chinese food? It could be done with a limited menu, with the more popular types of dishes that the general public was familiar with. Nothing too exotic, but limited to items like egg roll, chow mein, fried rice, sweet and sour pork, egg foo yung, orange chicken, fortune cookies, etc. To my knowledge, there were not any operations of this type anywhere.

After working out a business plan with my brothers, we spotted our first location in a middle-income area, in a former restaurant with plenty of private parking on a busy business street. It didn't take too much effort to remodel it to include a small dining room and a drive through lane and window. So in a short time of about four months we had the restaurant, named Ricksha Boy, ready for business. Our chef was an excellent seasoned cook who formerly worked at his father's Chinese restaurant in Boston.

We flooded the neighboring area with door-to-door menus announcing our Grand Opening. Good Lord! To my surprise, we were immediately swamped with people lining up at the door to dine in, and a long line of cars to get service through the drive-thru window. The line of cars stretched a couple of blocks down the street. Traffic was so congested that cops had to come to regulate the traffic flow. That was opening day, but I also knew a lot of the people were there on a "to try it out" basis. As the weeks went on, we established a more regular trade with a steady flow of customers.

After a year, we were approached by a property owner who saw our operation and said he had a vacant building that was suitable for a fast food restaurant in another part of town. He quoted a rental rate that was reasonable. After doing a survey on its location and doing our due diligence, we offered to rent on the condition that certain improvements be made with our lease. He accepted. So within a little over a year we owned our second fast food Chinese restaurant. By this time, the workload was beginning to take more of my time than I had expected. My city council work had to come first, so I handed over most of my responsibilities to my brother Albert, who before joining Ricksha Boy was a sales manager at David Produce Company. No question that was the right thing to do, for I could sure see my dad looking down at me and saying, "Tom, many people can work in a restaurant, but not many can serve on the City Council!"

By our fourth year in operation, we opened our third location on El Cajon Boulevard, in the eastern area of town. That was our largest and busiest location. Our employees were like the Jack-in-the-Box employees, mostly high school and college age students, except for the managers. Because our food was Chinese, my brother Albert wanted to give the image of greater authenticity by having the Chinese kids work in the front serving area, and the few non-Asian kids work in the back kitchen area. Well, this went on for about three years, until one day a dear Caucasian lady friend, who worked on my political campaigns and had a son, Walter, who worked at one of the Ricksha Boys, called me. She said, "Tom, I don't mean to run your business, but my son Walter just told me that he wasn't allowed to work in the front area of your restaurants because he wasn't Asian. He had to work in the back, chopping onions, cutting celery, cooking rice, and all those things. He wants to work in the front where the fun and action is." And she went on to say, "Isn't this, I hate to say it, discrimination and segregation?" I must say, that caught me off guard. I guess I didn't realize that Caucasians could be sensitive to being racially discriminated against or segregated.

All this time I had seen myself as a supporter of diversity and desegregation, but instead I was doing the opposite. My reply to my friend was, "Julie, I really want to thank you for your observation on this. We never realized we crossed the line on something that I don't approve of. The reason we did it that way was that we thought it'd help our business image. Now I'm beginning to think it'll hurt it instead. Besides, it's not right, and it's contrary to what I believe. We'll do something about it right away." We parted amiably, and before we did, she apologized for bringing this sensitive matter up. I'm glad she did. After all, as a minority I should have been more aware of these things. I thanked her.

Walter did get to work in the front, and it didn't seem to matter that he wasn't Asian. But within a few weeks, he said the front was too much pressure and he asked to go back to the kitchen where it was more sane and relaxing. Besides, Walter said he wanted to learn how to cook Chinese food, which he did, and he became an excellent assistant cook. Good kid.

We had one customer that came in to eat several times, stayed around for an hour or so, seemingly studying our operation. One evening, after business had slowed down, this gentleman introduced himself, and said, "Mr. Hom, I'm James Parker. I know of you but you don't know me. I'm an attorney here in town, and I've been observing your operation off and on for several days. I want to congratulate you on this innovative concept of a Chinese fast food restaurant. Your food is good and your prices are most reasonable. Have you ever given it a thought to eventually franchising this concept?"

"I never thought of it, but I eventually hope to have a small chain of them," I replied. "But as far as franchising is concerned, I know very little about that."

He described himself as an attorney who practiced in franchising businesses. That intrigued me, so we sat down and he gave me the ins and outs of franchising. After about an hour of discussion, he suggested I should first establish eight operations, to establish a track record, and to have a logo with a prototype building designed, a model business plan, along with other essentials.

Our first Ricksha Boy drive-thru; one of three of the restaurants.

This was all intriguing, but obviously we were not ready for that. He did not try to push himself on me, and we parted on friendly terms. He said, "Tom, here is my card, and if you should later want to pursue the franchise route, feel free to call me." As time went on, I often thought of Jim Parker, but I never made contact again, as we never reached a point of franchising.

With three restaurants now in operation, I left more and more of the major decisions to Albert and the managers. I loved being in business, but I thrived in politics. I felt it was a higher calling. One could make a difference and it was important to have a presence, especially as a person of minority background.

IN THE SPRING OF 1965, I got a call from Les Gehres, the chairman of the Republican Party of San Diego, regarding actor Ronald Reagan. "I need to ask you to make some time on the day after tomorrow to meet with Ronald Reagan." You can imagine my surprise. "As you probably have been reading lately," Chairman Gehres said, "he is thinking of running for California governor. He has been traveling the state meeting with some of the head honchos to get their feedback on his possible candidacy."

I responded, with a bit of pride to be noted as a head honcho, and said, "Sure, Les, I'd be glad to do that! Tell me, who else will be there?" He gave a list of about a dozen names, most of the people I already knew. And he gave me the time and place, at the Hilton (the hotel had a different name then) in Mission Bay, top floor suite at 11 a.m. on Wednesday.

Upon arriving for the meeting at the suite, out walked my friend Congressman Clair Burgener. After exchanging greetings, he said he had to run along as he had another meeting to go to. A bit confused, I said, "Aren't you going to stay and meet with Reagan?"

While walking away, he said, "I already did, for about half an hour. I think you're next."

"Me next? Does that mean we're meeting on a one-to-one basis?"

As I entered the living room of the suite, a well-dressed young man greeted me and asked me to take a seat and said that Mr. Reagan would be with me very shortly. Within five minutes I was escorted into a room with Ronald Reagan standing in the middle, then he walked toward me extending his hand to shake mine. My first impression was that he was an "aw, shucks" kind of guy, the kind that would fit into a Norman Rockwell painting.

As we exchanged greetings he guided me to the bar, which had coffee, tea, cocoa, and a variety of soda pops and a jar of jelly beans. He asked what I would like and I chose a Diet Coke. I thought to myself, I've been to a lot of political events and they always had an array of liquor available, but not here. This was different. That was all right with me, but I never figured out whether this was for show or he was a teetotaler.

We sat across from each other in two leather chairs with a coffee table between us that had a legal-size yellow writing pad, several pens, and pencils. He explained to me that many people had been urging him to run for Governor of California this coming election, and that he was thinking about it and wanted to get some consensus and opinions from people like me. He said, "Chairman Les Gehres recommended you as one of the people I should consult, along with several others in San Diego. I'm doing the same thing in many other areas in the state. I would like to share some of my views, issues, and philosophy in running a better government. And, of course, your thoughts on my candidacy and the chances of winning." According to some of the early polls taken, I knew that he was a popular figure, but to win was another matter. We discussed those possibilities, issues, who some of his main supporters were and about some of the main challenges that a candidate would need to address in order to win the support of the people.

Of course, I knew from my education in politics that meetings like this helped gather and consolidate support from the very beginning. This is what candidates generally do. Pretty standard, but effective. Nevertheless, I did like his views on many of the issues, not all, and I asked him to consider modifying some of them in order to broaden his base. He made notes as we talked.

Within a half an hour of our meeting, he laid down his pen and pad and spoke to me about my family. He already knew that my wife was Dorothy and I had six kids, and that I did very well in winning my election having had strong support from a broad cross-section of voters, Republicans and Democrats alike. As we walked towards the door, he stated that if he should run, he would like to have my support. Without hesitation I said yes.

As I was leaving, walking across the living room, I saw my friend Herb Klein, chief editor of the Copley Press newspapers. We greeted each other, and I said, smiling, "You're next, Herbert. I think we may have a winner!"

Of course, Ronald Reagan did run and he won the primary election over several opponents and went on to win the general election for California Governor with an overwhelming majority over the incumbent, Governor "Pat" Brown.

IN 1965 WHEN THE SAN DIEGO CHARGERS football team was playing at the old, decrepit San Diego Balboa Stadium located next to San Diego High School downtown was when I became involved in helping to build a new stadium to accommodate major league football and major league baseball.

A few years earlier the Chargers moved from Los Angeles to San Diego. They felt San Diego had a better potential market for them, since the big team of Los Angeles, the Rams, had already been well established for many years. So in accommodating the move, the city added a second tier of 10,000 seats to the old Balboa Stadium's 20,000 seats. In a short time that still proved to be inadequate. Aside from that, the offices, athletic facilities, public bathrooms, and food concession stands were totally antiquated, which created many health and safety issues. Also, the public parking facilities could only accommodate about 2,000 cars. The rest of the cars had to park in the surrounding neighborhood, and that created a lot of anger among many of the property owners.

Those issues and the desire of keeping the Chargers in San Diego meant the city had to think about building a new stadium to meet the standards for a major football team.

Before moving on to the next step of building a new stadium, the City Council wanted consensus by the citizens as to whether they wanted it or not, and if so, would they be willing to pay for it through a property tax base or sales tax.

Two propositions were prepared for the ballot. One asked whether the voters wanted a new stadium based on paying for it through property tax or sales tax. The other proposition asked if they supported the building of a new stadium if it could be built without raising these taxes.

After the votes were tallied, it was evident that voters were overwhelmingly against any new taxes. There was huge support for the other proposition, about building a stadium without raising taxes.

In so doing, the City Council passed a resolution to form a task force, and appointed me as chairman, to work with City Manager Tom Fletcher and his staff. We had the monumental task of exploring the feasibility of financing the stadium without raising taxes. Our first job was to get an estimate as to the cost of a new multi-purpose stadium that could accommodate football and baseball alike. To that end, we hired one of the big five accounting firms to do the feasibility study. It came back with an estimate of $30 million, for a seating of 65,000, based on land cost of about $25 per sq. ft. Building the stadium would be the largest and most expensive single project that the city had undertaken so far.

With that study, we had our work cut out for us. After a series of meetings and suggesting different scenarios as to how to raise the funds, we finally came up with a proposal that we believed could work, without raising taxes. The following is the general outline of that proposal:

1) The city had a lot of surplus vacant land, known as the Pueblo Lands, given to the city many years ago by the federal government. Some of the land was in the pathway of the expanding growth of the city.

Caltrans, the California Highway Department, was planning to build freeways in a number of these areas. We worked with Caltrans to locate the cloverleaf ramps in strategic areas for the growth of industrial, business, and housing developments. Later we would sell these parcels of lands through a bid process and use these funds to build the new stadium.

2) At that time, San Diego only had a triple AAA Pacific Coast Minor League baseball team, named the San Diego Padres, owned by banker and entrepreneur C. Arnholt Smith, who had his own baseball park, called Westgate Park, located in Mission Valley. For years he had been trying to get a major league franchise for the Padres, but to no avail, due mostly to the lack of the right kind of sports facility to fit the needs of a major league team. Knowing that, we approached Smith to become a tenant in our new proposed multi-purpose stadium, giving him a better chance of getting the major league franchise that he had sought for so many years. He jumped at the offer; the National Baseball League backed the new proposed stadium, and Smith got his major league franchise.

3) Next we approached the San Diego County Board of Supervisors for their support of the new stadium. With their support we would be able to work a better bond issuance for the financing of the stadium. The board passed a resolution that supported the new stadium.

4) The summary is that we would be raising several million dollars from the sale of the vacant surplus Pueblo Lands that the city owned. The revenue from the rental income of the San Diego Chargers and the new National League San Diego Padres, along with other incomes that would be generated from different venues, would be enough to pay toward the retirement of the revenue bonds that would be sold to finance the stadium.

The process of putting it together took about six months. Following, the Task Force Committee submitted a full report for the City Council to review. After the Council's review, a Council Conference was convened for discussion, and some minor adjustments were made here and there, but the overall concept of the proposal was well received. After a public hearing, the recommendation would be submitted for a referendum in order for the people to vote on it. Prior to going before the voters, a citizens committee was formed to spearhead support for the new stadium. We also hired the well-established Frank Hope architectural firm to draw preliminary plans of the multi-purpose stadium that would be located in semi-rural Mission Valley. The special election was held, and it was approved by an overwhelming vote of 76 percent.

Ground was broken for the stadium in August 1965 and completed two years later. Originally it was named San Diego Stadium. But later, when Jack Murphy, the chief sports editor of the *San Diego Union* who brought and promoted the idea for a new stadium to the City Council, passed away in 1980, the stadium was renamed Jack Murphy Stadium in honor of his efforts and dedication. However, as years went by, in 1997 the global wireless technology firm, Qualcomm, paid $18 million to retain the naming rights through 2017, and the stadium was renamed Qualcomm Stadium.

That's the way it goes, I guess, with more funds needed to promote sports along with tourism, cities get funding wherever they can. That seems to be the trend all over the country. The locals benefit too, so I can't knock it. It bothers me, though, that ticket prices to see a major league game have become so exorbitantly high for the average mid- to low-income family. Most of them can't afford it. It had not always been like that. One of the reasons price of tickets being so costly is that the major league entities, such as the National Football League, National Basketball Association, and others, have a monopoly and are exempt from the antitrust laws through an act of Congress. I strongly believe Congress should do something to rectify that.

CHAPTER 34

In the Deep South

THE GRAMBLING TIGERS OF LOUISIANA COME TO SAN DIEGO.

I T WAS THE YEAR OF 1966 WHEN I MET THE PRESIDENT OF GRAM-
bling College, Ralph Waldo Emerson Jones. He accompanied the
college's famous jazz marching band to entertain at the halftime event
of a San Diego Charger game. As Deputy Mayor, I was hosting the president and at halftime, before the sellout crowd of fans, I presented him the
proverbial Key to the City, something we often did with dignitaries.

To my surprise, a few months later I received a letter from President
Jones inviting me to be the commencement speaker for the class of 1967.
Grambling was such a famous Black college, I felt it was indeed an honor
to be asked. Of course, I accepted.

In spite of Grambling's fame, I didn't know it then, but found out years
later, that there were over 100 Black colleges in the country, which produced many outstanding leaders who were successful in many different
fields. Among them were Thurgood Marshall, Justice of the U.S. Supreme
Court; Andrew Young, former Mayor of Atlanta and U.S. Ambassador to
the United Nations; Rosa Parks, civil rights activist; Booker T. Washington,
educator; Rev. Martin Luther King, Jr., church and civil rights leader; and
Oprah Winfrey, television and humanitarian icon.

Up to the year of 2000, the Black colleges produced about 70 percent
of all the Black physicians and dentists, 50 percent of the Black school
teachers and 50 percent of the Black Congressmen and women. Considering
the many challenging conditions that Black colleges had to go through, I
would say they did quite well.

Upon landing at the airport in Shreveport, Louisiana, I was greeted by President Ralph Jones of Grambling College and his assistant. After gathering my luggage, we proceeded to journey about 65 miles to the little town of Grambling. I noticed the quaintness of the town, not very large, but very much like many other college towns, with many trees and well kept lawns and homes. The town was predominately Black.

I was taken to President Jones' home, where I would be staying, and met his wife, who had lunch ready for us. She was a charming and obviously well-educated person. Later I found out I was correct. She had a PhD in education.

After lunch I was given a tour around the campus by the president and his assistant, meeting some of the students, including the student body president and some of the outstanding athletes, who would be moving on to the professional level, subject to the draft season that would be coming up. It was common knowledge that Grambling was a school that regularly produced outstanding athletes. At that time, among the outstanding football players for the San Diego Chargers were 6′7″, 325-pound Ernie Ladd and 300-pound giant Earl Fasion, both Grambling alumni. The school's sports program especially excelled in football and baseball under the famous coach, Eddie G. Robinson, Sr. Along with touring the campus, we also watched the senior graduating class's rehearsal for the next day's ceremony.

That evening I attended a reception where I was introduced to the faculty. Although Grambling College was known as a Black college, not all the faculty members were Black. There were several non-Blacks of different races. Likewise, the student body was about 90 percent Black and the rest were white, Asian and, other races.

During the course of the evening, a tall, friendly, dignified gentleman said to me, "Mr. Hom, we're quite honored to have you, the Deputy Mayor of San Diego, be the speaker for our commencement. Tell me, what university did you go to?" Before I could answer that I never went to college fulltime, only night classes for some business courses, I was interrupted by an overly enthusiastic woman, who cried out loud, "Mr. Hom, we heard so much about you, and I want you to meet one of our lady professors, Catherine Tom. She's Chinese and would love to meet you!"

"Mr. Hom, we are so proud to have you as our speaker tomorrow," said the Chinese professor. "Tell me, where did your parents come from in

China? Since your name is Hom, same as the Tom family name, your parents must have come from the Canton area. Whereabouts in that area?"

The lady was eager to talk about family, so I looked apologetically at the gentleman with whom I'd been talking. He just shrugged his shoulders, smiled, and said to Catherine Tom, "Cathy, you may have found a new cousin. And, Mr. Hom, it has been a pleasure meeting you and please excuse me. I'll just move along."

"Yes, Catherine, my parents are from the Canton area," I said, returning to the conversation, "the Hoiping village, and we speak the fourth dialect, See-Yep. Yes, we really may be cousins." In response, she laughed out loud and gave me a powerful bear hug. She then went on and told me about her father who came over to the U.S. in the 1930s and went to New Orleans to work in his cousin's restaurant, and eventually went on his own to start his own restaurant, which was doing very well. There were five children, and she was the second oldest. I thought about her family as she talked; a typical immigrant story, they came with hardly anything, worked hard, made good and raised a big family, and the priority was to give the kids a good education and have the kids become more successful than they were.

The next morning, rather early, I got up to practice my speech, had breakfast with President Ralph Jones and his wife, and then went together to the campus for the graduation ceremonies. It was already hot and muggy that morning, which must've been part of the southern summer that was starting. They fitted me with a rather heavy colorful gown and cap to wear. That made me even more uncomfortable. But because of the excitement of the coming event and the band playing the prelude for the ceremony, I was able to overlook the hot discomfort. During the ceremony, the president shed his cap before he started his speech. I took that as a cue that it was permissible, so I too took off my cap, as several other faculty members did too.

In my speech I told the students of the major social changes that would be taking place in their time, so they must get involved to make a difference. I talked about the sacrifices that their parents and the school had made in giving them this education to make these differences and not to be afraid to think outside the box to achieve these goals. I acknowledged the high scholastic standards of Grambling, and also the outstanding athletes that the school had produced, such as Ernie Ladd and Earl Fasion with the San Diego Chargers. I also read a letter presented to me from the famous Charger Coach Sid Gillman, extolling many of the well-known and out-standing athletes that had come from Grambling. After my 20-minute speech, I got a standing ovation. I'm not sure if it was for my speech or my praising the outstanding athletes. Nevertheless, it was a surprise and it felt good.

On the way to the airport, I asked President Ralph Jones, "By the way, Ralph, as a curiosity, while I am deeply flattered, how is it that you decided to ask a guy like me to be your commencement speaker, from way out in San Diego, when you had so many other fine choices available to you?"

He said, "Tom, I am an historian. And I know the role the Chinese have played in early California, the building of the railroads, reclamation of the lands to make them productive, and the prejudices that they had gone through, including the Congressional act of the Exclusion Law in 1882 that prevented Chinese laborers from entering the country. The Chinese suffered through riots and lynching. We Blacks understand all of that."

He went on to say, "After I met you, as a City Councilman and the Deputy Mayor of a lily white city like San Diego, I said to myself, how did this happen, a Chinese, a minority, elected over a supposedly popular white man? I did some research on that. And the population of Orientals in San Diego is less than two percent. You are one of the very few Orientals ever elected to public office, especially for a big city like San Diego.

"To put it plainly, I wanted my students to see you as an example to achieve higher goals, in spite of the odds. Make sense?" he remarked. Now that I'm older, and that was in 1963 when I was first elected, a much different world from today, it did make sense. I hoped my appearance at Grambling did nudge the door open for making a positive difference.

As we arrived at the airport, President Jones handed me an envelope, and said, "Here is a little token of appreciation, your honorarium." I was surprised, and I replied, "Honorarium? I didn't expect this, and I have no need for it. And besides, it was my pleasure being part of this graduating class."

He responded, "Nope. Tom, you must take it. It's already budgeted. You have to take it!"

So on the flight home, I opened the envelope. Inside was a cover letter thanking me for the inspiring talk to the graduation class and a check for $1,000. The next day I sent a personal check for $500 to Grambling College for its student body activity fund.

GRAMBLING COLLEGE RECEIVED
R. W. E. JONES, PRESIDENT
GRAMBLING, LOUISIANA　　1967 JUN 29　AM 9: 35

CITY COUNCIL OFFICE
CITY OF SAN DIEGO

DIVISION OF APPLIED SCIENCES
AND TECHNOLOGY

June 28, 1967

Mr. Tom Hom, City Councilman
The City of San Diego
City Administration Building
Community Concourse
San Diego, California 92101

Dear Mr. Hom:

One month ago you were here with us in Grambling--and because of your visit we will never be the same. You gave new insights and added meaning to experiences which we shared. You helped us to see ourselves in a new light; as a group making contributions--perhaps, important ones--to the ever-changing way of life and culture of the United States. You also provided an incentive--an example of success--for higher goals on our part. Rarely has anyone so positively influenced so many people in such a short period of time as you did during your visit. We thank you sincerely for coming to Grambling.

We, the Stewarts, were delighted to have you as guest while you were here. You had a tremendous influence on each of us; especially Robert who has enjoyed the baseball glove so much. He is a member of the Pee Wee League and has played in one game which ended in a tie (14-14). Can you imagine such a thing?

You certainly know how to select useful and unique gifts. The book marks are perfect. They give me an excuse to read more so that another book mark can be used. Karen is excited about the stationery. I believe that she is using some of it to write a note to you. The tea is delicious and different. Thank you so much for remembering us.

we are in California. You know, of course, that you have a home in Grambling whenever you come this way. Please make our home your home.

Thanks again for the compliments and good wishes. It was a real pleasure to be your host during your visit to Grambling. Do come again soon.

Sincerely,

J. T. Stewart

J. T. Stewart
Dean

JTS:oml

SITTING ON THE CITY COUNCIL also put me in the position of being appointed to other boards and commissions in the county. In this case the mayor appointed me to the San Diego Health Department Board as one of the five commissioners; the other four were from other agencies. I attended several meetings and they were pretty much routine matters, mostly pertaining to better regulations of the health laws.

That was until the chief health officer of the county recommended that we pass a law for San Diego County to put fluoride in the public water system, in order to prevent tooth decay in children.

That seemed like a win-win proposal, to fight tooth decay on behalf of the children. But after some thought and further discussion, I decided to oppose it. I opposed it because the fluoride did not do anything for the purification of the water, like we do with some chemical substances to keep it purified and safe to drink. Putting fluoride in the system was only using the water system as a mode of transportation to carry a substance that had nothing to do with the purification of the water. What was there, I thought, to prevent a group from also wanting to use the water system to transport aspirin and vitamins C and D to the general public? We were told these were good for people, too. This could go on and on. I advocated that fluoride pills be dispensed free of charge through various health agencies, or other means, for those who wished to use them. We already had fluoride in toothpaste, and that was by choice.

The meeting was covered by the news media, and without realizing it, it became such a hot issue that it made the front page headlines and the leading TV news story, quoting me frequently as the main opposition. I was accused by the San Diego Dental Association that I was against children having good teeth, especially the low-income family kids who could not afford dental care. On the other hand, I got strong rallying support from many people who thought I made good sense and from groups who wanted to limit "big brother" government.

In any event, when the issue of fluoridation of the public water system was later put on the San Diego ballot for a vote, the measure was not approved. Ironically, the areas that stood to benefit by it the most, the lowest income families, were the areas that voted overwhelmingly against it, and the high income areas, like La Jolla, voted in support of it.

About 25 years later, in 1995, the powerful California Dental Association and its strong lobbying group took the matter of getting fluoridation
into the public water systems to the California State Legislature, who put
it on the statewide ballot for a vote. After a very volatile campaign, pro
and con, the voters approved it. In spite of the fact it passed in 1995, by
2011 there were still many public water systems that had not abided by
that ruling, citing some studies that fluoride had not been proven to prevent tooth decay. Others reasoned that the water systems should not be
used as a mode of medical transportation that has nothing to do with the
purification of the water.

Not too many of the issues were that controversial. Probably only about
10 to 15 percent of the issues provoked strong emotional reactions from
the public.

There are some propositions that seem frivolous to some, but important
to others. One in particular was when the U.S. Postal Service in Washington, D.C., decided to streamline the postal operation in San Diego. They
wanted to eliminate the postal marking of the word "La Jolla" to all mail
processed through the La Jolla Post Office, and have it postmarked as "San
Diego" instead, like the rest of San Diego, since La Jolla was not officially
a separate city, but a community within San Diego.

The people in La Jolla were incensed. In no time, the La Jolla Town
Council appealed to the City Council to do everything they could to
defeat that drastic change. A public hearing was held so the people could
be heard on the matter. An hour before the hearing the council chamber
was filled with hundreds of people, with an overflow in the hallways and
into several extra rooms.

The hearing went on for hours, with 99 percent protesting the change,
and a handful supporting it because they didn't like "the uppity attitude"
of the people of La Jolla.

After several hours, the mayor entertained a motion to pass a resolution
to retain the La Jolla postmark for the La Jolla Post Office. Of course, that
resolution passed unanimously without much debate. We all knew that La
Jolla was a distinctive community known internationally, so why not? In
response to the City Council's resolution, the U.S. Postal Service cancelled
its order to make the change.

This was one of the more volatile issues that was easy to resolve without making many enemies.

IN SPITE OF THE MANY PROBLEMS while serving in public office, there were many good moments, too. Like one day a good friend who was one of the largest general contractors in town called me and said, "Tom, I recently read in the papers that one of the areas you represent in southeast San Diego has one of the highest rates of juvenile delinquencies. Is there anything I can do to help?" He was one of the early pioneers of San Diego, who was born in Arizona, and came to San Diego in the 1890s while helping drive a herd of cattle to the coast when he was twelve. He never went back and later became one of the top citizens of our town. Small guy, always wore a cowboy Stetson hat and western clothes and spoke softly. He was fondly known as Roscoe "Pappy" Hazard, then in his eighties.

Hearing Pappy asking what he could do to help brought music to my ears. A few years earlier, I was one of the co-founders of the Southeast YMCA, which later was renamed the Jackie Robinson YMCA. I continued to be active in the organization and was asked to be co-chairman with Dr. Vell Wyatt to raise funds for a swimming pool.

I responded, "Pappy, if you have time right now, I can pick you up and we'll go down there and see what the needs might be." In my mind I knew it would be a swimming pool. "How about half an hour from now?"

So I picked up Pappy and drove around the southeast area and pointed out the places of interest, and finally ended up at the YMCA. "Pappy," I said, "in all of southeast San Diego we do not have a public swimming pool for the kids." As I pointed to a bare spot near the clubhouse, I added, "In our master plan, we dream of one day having a swimming pool right there."

His response was without hesitation, soft and clear, "Sure, let's do it. We'll get it done!" The next day he had his foreman meet with Rufus DeWitt, the executive director, to layout plans for the new pool. Within a week a bulldozer was on site to start excavation. Wow! Within a few months, the kids of the area finally had a swimming pool.

As the years went on, the Jackie Robinson YMCA continued to grow into a very popular gathering place for youth. I'm sure the pool was one of the major attractions in helping to keep kids off the street. Pappy Hazard did a lot of these types of kind gestures of concern, and without any fanfare. He was a small man in statute, only about 5 feet 4 inches, but mighty tall by all who knew him.

x. The Governor Called

AGES 40 TO 45

Me with then-Governor Ronald Reagan.

CHAPTER 35

Second Time Around

IN 1967 ISRAEL WON THE SIX DAY WAR OVER A COALITION OF ARAB NA-
TIONS, AND DR. CHRISTIAAN N. BARNARD OF SOUTH AFRICA PERFORMED
THE FIRST SUCCESSFUL HUMAN HEART TRANSPLANT. OUR COUNTRY
WAS COMING OUT OF A RECESSION. THE ECONOMY WAS PICKING UP
AND PEOPLE WERE SPENDING AGAIN. GOOD YEARS WERE LYING AHEAD.

IN THE SPRING OF 1967, I STARTED THINKING ABOUT THE FACT that my four-year term on the City Council would terminate at the end of December. It had been over three years since my last election. With the primary elections taking place the coming September and the general election two months later in November, I had to seriously start thinking about whether I wanted to run for re-election or to run for another office, such as the San Diego County Board of Supervisors.

After discussing this with Dorothy, who always offered very good insights, we decided that I would run for re-election, where I could have a good chance of winning. And depending on how well I did, we would decide from there as to whether my running for a higher office would be feasible in the future. So I filed my re-election papers to again run for the City Council. Aside from serving in a high profile and important position, it would give me a good chance to see how people in San Diego felt about my representation so far.

It was at this time when the City Council received a study and report from Walter Hahn, our highly capable city manager, who recently moved up from assistant city manager, stating that it was time to reevaluate the taxi fare rates for the City of San Diego. The report said that the city's rates were the lowest of all the other major cities on the west coast, such as Los Angeles, San

Francisco, Oakland, Seattle, and others. The taxi companies, led by Yellow Cab and the taxi drivers, were pushing for the adjustment to be in line with the other cities. After a public hearing on the issue, with no opposition, and with the recommendation of the City Manager to approve this adjustment, the City Council and the Mayor voted unanimously for approval.

The issues were simple enough, to equalize the rates with other major coastal cities, but little did I realize that later on this single issue would come to haunt the City Council members, including me.

Having decided to run for re-election, a committee was formed to start the campaign and to raise funds. Getting all this together was much easier than my previous election, because I had the advantage of being an incumbent and also being better known.

In the September primary election there were three other candidates running to oppose me. As it was the law then, the primary elections were held in each of the different districts, and the two candidates to receive the most votes would run off in a citywide general election in November.

In the September primary election I won with 68 percent of the votes. In November in the citywide general election, I won, to my surprise, an astonishing majority vote of 87 percent, which at that time was the largest plurality in the City of San Diego's election history.

Of course, I was astonished. Either my opponent was so bad ... or I was so good. In either case, I won big. But in reality, it was a combination of many things, especially having an abundance of dedicated volunteers. Many of the volunteers were just as surprised about the huge margin of victory, but there were a few that said they knew right along I would win big. I felt mighty good about that, but while thinking that, I had a fleeting thought that went back to almost four years earlier, when I was first inaugurated into the City Council. I'll never forget my 80-year-old friend Don Campbell's words of warning while I was walking out of City Hall: "Tom, I know you worked hard on this campaign, but remember, it'll be harder yet for you to steady yourself now that you have won." With that in mind, I celebrated with the rest of the supporters, but not boastfully nor flauntingly.

The campaign office was full of joy and we whooped it up with champagne and snacks. I soon got a call from my friend, Tommy Sheng, congratulating me, and he offered once again to send food over to the campaign headquarters as he had done four years before. All he needed was a head count, and I told him 100 to 150. In less than an hour the delicious food was delivered. As time went on more people kept pouring in, and I started to worry about running out of food. But at the end we still had enough, which was characteristic of the Chinese to always provide much more food than what was generally needed. Nothing is worse than running out of food. That would be a loss of face. Nevertheless, I was thankful for that generosity of the Chinese culture.

The next few days were very hectic. I was swamped with calls and letters congratulating me, and I was busy responding to the attention of the news media. Many of the common questions asked by the media were, "What's your next move in seeking higher office?" I had been advised by some of the more astute political people that the proper answer, so as not to appear too ambitious, was, "At this point, I just want to do a good job for what I was elected for."

With that, Dorothy and I took the six children up to Disneyland and visited my orthodontist brother, Allen, in Los Angeles for a week. This gave us some much needed quality family time together, which had been so scarce during the campaigning months.

Allen had helped in my campaigns since the very beginning. So taking a break, spending time together, was relaxing and fun. We enjoyed reflecting about what the future might be for both of us. For me, perhaps a higher office. And for him, aside from his orthodontist practice, to get involved in investments. As life would have it, I did later seek a higher office. And as for Allen, he did get involved in investments, such as banking, television ownership, and real estate, becoming very successful in doing so.

The following month, December 1967, I was sworn in for my second term on the City Council. As usual, I had members of the family there along with a number of supporters. There were not as many as when I first won that seat with all the newness and fanfare, which was understandable. But for me, the second time had something special about it. Because I won by a big margin, it gave me a boost in confidence that I could do a better job and even possibly move on to a higher office later on.

In the ensuing months I noticed some positive changes in my working relations with my fellow council members. It dawned on me that whenever

I advocated on issues, it had an influence on them that I did not have during my first term. Of course, more experience had something to do with it, but it was more than that.

As the days went on, I came to realize that the impact of my winning by such a large majority in a citywide election meant I also won quite heavily in each of their own council districts as well, which left some degree of an impact on them. On many occasions, with issues which were heavily debated, some of the council members would defer to me and want to know my thinking before they would take a strong position. It was not always so, but it happened enough times that I realized I had arrived, that I had some leadership and influence on the Council.

I suppose I gained some sense of pride in all this, but I had already understood by then the vulnerability of self-importance and the volatility of politics on the day-to-day basis. "Stay on steady ground," I said to myself, "and don't go flaunting yourself as though you are the anointed one." Besides, I would probably make a fool of myself if I tried. A guy almost has to have an image of a John Wayne to get away with it. That, I didn't have.

Republican Chairman Les Gehres called me about three or four months after my re-election. He told me he wanted to have lunch to discuss a recent meeting he had with Governor Ronald Reagan. It was important, just the two of us, he said.

So we met at the Cuyamaca Club downtown. He reiterated how elated he was with my winning re-election in such a convincing manner. He expressed that I, along with others, like State Assemblyman Pete Wilson, were part of the new blood that was badly needed in the California Republican Party. His remark regarding Pete Wilson came to fruition in a big way in later years, when he was elected Mayor of San Diego, then U.S. Senator, and ultimately Governor of California.

Chairman Gehres also told me about his recent meeting with Governor Reagan, along with the Republican chairmen from other state counties. The important issue was that in two years, the U.S. Census would be taken and new Legislative Districts would be redrawn two years after that. How the new districts would be redrawn was mostly influenced by which party controlled the state legislature. At the present time, the Republicans were three short of control.

Chairman Gehres went on to say, "I told the Governor of your background and how you came across so well in the citywide election with the largest plurality in the city's history, 87 percent against your opponent's 13 percent. He was impressed, and said for me to talk to you. Tom, along with having lunch with you, I'm here to ask you to consider running."

"Well, Les, this is a surprise," I said, "especially because I have hardly caught my breath from the last election, and here I am, to consider running again so soon. This is something I need to really think about and discuss with my wife Dorothy. I've got a business here, six children in school, and other things to consider. I need to think this out."

Chairman Gehres said, "I don't expect an answer now."

That evening I talked to Dorothy about my meeting with Gehres. After a discussion of the pros and cons of such a move at this time, we decided to think more on it and evaluate it over the next few days.

Meanwhile, I got a call from Sacramento. The caller, a lady's voice said, "I am calling from the Governor's office in Sacramento, and I wish to speak to Councilman Tom Hom."

"Yes, this is he," I said.

She responded, "Hello, Councilman Hom. Governor Reagan would like to speak to you. Please hold the line while I connect you."

"Oh my gosh," I said to myself, "don't tell me the Governor is calling to put pressure on me to run. I'm not ready to give an answer." In that moment, it seemed like a hundred things were going through my mind as to how I would handle this, without giving an outright answer. After all, the Governor himself was calling.

Then Governor Reagan came on the line and said, "Tom, I want to say that it is good to talk to you again. The last time, as you will recall, was when we met at the hotel in Mission Bay to discuss the possibility of my running for governor. Thanks to you and people like Herb Klein, Malin Burnham, and many others, we came out winners. We've been hearing great things about you. Tom, tell me about some of the things you're doing down there."

I told him about my recent re-election, trying not to blow it out of proportion, and about working with some of the San Diego legislators in Sacramento, like Assemblymen Pete Wilson and Dick Barnes, and others.

I also talked about my growing family, wife Dorothy, and even about my hobbies. He was easy to talk with.

After a few more minutes, he closed by saying, "Last week Les Gehres praised you to high heaven as a possible candidate to help us gain a majority in the Assembly. I know, at this point, you haven't made up your mind. You have to do what's best for you and your family. So, Tom, think about it. It's going to be very important for the state of California in 1970." He never really pressured me—just by calling me was pressure enough. Yes, there is a reason why he is referred to as the Great Communicator.

After I hung up, I recalled the first time we met, how he was a regular guy as in a Norman Rockwell painting. But, in reality, he was much more than that as I got to know him better in later years. He was a person with no airs at all for being a famous movie star and governor of California.

Later that evening, I had a serious talk with Dorothy about this. She, forever an optimist, ready for new challenges, felt it was up to me as to whether I wanted to run or not. She outlined it by saying, "If we should go, the logistics of relocating the family to Sacramento would not be a problem. The kids are all in school, from kindergarten through high school, and they can adjust, by having two sets of friends, in two different environments. One in Sacramento, while the Legislature is in session, and the other back in San Diego when it is out of session." She said to the kids, "You'd be lucky, not all children have that opportunity."

I shared what was transpiring with my brothers, and they felt as Dorothy did, that this was an opportunity to move on to a higher level to be more effective in working for better government. That was noble of them to think of me like that. I was beginning to feel overwhelmed.

A week later, Chairman Gehres called me to have lunch with him along with several of our friends. There were ten of us altogether. The upshot was that they wanted me to run. Near the end of the luncheon, I felt like the anointed one, and said, "Folks, I would consider running if you can give me assurance that you can help raise the funds to run a decent campaign!" Several of them spoke up and said that they would if I should decide to run. Chairman Gehres did not ask for any commitments at this point.

In a couple of weeks, I again was invited to a meeting, this time at the conference room of a construction firm, where there were about 25 men and women of different backgrounds. There were doctors, lawyers, businessmen, community activists, socialites, and others present at the request of Chairman Gehres. I knew about half of them.

Chairman Gehres opened the meeting by introducing me and talking about Governor Reagan's strong desire to have me run for the 79th Assembly District in order to help capture the majority he needed in the State Assembly. Equally important was the upcoming reapportionment of the districts in 1970. Chairman Gehres went on to say, "Tom, as you know, won his re-election to the City Council by a large majority not long ago. The people in San Diego need him in Sacramento. After a hard campaign recently, he is not about to gear up again to have to raise funds for another campaign. It is very time consuming. If we want him to run, we need your support and financial help to show that we are behind him." He elaborated further and later answered questions.

After about an hour, Chairman Gehres asked for commitments to help raise funds for me if I should run. At the end, the tidy sum of $68,000 was pledged. This was not really enough to run a hard Assembly campaign—that would be about $100,000, a hefty sum at that time—but that commitment was enough to convince me that my efforts were needed.

That evening I described to Dorothy the tone of the meeting and all that happened. After some shared thoughts and discussion, Dorothy said, "Tom, you have been effective at the City Council level, so why not on the state level? I think you should give it a try. After all, to get elected at the state level would set the tone to opening doors for other minorities too."

Dorothy was always full of common sense and wisdom. She was that way when I first met her when she was 18. I supposed that's why I married her when she was 19.

The campaign for the State Assembly seat against an incumbent, who had an advantage of a 65 percent Democratic registration against my 32 percent registration of Republicans in the district, seemed insurmountable. But in my case, I grew up in that environment and was not fearful of the odds. I had learned that people, regardless of party affiliation, generally were flexible in their voting if they liked how the candidate came across on a personal basis.

After about eight months of campaigning, I did win the election for the State Assembly with 52 percent of the votes. Of course, the press, as well as many others portrayed this as a major upset. My opponent, Assemblyman Jim Bear, probably had gotten a little too complacent in his efforts because of his huge plurality in registration.

Aside from that, some of Jim Bear's campaigners installed a large sign in the rear of his campaign headquarters, away from public view, with the words, "Hom Doesn't Have A Chinaman's Chance!" Whether that was in jest or done in seriousness, I don't know. But when word got around to my volunteers about that sign, they were so incensed and aroused to the point that they started doing double and triple time in their campaign efforts. Yeah! Sometimes a knock is a lift.

The morning after the victorious election, I got an early call from Governor Reagan congratulating me for what he called an outstanding victory. He also shared that in Los Angeles and in the Fresno area another two Republican candidates were elected, thereby giving the Republicans a majority, 51 to 49, in the State Assembly. This meant that the present speaker of the Assembly, powerful Democrat Jesse Unruh would be replaced with Republican Bob Monogan.

Before closing, the Governor said, "I want to personally thank you and the two other newcomers to the Assembly. So I'd like you and Dorothy and the other two with their wives to have dinner with Nancy and me this coming Friday. I hope you can make it." I immediately accepted.

That Friday we arrived at the Sacramento Airport, and as we were descending from the plane along with the other passengers, a black sedan drove up and parked under the plane's wing. I drew Dorothy's attention while nodding towards the car, and said, "Looks like someone important is being picked up."

As we were walking on the tarmac nearing the terminal, a well-dressed young man excitedly came running up, and said, "Sir, sir, by any chance are you Mr. Hom?"

I replied, "Yes, I am."

"Right this way, Mr. Hom. I'm sorry we missed you, sir," pointing to the black car underneath the airplane wing.

After we were dropped off at the well-known Hotel Senator, while unpacking, I chuckled and said to Dorothy, "I felt sorry for that young man. He looked so confused and apologetic. I think I understand why. After all,

I'm only the second Asian ever to be elected to the State Legislature. The first one was Assemblywoman March Fong, who was elected only two years ago. I guess he wasn't expecting an Asian person. Staff probably just gave him the name. Besides, I don't think I come across, physically anyways, like a powerful and important politician." We laughed about that.

Then Dorothy playfully said, "He could have seen you and thought you were an owner of a small Chinese restaurant ... or maybe even a hand laundry." We had a good laugh over that.

In the early evening we were picked up by the same young man. He drove us to the Governor's home in East Sacramento, an older, but well-preserved area of large, stately homes, with so many leafy green trees lining the streets they formed a canopy.

We were met at the door by the maid and escorted into the library lounge, overlooking a beautiful garden. The Governor and his wife Nancy were the first to greet and welcome us. There were several other people of which two of them were the newly elected Assemblymen, like me, with their wives. Ed Meese and Cap Weinberger, members of the Governor's cabinet, were there too, among others. Apparently we three newly elected Assemblymen were the special guests, so we took it all in and enjoyed ourselves.

After cocktails, dinner was served, with a combination of filet mignon and lobster thermidor. Early in the evening Dorothy and Nancy Reagan got along quite well, especially talking about Hawaii, where Dorothy was from. In seating the guests at the dining table, Nancy placed Dorothy on her left and me on the right of the Governor. The dinner went well, with a lot of conversation. Interestingly, very little of it was on politics, except when the Governor made a toast to honor the three freshmen for making a difference in the State of California. The majority of the conversation was mostly about each other's family, personal stories and experiences in life. The evening was very pleasant, and went by quickly, in spite of the fact that we were there for over three hours.

IMMEDIATELY AFTER THE ELECTION, I had a lot of planning to do. One was to figure out who would replace me on the City Council to fill the balance of my term. This would be done by appointment. My colleagues on the Council asked me for a recommendation. Since my Council district had a sizable minority population, they were looking upon me for some guidance. After some soul searching, and inquiries with people I knew, including Latinos and Asian Americans, I finally recommended a fine, middle-aged African-American gentleman named Leon Williams, a person who was employed by an organization that interacted frequently with government.

My colleagues accepted my recommendation and Leon Williams was appointed to take my Council seat for the remaining three years. He served very effectively and later ran for election and won to serve four additional years. Later he ran and won a seat on the San Diego Board of Supervisors, the first minority to do so. He served all this time with great distinction. I think that was one of the best political choices I have ever made.

Another major transition was to mobilize our efforts to move the family to Sacramento. Dorothy and I had decided that keeping the family together was important and I shouldn't have to commute back home to San Diego each weekend.

Besides, the kids had already been apprised of the fact that to live in Sacramento during the legislative session, from January through August, and then the rest of the year in San Diego would have great benefits. This would mean going to schools in two places. At first there was some apprehension. But shortly after, living in these two different places, and having two sets of school friends, they came to love it. It didn't hurt their school grades either. And it sure did help their social skills, with going away parties and welcoming parties on both ends.

Dorothy and I went up to Sacramento in early December to find a house to either buy or rent. I didn't trust myself in picking something as important as a home for the family without the input of the lady of the house. It had to be her nest. Luckily, within four days we found something that was in a decent neighborhood, near good schools, with five bedrooms from a family that had lived there for 30 years. The owners were an elderly couple who were formerly in the nursery and landscape business. It had a beautifully landscaped garden with many exotic plants and fruit trees. And it was priced right at $36,000. They already had an offer on the house, pending for the past two months because the buyers couldn't get financing on it and their window of time to complete financing had already expired.

It so happened that I had a stockbroker friend, Young Lee, a childhood buddy, who married and moved to Sacramento, and had friends in the banking business. The day we saw the house, he took us to one of his banker friends, and, on the spot, the banker gave us a written commitment to make the loan. I took the commitment to the seller, and the next day he cancelled the pending expired offer and sold the house to us. Dorothy was elated, for now she knew where home would be.

We moved into the house on New Year's Day 1969. It was an extremely busy first week. We had to move in, get the kids registered at their new schools, all six of them, and do shopping for supplies. I had several meetings to attend to prepare for the opening of the Legislative Session on January 5TH. It was hectic, yes, but gratifying. We were accomplishing a lot.

AS THEY NORMALLY DO UPON opening the session, the newly elected legislators were welcomed, of which I was one. Next, the Speaker of the House, in this case, the powerful Jesse Unruh who served for many years with an iron hand, called for the election of the Speaker for the coming session.

The roll call of votes was taken for a new Speaker of the State Assembly of 80 members. The final vote count was 41 for Republican Bob Monagan and 39 for Jesse Unruh. After several years of trying, the Republicans were finally able to remove Jesse Unruh. Following a big roar of approval, the gavel of change was handed over from House Speaker Jesse Unruh to Bob Monagan. In so doing, Unruh made a few friendly and kidding remarks, which included the dark horse, Tom Hom, and then departed from the podium.

The interesting thing about all this was that many people felt I was the pivotal point in making this change. This was mainly due to the fact that I had such odds against me, twice as many registered Democrats than Republicans, and was still able to beat an incumbent Democrat. I guess I was the hero of the day for the Republicans. I was also aware, come the next election in two years, that kind of registration also made me a strong target for the Democrats to challenge.

That day, during the recess, a number of fellow legislators, both Republicans and Democrats, came over to congratulate and welcome me to the State Assembly. Among them was second-term Democratic Assemblywoman March Fong from Oakland, who was the first Asian elected two years earlier. She was helpful by giving me some advice as to the overall workings of the Assembly and also said for me to call her anytime for help. I was pleased with that kind gesture.

In time I found that with my fellow legislators, in spite of differences between our political parties, more often than not would find common ground in solving issues. I would say 85 percent of our voting issues were really non-partisan and we could work out these differences on a bi-partisan basis. I liked that, as I considered myself to be a Republican who was basically liberal on social issues and rather conservative on fiscal matters. I think both parties had many moderate members leaning closely to that overall philosophy.

I think the general viewpoint of the average citizen was that the Democrats and Republicans are always at each other's throats and that we never talked with each other on friendly terms. Not so. It was not unusual when the business of the day was done, issues set aside, we legislators, regardless of party, got together socially, and often with our families as well.

I think 15 percent of the partisan issues were played up through the headlines in the news media exaggerating our separation more than really existed. I can understand the headlines though. They generally reflect the more important and hard line issues that have the biggest impact in our society, making partisanship more evident. That's all part of our democratic structure, checks and balances, as well as bipartisanship on most issues.

THAT'S STRANGE, SO MANY DEAD TREES in Sacramento. That's what Dorothy and I first thought when we got to Sacramento in January, wintertime. With the cold wet weather and super thick Thule fog, we weren't sure how the children and we would adjust to living there. And everywhere we looked there were so many seemingly dead trees without leaves—in parks, lining streets, in front yards—we weren't used to seeing that kind of landscape. Especially being from southern California and Dorothy originally from Hawaii where we always had sunshine and mostly evergreen trees year-round. We thought these dead trees should be cut down—we were that naive about this new environment.

That confusion only lasted a short while, until someone explained to us that they were dormant just for the winter. Two months later, sure enough, when the trees started to sprout new leaves, some in different shades and colors and some with beautiful flowers of many shapes, we were astonished how majestically and quickly it transformed the drab surroundings. The parks and front yards dazzled us with an array of blooming flowers of every color of the rainbow. Everywhere became gorgeous. The outdoors had a different new freshness that we were not used to in San Diego, and it all happened so quickly. It had a positive effect on the children in helping them to adjust in this surprising new environment.

Now the summers, that was another thing. Sacramento was hot and humid, whereas San Diego was mild, not as humid and mostly in the 70s, which made it ideal summer weather. In the autumn, Sacramento became more pleasant with cooler weather and very beautiful with the tree leaves beginning to change to a different hue with spectacular colors. Fall foliage, it's called. And the fall in San Diego remains almost just like summer except a little bit milder in the evenings. Not as dramatic but most pleasant. And the winters in San Diego, I would say, are probably the best climate in the country, normally in the 60s and 70s. San Diego weather is pretty temperate year round.

AFTER BEING IN THE ASSEMBLY for about two months, the Governor asked me to carry a legislation bill especially intended for the education of immigrant children, mainly those living in the Central Valley, Imperial Valley, and certain urban areas where there was a heavy concentration of immigrant working families. The bill was to help teach these children who spoke little or no English to learn English and help them assimilate into American society. It was known as a Compensatory Education bill, with a financial appropriation of $15 million. I sought out a Democrat as the other principal author with me on the bill, plus a number of co-authors from both parties. After hearings on the proposed legislation through several committees, it was approved by both the Assembly and Senate, with Governor Reagan signing the bill before the news media. This was the largest bill of its kind in the country, and set a new standard in this type of educational program. We got good statewide coverage, as well.

As the years went by, even after I was out of government, I continued to follow the progress of the effectiveness of the bill. Within about 10 years, the program became so successful that it was renamed the English-as-a-Second Language (ESL) program. With added funding, it started to be extended so students could stay in the program, from grammar to high school. The original program's intent was not to extend a student's ESL for that long. Many of the students who stayed with the program for years had become so comfortable in their English-as-a-Second language classes that they continued to have trouble communicating adequately in English. For some, ESL became counterproductive and a crutch, and actually stymied their English proficiency.

The original bill I introduced was to work with the students for two to three years only, and then have them join mainstream classes with the regular English-speaking students. It was to be, from there on, English by immersion. As time went on, the leadership in education came to realize this and the ESL programs were modified to again address and concentrate on children for only a limited time, to prepare them for the immersion.

I always believed that if we gave children the basics in English and thereafter English by immersion, it would facilitate them to assimilate into the American mainstream productively.

I say this because of personal experience. Four of my brothers and I were born in San Diego Chinatown along with other Chinatown kids who spoke only Chinese until we went to kindergarten at public schools. We did not have ESL programs then. We just winged it and learned English by immersion. The end result was that all of us kids turned out pretty well, acclimated into society, and many succeeded in the business, professional, and academic fields.

There were, however, and always have been, programs for handicapped and special needs students. Those always had good bipartisan support.

During the legislative session, I occasionally would have to return home to San Diego to attend meetings either with government officials or constituent groups. I flew most of the time, but on a number of occasions I would drive with the family because the kids always wanted to see their friends. They also enjoyed going across the border to Tijuana, Mexico, 20 miles from our San Diego home, where they could buy souvenirs for their friends in Sacramento. We'd leave Sacramento on Friday after school, and drive for seven to eight hours and return on Sunday afternoon. It was a 450-mile drive each way. It was not too bad or tedious, because I learned that in driving long distances, it was easier if I factored in various destinations along the way, like a certain pit stop or a favorite hamburger stand.

While in town, there were family dinners and visits with friends. There were some advantages in having two homes with family and friends at each end; it's like a homecoming every time we came into town. After getting back to San Diego and quickly repacking to return to the north, Dorothy and the kids always had things to take back with them that they had left behind in moving to Sacramento. On top of that, my brothers at David Produce would always load us up with all kinds of fruits and vegetables to take. Our large Chrysler station wagon with a rack on top of the roof was loaded from top to bottom with boxes, six kids, a dog, not to mention Dorothy and me. Sometimes I felt we were so overloaded and top heavy that we might even have a rollover. Thank God, nothing ever happened.

AS A FRESHMAN LEGISLATOR, and in a new exciting environment, I had no complaints. Our legislative session ran from January through August. During the rest of the year, our legislative work continued through committee meetings. I served on four committees: Vice Chairman of Local Government; Commerce & Public Utilities; Urban Affairs; and the Commission on Aging. Meetings were held in different cities throughout the state, requiring me to either drive or fly leaving early, finishing in the late afternoon, and arriving home by early evening. In addition, there were also meetings with local groups to hear about their needs and issues. At times, those could be pretty challenging. Nevertheless, I loved it. Knowing that I was one of the 80 Assembly members in the state motivated me to stay fully engaged and not slack off. In most cases, I could help and do some good.

During my first term, I introduced four bills of which one passed, that being my $15 million Compensatory Education bill. The other three never made it through the necessary committees. I did co-author several that did pass, of which one was to eliminate pay toilets in public places, like airports, libraries, restaurants, and such. The principal author of this bill was my friend Assemblywoman March Fong. A lot of statewide jokes were made about that bill. In spite of that, it was needed. If nothing else, I would say it was a sanitation bill. It was especially helpful for the older people who had more urgency, and might not have the right coin available when it was most needed.

The Assembly election terms were for two years and in November 1970, I would be running for re-election. In order to know how I stood with my constituents during my first year as an Assemblyman, a poll was taken. The results were encouraging with 68 percent being positive. That was good. During the Republican primary elections, I had no opponent. There were several Democratic candidates which included a retired public school principal, Peter Chacon. Two months before the general election in November, a poll was taken as to the voter's preference between Chacon and me. The results showed me winning by a large margin.

However, some things are unforeseen because sometimes the past creeps up and that can be devastating to one's career. In my case, a vote I cast in 1967, along with the rest of the San Diego City Council and mayor, came back to affect my campaign three years later. It also impacted my future political career and those of my former City Council colleagues and mayor. The issue had to do with the increase of taxicab fares in order to align them with the other large cities. This had been recommended by a study from the city manager and his staff, and we had all supported it.

To my shock and surprise, only three weeks before the general election and three years later, the district attorney indicted the entire City Council and the mayor for conspiracy and bribery. Needless to say, I was dumb-founded and quite angry at that charge, especially when it was not true and it was so close to election time.

This issue became major news for all the news media, with headlines blaring out continuously for weeks. Needless to say, this had a damaging effect on my re-election campaign. In spite of my campaign committee and supporters working hard to try and overcome this negative issue three weeks before the election, we were not able to do that. I lost the election with 48 percent of the votes, to my opponent, Peter Chacon, winning with 52 percent. On the eve of my loss, I sent a congratulatory telegram to my opponent acknowledging his victory. It was difficult knowing that just three weeks prior, my chances of winning were extremely positive.

My big challenge after the election was to hire an attorney. I interviewed several and finally chose an attorney by the name of Louis Welsh, a brilliant man who was a civil attorney, not a criminal lawyer. I picked him because when I finished interviewing him, he said he was also interviewing me and was convinced that I was not guilty of the charges. He said that he had confidence that he would be able to break down the credibility of the opponent's witnesses.

Since the holiday season was approaching, the earliest trial date we could get was in the first week of the next year, January 1971. We wanted the earliest date possible, before any of my other colleagues, because we weren't sure who was guilty or who was not, if any. We didn't want any one of them to be found guilty, thereby possibly setting a trend for the following trials. The mayor also felt the same way.

The mayor and I were the first to go on trial, both separately. My trial started in the first week of the New Year, and it ran for three weeks. The trial became more ridiculous and preposterous as it went along. It seemed the guidepost for the conspiracy and bribery charges stemmed mostly from the Internal Revenue Service's auditing of the Yellow Cab Company's books showing that it gave us major gifts in order to influence the increase in taxi fares. That counted as bribery and conspiracy. The books described them as business expenses.

The books showed that I was given ten cases of Mumms Champagne, jewelry for my wife, and a two-week cruise on the Yellow Cab president's yacht to Acapulco, Mexico. Of course, these things never happened. Aside from these charges against me, there were other similar charges alleged against the mayor and others.

On the witness stand, under the interrogation of my attorney, the president of the Yellow Cab Company broke down and admitted that these charges were falsified in order to have them written off as business expenses. The reality was that the Mumms champagne was for his own parties, the jewelry was for his girlfriend, and I never went on a cruise with him. He also said that he never expected the matter to amount to much because he thought the elected officials were too important and influential to be indicted. Apparently, he never thought about the IRS which had a different agenda. They thrived on high profile cases of tax evasion and partly used that as a warning to potential tax evaders.

After about three hours of deliberation, the jury determined that I was not guilty of any of the charges. What a relief! My wife Dorothy shed some tears but was otherwise quite composed. My supporters in the courtroom who followed the trial closely came forth to hug me and cried with a sigh of relief.

Interestingly, about an hour after the announcement of my not guilty verdict, the jury of the mayor's trial in a courtroom just up the hall from ours also announced a not guilty verdict. And the next day, another colleague on the council, Mike Schaeffer, was given a not guilty verdict.

With the headlines of the news media playing up the exoneration of the trials, within a few days the district attorney dropped all charges against the rest of the council members who had not yet gone to trial.

After the trial, it took a few weeks to gather my wits back together. It was a traumatic episode, the likes of which I had never experienced before. I grew up a lot wiser regarding politics. To this day, I am convinced that politics were behind the indictment process, from the powers in Sacramento to the rivalry of the district attorney race that was taking place during that election year. To declare an indictment three weeks before the election was perfect timing to sabotage and change the election outcome.

There always seemed to be a flip side to a bad experience, though. A couple of weeks after the verdict by the jury, a lady member of the jury called me and said, "Tom, I'm calling on behalf of several of the jury members on your trial and we want to invite you and your wife to lunch. We just want to say how happy we are about how it all worked out and how well you and your wife Dorothy handled yourselves." In hearing that, I immediately thought to myself, I probably looked like I felt, scared and concerned in not knowing what the final outcome would be. Apparently, to others, I may have looked cool and collected with a convinced air of my innocence. Yet, one never knows the outcome of a court trial. I appreciated her comments. I readily and happily accepted that most considerate invitation for my wife and me.

After all the years in politics, it was hard to just hang it up and divorce myself completely from it. After the trial and a few weeks of moving back to San Diego from Sacramento, along with taking the kids on a vacation, I decided to give it one more shot. With the local elections coming up for mayor, I decided to throw my hat in the ring to run. At the end of filing, there were 14 candidates, of which I was one. At the final outcome in the primary election, I came in fifth. That left me out of the running, as only the two top winners would be in the runoff.

Interestingly, among the 14 candidates, the mayor was running for re-election, along with some of my former colleagues on the city council, who were also indicted and their cases later dropped. None of them made the runoff either. Obviously, the voters wanted a change.

Although I lost, one good thing that came out of this election was that my former Assemblyman colleague, Pete Wilson, won the election for Mayor of San Diego. Pete served three terms as mayor and from there, as I mentioned earlier, he went on to be elected to the U.S. Senate and later, Governor of California for two terms. He served effectively in all of these positions.

I've always taken special pride in having known Pete when he first came to town and served as the Executive Director of the Republican Associates, an organization of mostly businessmen and women. When I first ran for the city council, Pete occasionally took time to do some campaigning for me.

After losing in the Mayoral primary election, it was a solidifying factor for me, telling me to start thinking of doing something else. Yes, I had my run. No regrets. It was a signal to move on.

In closing my book on serving people through elective office, I thought what my dad would say about that. I venture to think he would have said something like, "Tom, you've done well. You have broken through a social barrier that shall be beneficial to the American people from here on. Move on to new challenges. Remember, always be a gentleman!" Yes, those are my words, but knowing Dad, I think they're pretty close.

WHEN ONE DOOR CLOSES, TWO OPEN. In planning for my future, my loving wife Dorothy, an eternal optimist, said, "Tom, you have always done well in real estate. There is where you belong! Aside from that, you can still get involved in community affairs like you've always done." She went on to say, "And not to mention it, we now have a bunch of teenagers on hand, and they become more expensive each day, and they'll be going on to college shortly. More income would help. Real estate! You've always been good at that!"

So be it! I had been thinking along the same line, but hadn't said it. By her saying it first, I figured that she would feel part of the decision making. I always needed her help, especially with major decisions. In many ways, I always felt she was a lot smarter than me ... except in the field of sports.

XI. Honky-Tonk Skid Row

AGES 45 TO 50

一只兔子崎岖的心路历程

The Gaslamp Quarter District. Photo courtesy of San Diego History Center.

CHAPTER 36

Gaslamp

1972 WAS THE YEAR PRESIDENT RICHARD NIXON WON RE-ELECTION BY A LANDSLIDE. AND ALSO, SADLY, THE NATION MOURNED THE PASSING OF THE FEISTY FORMER PRESIDENT HARRY TRUMAN.

NOW THAT POLITICS WAS OVER FOR ME, AND AFTER HAVING a short two weeks' vacation to Hawaii to visit Dorothy's relatives, we came back with a fresh outlook on life. To start a life without constant calls from constituents seeking help with their problems seemed strange at first, but in time I got used to it. I especially didn't miss those calls that would come in at all odd hours of the night. Overall, I enjoyed those years serving in public office, but with the wind having shifted for me, I was ready to take on new challenges.

As time went on, I did get involved in supporting certain candidates that I liked, making speeches for them and supporting them financially as well. I guess it was one of those things, where you can get a guy out of politics, but you can't get politics out of the guy.

My first priority was to once again find a location and establish my real estate office. My brother George, the eighth of the Hom family children, also wanted to relocate his thriving orthodontic practice. After looking for two months, we finally found a building in the North Park area that fit our needs. Location-wise it was central and convenient, by far large enough for us to share, and it had adequate parking. It was a vacant medical center building, perhaps about 30 years old, that needed some remodeling. We had our contractor friend, Fred Gruner, look it over to determine the feasibility of dividing it up into different offices. He told us, "No problem! We can do it on the cheap and have it done in 60 days."

Based on that, we formed a partnership and bought the building. True to Fred's words, the building remodel was completed on time. Everything looked new and we were ready to do business. I must say, the cost of doing it was much less than we had expected. Fred was a one-man operation. He worked at a fast steady pace, putting in at least 12 to14 hour days. He was honest as the day was long. Fred was a very opinionated man and would do anything to help his friends. Our family felt privileged to be among them. He worked for the Hom family for many years doing the one to two-men projects.

I was excited about starting back into business. After the new office was ready, I sent out an announcement to everyone I knew—a rather sizable number—mainly friends and people at the church and the people I knew from my involvement in public life.

Within two months, I was back in business with four salespersons. It had been about 15 years since I first applied to join the San Diego Board of Realtors, when ethnic membership was not encouraged. I applied again. This time, the attitude about the acceptance of minorities in the real estate business had loosened up quite a bit, especially with laws passed by the State of California and the U.S. Supreme Court's ruling that housing discrimination was unconstitutional. My application was readily accepted and I was welcomed into the fold. The cordial acceptance was probably partly due to my name recognition in the community as well as the many realtors with whom I worked and befriended when I was in public office. Yes, life was full of twists and turns and in time true righteousness won out.

It didn't take me long to get back into the swing of things. A year later I was elected to serve as a member of the Board of Directors. The following year, I was given special recognition for my chairmanship of the newly formed Governmental Affairs Committee, for accomplishing many positive results for the real estate industry through various government agencies. As a matter of fact, I was displayed on the front cover of the monthly *Realtor* magazine, with a full-page story of our work. To this day, I'm not sure if it was to make up for the injustice of the 15 years earlier, or that I affected change in providing a good service for the industry. Most likely both.

The best part of this time was that my business was thriving and my office was fully staffed now with eight salespeople. In my previous real estate office, we generally dealt in residential properties, but this time around, we added a department handling commercial and industrial properties. It worked out very profitably, as the commercial and industrial properties were generally much larger transactions, thus our commissions were much larger.

Time went by quickly, especially because I enjoyed the challenges of creating and growing a business. Within a year, I had enough surplus funds to once again start looking into investing in real estate.

At a later point in the life of our large Hom family, with all the younger siblings having gone on and graduated from universities, established successful career paths, and earning good money, some of them were looking for opportunities in real estate investments. Of the twelve of us siblings, there were three orthodontists, two teachers, a chemist, a medical doctor, and five businessmen, including myself. With our extra funds, we decided to pool together to form our own little syndicate partnerships to invest, mainly in real estate. Since I was in the real estate business, I did the preliminary groundwork to look for any good buys. This was kind of exciting, having our own syndications. Some of us were able to invest more, some less.

Within a month I found something for us to buy. One of our first investments was the purchase of a landmark three-story bank building with a finished basement in downtown San Diego. It was an older, majestic-looking historic building built in 1893, situated at 5th and E Streets, an older part of downtown that had seen better days. The price was very reasonable because of its obsolescence, but it was still in excellent shape. It had been structurally upgraded to meet modern seismic standards, with the old historic lines retained. It had a lot of marble staircases, hallways, floors with artistic designs of marble, and walk-in vaults. The offices were walnut and mahogany paneled and had a large open space lobby with beautiful chandeliers. It was very rich in quality and antique décor.

Obviously, we were not bankers, so the big challenge was how to use the building and make it generate revenue. Since we bought it at a good price, we had some flexibility. My brother George, a homespun entrepreneur who was always full of business ideas, wanted to rent the spacious ground floor and open an Asian import gift store. Several of us invested with George in what became the Far East Trading Company. George often took time off from his practice to attend trade shows to stock the inventory. The store was filled with all kinds of goods from Asia, especially from China, Japan, Singapore, and Malaysia. He hired a staff and had a grand opening that attracted good media publicity and a large crowd.

The business started out with a bang, and my mother Ah Nuing wanted to get involved. At this point in life, she lived alone in the same three-story family house with six-bedrooms, and wanted something else to do besides gardening and visiting her friends at the Chinese laundries. Before long, she joined the staff and in a short time took over running the store. Mom was a smart and educated woman from China and you could see that by how well she organized and handled the operation. Customers loved her.

She had an eye for catching shoplifters. She would reprimand them and tell them not to come back into the store until they had learned to behave. She treated them civilly and respectfully. One time after she caught a man shoplifting, he confessed that he stole things twice before and later brought the two items back to her.

She was tough, too. Once a guy pointed a gun in her face and demanded all the money from the cash register. She gave it to him but not before she told him his parents would not approve of what he was doing.

The robber took the cash and ran up the street towards Broadway and she followed him. The crook hopped on a bus and she hopped on too. But before doing so, she flagged down a police car and, pointing to the bus, shouted, "Robber, robber. Bad man!" The cops pulled in front of the bus and followed her as she pointed out the robber, shouting, "He is bad man!" in her broken English. As the police arrested the man, she asked for her money back. The police said they couldn't give it back then because they needed that for evidence. After the police got her name and other information from her, she asked the policemen for a receipt for the cash taken by the robber.

Later she told some of us that when she got back to the store and thought about what had happened, she almost fainted. A few weeks later she was called to court to testify against the robber and had her first courtroom experience in American justice after 40 years in America. She thought it was pretty neat. She did get her money back, too.

On Sundays the Far East Trading Company was closed. This was so my mother could continue to do what she enjoyed most of all, and that was to have the kids and grandchildren over for dinner. There would be anywhere from 15 to 25 people at the house each Sunday, depending on the schedules of the families. Starting Saturday evening she'd start preparing a wide assortment of delicious Chinese dishes for the Sunday get-together. At times I would help, which gave me a chance to learn some of the secrets of her good cooking. Along with painting, cooking was one of my hobbies and I never felt it was inconvenient to help in the kitchen. No doubt, Sundays were among the highlights of my mother's life.

The bank building turned out to be a pretty good investment. The total square footage of the building was 20,000 sq. ft. and we rented out the top floor to the San Diego County Republican Central Committee, the second floor to various small professional firms, and the full basement with its 2,000 sq. ft. vault, to a wholesale jeweler. We were lucky. We turned a white elephant into a soaring phoenix.

A FEW MONTHS AFTER WE BOUGHT the bank building, a group of property owners in the surrounding area asked me to join them in cleaning up problems in our old and deteriorating part of the Fifth Avenue area. One of the property owners, David, who operated a well-known men's clothing store, said, "Tom, we're coming together to see what can be done about the porn shops, Go-Go places, and honky-tonk bars that are in our area. Prostitutes are all over the place. It's hurting our businesses and property values! You used to be on the City Council, we need your advice and help."

Another man explained, "Lately, the city has been inspecting our buildings for building code enforcement in order to bring them up to earthquake seismic standards. If we don't make these expensive repairs, they will be making us tear down some of the upper floors. We can't afford it! Matter of fact, they are already having some torn down. What can we do?"

Since the Homs were property owners now, I thought I should meet with them and go from there. My wife Dorothy joined me. We met in the 1890 four-story Keating Building a block away from our building. During the meeting, most of the discussion was about the need for more police protection and what it would take to close up the so-called unsavory places like the porn shops, arrest the prostitutes, and relocate the homeless.

People even suggested raising funds to pay for a one-way bus ticket plus a little spending money for the prostitutes and homeless to relocate to San Francisco. I sensed their frustration.

After the meeting, with many notes taken by Dorothy who was an obsessive note taker whenever there was a meeting, we reviewed them during dinner. We concluded that shipping out the prostitutes and homeless was not practical, and closing the Go-Go places, porn shops and honky-tonk bars would be extremely difficult because of constitutional rights. I knew that from the City Council experience. How could we get around this?

In trying to digest all this, I randomly and fleetingly thought back to the time I was a youngster working at the David Produce Company located at lower Sixth Avenue where all the wholesale produce warehouses were located extending over to lower Fifth Avenue. So the strip of Fifth Avenue, stretching from lower Fifth to the upper part where it reached Broadway, was very familiar to me. I had walked this area hundreds of times, from the time I was twelve with my shoeshine box, selling *The Saturday Evening Post*, going to the movie theatres, to working the small produce stand that my father set up for my brother Allen and me. I knew the area almost like the palm of my hand.

I also knew the many prominent unique buildings that housed wonderful stores and knew about the important civic leaders who had offices there, the old city hall building and many of the vintage buildings of the late 1800s and early 1900s. Many of these buildings were either vacant or partially vacant. Most of the anchor businesses and leading citizens moved away to the upper Fifth Avenue area, north of Broadway. Thus, in the following years, the lower area started to deteriorate.

It even got to the point where that area, especially the lower part, was referred to as the S.O.B. area, South of Broadway. It was there where most of the controversial elements were the thickest. The area where our property was wasn't bad but we could see it could spread in time.

In thinking out loud, and sharing my thoughts with Dorothy, I felt I might have come to a possible solution. I wanted to shout, "Eureka! I found it!" But I refrained from that. Too premature. Moments before that, I recalled when I was on the City Council and we had the same deteriorating situation and problem in a community called Old Town San Diego, an area

A lower 5th Avenue building before the revitalization and development of the Gaslamp Quarter District.

The bank building at 5th Avenue & E Street that the family bought and rehabilitated, and later opened the Far East Trading Company managed by Ah Nuing.

Dorothy and I were active in creating the famous Gaslamp Quarter in San Diego.

HELPS BUILD GASLAMP QUARTER

Tom Hom's Vision, Chinese Heritage Bring Success

By ROGER SHOWLEY
Staff Writer, The San Diego Union

Tom Hom is a dreamer. He can see a dilapidated warehouse and envision a bustling marketplace, look at a pornography-plagued section of town and predict an urban renaissance, view a weed-covered wasteland on the Mexican border and propose a city.

His philosophy of Chinese patience and American pioneering has propelled him to leadership roles, not just in the local Chinese community but in San Diego and Baja California as a whole — seven decades after his father, Hom Chong, arrived here at the age of 14, changed his name to David Hom (because he liked the story of David and Goliath) and opened a produce company downtown.

"Tom is one of those people I call visionaries," observed Dan Pearson, a developer and consultant in the Gaslamp Quarter, which Hom has helped bring back to life. "He can see a thing and have the vision to see what it will be like three or four years from now."

Hom, 53, former councilman and former assemblyman, said his secret is to grab an opportunity and wait for the right moment to make a dream come true — after gleaning trends in other cities from the 15 to 20 trade magazines he reads.

"I'm what you might call a history buff," says this real estate broker operating out of an unpretentious North Park office that matches his self-effacing personality. "Cities go through cycles of between 90 and 100

years. They reach a plateau, go down slowly and all of sudden drop off. Then they start back again."

Hom family fortunes also have followed a cycle of their own. David Hom Chong arrived here in 1913 from China, where the demise of the Manchu dynasty had thrown the country into chaos. The teen-ager's mission was to make money, send it back home, to Canton and return eventually to claim a bride.

He returned in 1920 for an arranged marriage, but came back to San Diego to found the David Produce Co. downtown. The first Mrs. Hom died after bearing five sons and Hom returned to Canton to marry again. His second wife had four sons and three daughters and now manages the Far East Trading Co., the Homs' import store at Fifth Avenue and E Street.

David died of tuberculosis in 1943, leaving the family fortunes in the hands of teen-age sons.

"That was the hardest time," the second Mrs. Hom recalls, in between helping customers. "My youngest son was 10 months old and my oldest was away at war. There was nobody to run the business."

Tom, then only 16, dropped out of San Diego High School to manage the business until James, the oldest son, returned from the war to care for the family. Tom graduated in 1946 by taking night classes.

The family's Chinese background was never forgotten. The Chinese Community Church was the social center of Chinatown. Chinese was spoken at home. Childhood earnings

were always handed over to mother to help with family expenses.

"I sensed a difference (with other children)," Tom says. "I don't recall any real problems, but, you know, children are children. We were taught that we were from a rich culture and that we should accept that even if some people didn't understand."

Today, the family has grown to encompass about 60 members occupied in fields ranging from dentistry and law to real estate and retailing. But financial interests remain interlocked through a series of informal investment partnerships that allow major projects to be wholly family-financed.

The third son of the founding father, Tom Hom has chosen to operate in the public spotlight and thus becomes an example of an immigrant's son who has risen to high levels of the city's political and economic spheres.

In 1956, Hom learned he had tuberculosis, left the produce business, recovered his health and took up real estate, becoming one of the first Chinese-American realtors in the country. This change of career is all the more significant, because Hom said he had been unable to buy a house in 1947 for his widowed stepmother because of discriminatory deed restrictions.

In 1963, Hom became the first person from a minority group to be elected to the City Council, to which he was re-elected by a 6-1 margin four years later. In 1968, he won a

(Continued on B-4, Col. 1)

Tom and Dorothy Hom join their family in a portrait at their Golden Hill home, seven decades after Hom's father arrived in America. In the front row, from left, are Cindy, Gayle and Jennifer Hom. Behind them, from left, are Will Newbern and Nora Hom Newbern, and Winthrop and Phillis Hom.

— Staff Photo by Dennis Huls

seat in the Assembly.

"I had a meeting with my brothers," Hom said, "and they wanted me to go into public life. They said not to worry about the income (the council salary was only $5,000 per year then), so I drew an income from the produce company and went there at nights sometimes. I also had some small investments."

But Hom's fortunes suddenly dimmed in 1970, when he was indicted weeks before the November election for allegedly accepting bribes in exchange for raising the taxicab minimum fare.

He was acquitted, as were the other defendants who served on the council in 1967 when the rate was raised, but not until after he was trounced at the polls. He failed at a comeback in the 1971 mayoral campaign and gave up a bid for an appointment to a council vacancy in 1974.

"It was a blow; it hurt us," said his eldest brother, James. "But sometimes a kick is a boost. If he had stayed in politics, we probably would not have emerged as strong a body as we are now. We could do a lot more."

Tom returned to real estate. He looked from his Golden Hill home toward downtown, and based on the success of historic preservation projects in Sacramento, Seattle and Denver, he decided there was money to be made in old buildings.

Hom merely had to call one of his brothers or other relatives to raise funds to purchase properties. He began in 1973 with a former bank building at the corner of Fifth Avenue and E Street, where his mother

Among his other talents, Tom Hom, above left, plays the piano while his wife, Dorothy, works on the budget. Hom's mother, Yee Law Ho Hom, arranges miniature trees called bonsai in their Far East Trading Co., store.

is to be rehabilitated into a restaurant and office complex.

The next big investment was the Western Metals Co. building on 2½ blocks be-

nues; it became a farmer's market and is destined for office and commercial development. Of the family's 18 property holdings, 13 lie in and around downtown.

future trend (of economic growth in Mexico. They lie in a free-trade zone. Baja California is a natural area for development."

The county's Environ-

tion, acknowledged he had his differences with the Homs. But he praised them for being able to direct family resources to individual projects.

The old Chinese Mission being relocated to its new home in the Asian Pacific Thematic Historic District, later becoming the San Diego Chinese Historical Museum.

Here I am with Dorothy, co-founder of the Chinese Historical Society of San Diego.

The former Chinese Mission is today the San Diego Chinese Historical Museum.

Speaking at the San Diego Chinese Historical Museum's garden. L to R: Loretta, Executive Director Dr. Alex Chuang, me, and President Dr. Lilly Cheng.

Receiving a Distinguished Contribution Award from the Mexican American Business Association, 1987.

Banking days, as Vice Chairman with Chairman of the Board James Brown of BSD Bank Corp., which included the Bank of San Diego, American Valley Bank, and Coast Bank.

A bustling Farmers Bazaar in one of the old Western Metal Supply buildings.

Farmers Bazaar opened in one of the Western Metal Supply buildings that was built in 1886.

One of the historic Western Metal Supply buildings was converted into the Farmers Bazaar that unfortunately burnt down. The main Western Metal Supply building was saved by firefighters and was incorporated into Petco Park, home of the San Diego Padres.

A fire destroyed the Farmers Bazaar.

What was left of Farmers Bazaar following the fire.

Western Metal Supply building restored and incorporated into Petco Park (ballpark), San Diego.

A few Hom Family members at the dedication of Hom Plaza, Petco Park.

Chairman of the Board of the new television station, UHF Channel 69 KTTY, Cable Channel 5.

Enjoying one of my passions — painting with oil and watercolor.

Getting Ready *(watercolor).*

1880 New Roots *(watercolor).*

While writing my book, I painted this watercolor. This little boy is me.

Learning to play piano at age 65.

A later picture of my brothers and sisters. L to R, front row: George, Margaret, Helen, John, James; second row: Allen, Albert, Herb, Wellman, and me; missing are Beatrice and Paul.

Hom Family Reunion on our Mexican Riviera cruise 2005.

Three generations of Homs. L to R: Loretta, Tommy, Winthrop, and me.

Loretta and me on our wedding day.

Loretta and me with both our immediate families together on our wedding day.

Traveling in Asia with Loretta on our honeymoon with two of Loretta's friends who had booked a cruise together months prior to Loretta and me meeting each other.
L to R: me, Margaret, Loretta, and Grace.

Loretta and me at a San Diego Foundation event.

New wife will travel: Loretta and me at the Great Wall of China.

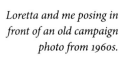

Loretta and me posing in front of an old campaign photo from 1960s.

Helping to cook at the Chinese Community Church luncheons.

New Chinese Community Church completed in 2006.

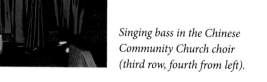

Singing bass in the Chinese Community Church choir (third row, fourth from left).

Admiral Les Gehres, a prominent Republican Party leader, was a major influence in my political career. Photo courtesy of San Diego History Center.

A major influence in my life, Memorial Jr. High School Principal William J. Oakes.

Celebrating 80th birthday with my children and grandchildren.

that was first established by mission founder Father Junipero Serra in 1769. In 1850 it became chartered into the City of San Diego, only to have the official city moved to its present downtown area in 1871.

During my time on the San Diego City Council, a group of citizens, property owners, and businesses from the original Old Town San Diego area came to the City Council asking for help in saving and restoring some of the historical buildings in the area. In so doing, we created a historic district for part of Old Town San Diego. In time, the historic district became very successful, thriving after the restorations and later becoming a California State Park. Today it is one of the highlights for tourists and local citizens to visit, and known as a place where San Diego and California history started.

In lower Fifth Avenue where the older downtown San Diego was located, was basically where Old Town San Diego moved. That move followed the pioneering efforts to build a new San Diego by people like William Heath Davis who arrived in 1833 and Alonzo Horton arriving in 1867, who promoted the growth for a new San Diego. Of course, after about 100 years, this part of new San Diego was no longer new and attractive, which accounted partly for its eventual decline.

The following month the property owners met again. During our discussion I proposed that we look into the formation of a Historic District, describing something similar to the Old Town Historic District that was established several years prior. I explained my role in the process while serving on the City Council. After some lengthy discussion, we decided to have a planner from the City Planning Department meet with us to explain the process of forming a historic district. I thought this was a good idea for I didn't want them to take my word on all this. It's good to get an outside view. So I was asked to contact the City to have a staff planner meet with us at our next meeting. Before adjourning the meeting and to my surprise, the president of the group, a lady who owned the Casino Theatre, suggested that I replace her as the new president of the group. I thought about it. Since I had experience in matters like this, I accepted, with the approval of the group.

In two weeks we had two city planners meet with us, Max Schmidt and Michael Stepner. They explained the pros and cons of such a district and the process of obtaining an ordinance to become law. Many questions were asked. The end result was the group unanimously voted to move forward. The next phase entailed getting official approval by the City Council to have the planning department review the feasibility of such a district to eventually become the Gaslamp Quarter Historic District.

In another two weeks, we were placed on the City Council docket requesting approval to refer the historic district to the planning department for its review and recommendation for the feasibility of such a designation. I appeared with others to advocate for the approval. It was approved unanimously. After three months of studies by the planning department, it recommended that a historic district designation be approved, subject to approval by the majority of the property owners that would be in the district.

At first, the boundary of the district was to be just six blocks. Then when word got around to other property owners who had vintage buildings, they wanted to be part of it, so eventually the boundaries expanded to sixteen and a half blocks. During the process of creating the district it got a lot of publicity and coverage by the media.

Not all downtown property owners and developers were in support of the district. Some of the downtown people felt that all of the old and nonconforming buildings should be demolished and new structures built to take their places. It was down with the old, up with the new. To appear merciful, they advocated for a handful of older historic buildings to be saved. But not as a district. Also, strong opposition was coming from the Adult Book Store group, Go-Go bars, and the Girlie Peep Show places.

To counter that, we got endorsements from many organizations in town, including the San Diego Chamber of Commerce and San Diegans, Inc., a powerful business group composed of top executives of most of the largest corporations in town. Also groups like SOHO, Save Our Heritage Organisation, and the San Diego Historical Society were strong supporters.

For final approval, the public hearing was held before the City Council with supporters and those in opposition speaking, but in the end the Council unanimously approved the proposal. We were elated. But the hard work was just beginning.

Now that we had gotten through the first phase of a long journey with approval by the City Council, we knew we had our work cut out for us. At our meeting following the city's approval of our Gaslamp Quarter ordinance, the big question was where do we go from here? We all agreed that around the country there had been several successful revitalized historic districts like ours. Places like Seattle's Pioneer Square, Vancouver's Gastown and Granville Island and Denver's Larimer Square. These areas went through similar dramatic changes that we in San Diego were experiencing. After some discussion, Dorothy suggested that she and I take a couple of weeks off to explore these revitalized places and learn what they did to turn the areas of abandoned buildings and a skid-row environment into something that later became a source of community pride.

Everyone thought it was a good idea, especially when Dorothy said, "Since the Gaslamp Quarter Association does not yet have adequate funds, we'll pay for it ourselves." Which meant to me, no problem, a worthy cause, and since I had heard so much about these places, it would be a nice little vacation as well as a good fact finding trip.

One thing about Dorothy, apart from most people, is that she could put difficult things together with such ease that it all came out to be very palatable and acceptable. For instance, in the Gaslamp area there were four adult book and toyshops. Each of them had displays in their front windows of provocative and sexy near-naked women. It cheapened the area, of course. To help remedy that, Dorothy, dressed prim and proper as always, walked into the store saying hello to the clerks and everyone else and politely asked to see the manager. Upon meeting the manager, she spoke in her respectful tone and told him what the city had done to help improve the area and we needed everyone's help. She suggested how they could help, since they were part of a larger community family.

In a non-threatening voice, she said, "If you remove your big girlie photos from your front windows and cover the windows with either drapery, blinds, or have them painted over, people cannot look inside from the outside and it will go a long ways toward making our Gaslamp Quarter a more pleasant and viable area. I'm sure some of your clients are respectable people. I'm not here to judge, but this may help them as well."

Amazingly, they thanked Dorothy for her concern and readily agreed to do what she suggested, and all this was done without any malice, threats or intimidation.

About a month later, I got a call from one of the owners of the adult stores who said, "Mr. Hom, I met your wife Dorothy. A fine woman. And I want you to know that since I've owned my property where I have the adult bookstore, I want to tell you that I never really wanted to have this kind of business. I really wish you luck in changing our area around. My wife and I are willing to volunteer to help wherever we can! Count on us!" Wow! Sometimes I think Dorothy would have been a good preacher.

Within two weeks, Dorothy and I made arrangements to tour the four revitalized historic districts. Prior to leaving San Diego we contacted each of the districts' associations, informing them that we would be visiting and would appreciate any help they could give us about their restoration and preservation program. All acknowledged that they would be glad to help.

My experience with the San Diego Old Town Historic District gave me some background for a starting point, yet I realized that each project was uniquely different, culturally and physically. Restoration would bring new uses, but the historic building façades of the past would remain and would dictate the work around that theme.

Our visits with the historic districts were extremely helpful. Each one indeed had its own uniqueness. In speaking with some of the tenants in these historic districts, we got many comments, both pros and cons, but over all, they said that it was now a lot better than it had been prior to restoration. Each one of the districts was continuing to make the district better, with improvements from the private and public sector. Tax benefits were big incentives for the investors, too. We came home with loads of material, like city ordinances, building and business plans, and how each of the districts was initially started.

We were excited about all of our findings, and were anxious to share them with the Gaslamp Quarter members. Within a week we held a meeting, and the information we shared was enthusiastically received by most. Still, there were some skeptics, concerned that the area had gone too far downhill for such a program. "And it'll be too expensive, and what about the homeless and wino derelicts, how will we get rid of them?" a member said.

"We'll chip away at it," I replied. "Every one of the historic districts that we visited had those same problems, and they managed. It'll mean working together with the social organizations, police department, and the city. It is a known fact that once we build the district into something viable that will draw people to the new and attractive businesses, those negative elements will drift away." And I added, "As for funds, we can be part of the Urban Renewal Redevelopment Program as a joint effort between the private and public sector. People who want to rehabilitate their historic buildings can take advantage of the Tax Credit Programs from the state and federal government that applies to approved historic districts, which will come through the support of the city." After that spiel, I thought, boy, good thing I served in government to know about these programs. In spite of that, I knew that we still had a long ways to go.

As to the homeless, I made a point to meet with the people at the San Diego Rescue Mission, currently a three-story facility in the Gaslamp area. The mission was working with the city to find another location that would better serve their program. One was found about a mile away, encompassing about half of a city block and was much larger than what they presently had. Redevelopment funds and private donations eventually built a new and expansive building, for one purpose only, to help rehabilitate the homeless.

There was still the matter of the derelict winos that left empty wine bottles and other debris around, often urinating in the business doorways. Dorothy and I took on a "martyr" effort to show that the area could be cleaned up. Dressed in our normal business attire, she in her high heels and I in my coat and tie, every morning for about a month, except Sundays, at about 11 a.m. when more people were around, Dorothy and I would deliberately walk the Gaslamp streets picking up wine bottles and debris and put them in the public trash receptacles. We'd do this while we would intermittently visit with the proprietors and friends we'd meet along the way. We wanted to leave the impression that Gaslamp was for real and it would eventually happen. In a short time, there were others doing it, as well. It caught on to the point where proprietors would sweep and wash down the sidewalks in front of their stores frequently to keep their frontage neat and clean. This included the adult bookstores too. After about six months, I'd say about 80 percent of the winos drifted away.

At the same time, we had a committee working with the landlords who had vacant space, especially those with upstairs for which it was hard to find tenants. We asked the landlords to donate the space to a responsible party for one year, and then to modestly rent to them thereafter, gradually increasing the rent while still making it affordable to the tenants. I, in turn, contacted some of the art associations around town telling them about the proposed terms. Before we knew it, there were painting artists, sculptors, and designers applying for space. A number of them were quite talented and fit in very well into the emerging Gaslamp avant-garde environment.

When word got around that artists were moving into the Gaslamp Quarter, I got a call from a friend that had an automobile agency, and said, "Tom, my wife graduated from UCLA majoring in art. I call her a frustrated artist, and I've been thinking, she might like to set up a studio of her own, among the other artists there. Would you by any chance know of a historic building, not too large, that I might buy for her art endeavor?"

I put one of my salespersons on this and within a month we were able to find exactly what his wife wanted. It was large enough for her to have a studio and to rent to four other artist friends at a modest price. In a short time they decorated the studios into something that only artists can do, colorfully and with a touch of class.

I consider the artist community one of the forerunners in the renaissance of the Gaslamp Quarter, just as they had been in other historic districts. They brought vitality, imagination, and life to an area in a way others could not.

That reminds me of that saying, "Most people see things as they are. But artists see things as they should ... or can be!" Yes, I did enjoy working with artists, even with some that may be a little offbeat, because they had such great ideas.

I learned from one of my visits to the other historic districts that in order to kick off a successful renaissance project, there had to be a catalyst tenant. Something big, nice, and exciting that would attract people and would be a talk of the town. It needed to be a catalyst that was able to sustain attracting people. I thought of The Old Spaghetti Factory, a restaurant that served hundreds of people every day, with its turn of the century motif in Pioneer Square, Seattle,. The motif fit right in with our Gaslamp Quarter theme.

To follow through, I prepared a package that included information about our Gaslamp Quarter Association, the city's ordinance and plans for the area, photos, district history with maps, demographics, and plenty more, filling a storage cardboard box. I took it with me and met with The Old Spaghetti Factory's management team in Seattle, outlining our goals for the coming years. They were interested, but made no commitments, other than they would look over the box of information I presented and share it with their associates.

I didn't hear from them again until about six months later, when a man named Bob, one of the vice presidents of The Old Spaghetti Factory, called and told me they had just purchased a warehouse at the southeast corner of 5th and K Streets. They would remodel it and open The Old Spaghetti Factory in San Diego. He thanked me for giving them the opportunity to be part of the Gaslamp Quarter and invited us to join them at their future Grand Opening.

As I'm writing this now, about 35 years later, I must say the advice given to me about getting a catalyst tenant first was the one thing that really started the ball rolling to rejuvenate our Gaslamp Quarter Historic District. Today, after all these years, The Old Spaghetti Factory is still thriving, serving up to several hundred meals a day. It has been one of the busiest, if not the busiest restaurant in town. Even one of my granddaughters, Chloe, waitressed there, working her way through college.

From then on an array of restaurants moved in, some high end to the more modest types. Eventually, boutique and international hotel chains opened for business, along with shops of different types, entertainment night clubs, specialty shops like the Ghirardelli Chocolate & Ice Cream Parlor, and much more.

In time, with the economic and cultural changes of the area combined with the attraction of higher-end businesses and tenants, the rents and property values went up. The Gaslamp became an economic stimulus for San Diego. Many of the less desirable businesses started to move out, including several of the adult X-rated stores. To this day, only one of these types of businesses remains in the district after the owner, an active member of the Gaslamp Quarter Association, did extensive remodeling of the building.

In working to make the Gaslamp Quarter a decent family destination, there were a few anxious episodes that could have been a real setback. During the early stage of the district's development, a group of mothers from the Kensington community, led by a vocal mother crusading against pornography, picketed an adult X-rated store. The television stations and newspapers covered the story, with the leader raising her fist, speaking against these adult stores and vowing to do this each weekend until they closed up. A couple of weeks later, the leader issued a press release, stating, "That because of illness in the family, I can no longer lead the charge of eliminating adult X-rated stores." It was short and to the point.

Later I was told that an unidentified man had cased the family of the crusading leader, found out where the husband worked and learned that they had three children of school age. During the time the husband was at work and the kids were in school, the man knocked on the door of the their house and said to the crusader, "Lady, if you don't stop your picketing of the adult stores, your husband or one of your kids might have an accident!" And he left.

We never knew who he was and we really didn't care to know, for we already had enough challenges just to get things going, like working with the city's planning department for more public improvements, and promoting the district to new local and out of town people to move into the Gaslamp. We were carrying a full load, double time.

Shortly after, we started a newspaper called the *Gaslamp Quarter Gazette*, which included many historical stories of the area at the turn of the century, as well as news of current happenings in the Gaslamp. To distribute the papers, we had a couple of teenage boys, wearing knickers and flat-visor caps, hand them out to stores and passersby. It went well, with the advertising taking care of the cost. People responded well to the nostalgia, especially the old San Diegans, and the young people seemed to enjoy reading about their hometown during the earlier years. Later, there were even ladies dressed in period fashion wearing high collared long dresses passing out pamphlets for various businesses.

There also was a classy Gay Nineties nightclub that had a buxom blond in a tight black and red figurine dress passing out cards announcing their floorshow. For a moment, when I first saw her, I thought she was working for the adult stores, and my next thought was I better get Dorothy on this case. When I related that moment of anxiety to one of the adult store managers, he said, "Man, we're doing all right as it is. We're not looking for any trouble!" I do have to say, the adult stores had been very cooperative in working with the Association.

As the Gaslamp Quarter continued to improve and build its reputation as a desirable destination, the Association was honored with a number of awards for turning an area from blight into a positive economic engine and a source of civic pride. Upscale businesses and proactive property owners upgraded their historic buildings, and the district and the San Diego Convention & Visitors Association promoted it as a great attraction.

While maintaining a balancing act of running my real estate business and serving as the President of the Gaslamp Quarter Association for four years, I felt it was time to pass the gavel. We were able to continuously increase membership in the association because of the positive direction that the district was going, and also the birth of new interest in what was happening there. It was a new generation of leaders and I was all for that. It coincided with my philosophy that growth of a good movement must constantly refresh itself with new ideas and new people. This new generation of leaders did provide that and the others that followed thereafter. Following my presidency, I agreed to serve on the board of directors and continued to do so for the next four years.

When the Gaslamp Quarter first started in 1974, the real estate prices were as low as $10 per sq. ft. Today, in 2014, values are ranging up to $500 per sq. ft. Some say the Gaslamp Quarter was one of the major parts of "the tail that wagged the dog" in the rejuvenation of the San Diego downtown resurgence.

Today, the Gaslamp Quarter is internationally known and is constantly referred to as one of the most visited destinations in San Diego, attracting both tourists and locals. It remains a vibrant, exciting, and safe place to visit.

CHAPTER 37

Bienvenido!

URING MY TENURE WITH GASLAMP, I MET A GENTLEMAN named James Brown, a real estate investor, who attended some of our open meetings. A short while after I left the presidency, he contacted me and invited me to join with him and several of his friends in forming a new independent bank in San Diego. I found it interesting, and I thought being involved in banking as an investor wouldn't take too much time from my real estate business.

After an in-depth discussion with James Brown and meeting with some of the other potential investors, I agreed to participate. In so doing, I was offered a board of director's position. Since my knowledge of the banking business was limited, I thought it was slightly over my head at the time. But, on the other hand, I already knew banking pretty well from the customer side that included borrowing, checking, accounting, regulations, depositing, loan-to-values, and compensating balances and other requirements of a bank customer. I was pretty good at math and I trusted my judgment in business matters fairly well, so I felt confident enough that I could learn the other side of banking as I went along. Like the Boy Scout's motto, "Be Prepared!" I read a couple of books on banking. I found it fun and challenging to learn more about it.

After about six months of working with the bank application attorneys, the Banking Commission of California approved our application for a chartered bank. We named it The Bank of San Diego. The main branch was opened in downtown San Diego in a newly built high rise, occupying the main floor and part of the second floor. It was located at the corner of Third and Broadway, across from the city's historic Horton Plaza Park and the new regional Horton Plaza Shopping Center. It was here at the Horton

Plaza Park where I used to shine shoes when I was twelve.

With the help of some of the banking veterans I learned quickly, and I was elected Vice Chairman of the Board of Directors. I found presiding over a bank board meeting was not much different from some of the other boards on which I had served.

As The Bank of San Diego grew to several branches under the direction of Chairman James Brown, we formed a new entity, BSD Bancorp, to be the holding company of The Bank of San Diego. In its formation I was also elected as the vice chairman. Within the following year we, through the holding company, bought out the American Valley Bank, with the target market serving mainly the eastern part of San Diego County. A few years later I was also asked to serve on that board.

With these two banks doing well, we embarked upon chartering another new bank, to be in the greater Los Angeles area, in Long Beach, named Coast Bank, which eventually expanded with several branches.

With my involvement in the banking business, one would think it would have been extremely time consuming. But it was really not. Board meetings met for two to three hours normally only once a month, and the loan committee meetings once a week, about an hour or two at most.

On that schedule, it still gave me adequate time to work in my real estate business and to do other things as well. I worked closely with my son-in-law, Will Newbern, whom I had made a partner. He did most of the grunt work and I did most of the oversight. It was sort of a Mister Inside and Mister Outside relationship, working together. We were not only involved with the real estate marketing, but also buying and selling properties for the Hom family entities and also in the business of developing apartments and commercial properties.

Aside from business matters, I even had time to keep up with our social life, as well as stay active in serving on committees at church and other organizations. In spite of our heavy schedule, Dorothy and I still adhered to our philosophy that it was important to spend as much time as we could with our kids, especially having dinner together each evening, where we shared our day's activities together, and having vacations together.

Our better family outings would be hopping into our self-contained motor home and taking a trip into Mexico. We did that frequently. We packed up our fishing poles and crossed the border and shopped for some of our provisions in Mexico, where we bought tamales, tortillas, and other Mexican food. Our destination would be about 200 to 500 miles south of the border, to get away from the tourist towns. It wasn't unusual for us to venture off the main road and drive into some of the smaller villages in rural Mexico, completely non-tourist destinations. We'd park and establish camp on the fringe of the village in our camper. In a short time, inevitably, the friendly people of the village would drop by to welcome us and offer food and drinks, especially tequila and beer, to Dorothy and me. Along with that friendship, the villages always seemed to have musicians with their guitars, accordions, and what have you, playing and singing rancho songs. With such a festive atmosphere, we frequently ended up cooking a big amount of Chinese food, sharing it with the locals. In most cases, this was their first experience with Chinese food. They loved it! I frankly never saw a Mexican person not like Chinese food.

Some of the seaside villages were great, too. We were never short on having all the fish we wanted by fishing off the surf. It was always more than enough. But we were not equipped to catch lobsters and crabs. Luckily for us, the village fishermen went out in their boats each morning and returned with a big supply of lobsters and crabs that we bought for 50 cents apiece.

Once I invited a lobster fisherman and his family of seven for a Chinese dinner. In appreciation, they brought a bottle of tequila and three dozen huge live lobsters for us. The next morning we cooked them, and refrigerated the tails. Needless to say, for the rest of the trip we ate lobster tacos, lobster omelets, lobster Newburg, lobster grilled and Chinese style. After a week of this, we traded our lobster tails for carne asada tacos from a taco roadside stand. The stand owner thought he got a great deal ... as we thought we did too. I think neither Dorothy nor I ate lobster again for at least a year.

My experience in visiting and traveling in Mexico has been good and we've had very few problems, no more than we normally would have traveling in the U.S. The first time I crossed the border into Mexico was into Tijuana, which was about 25 miles from my home, when I was sixteen during World War II. At that time our country had gasoline rationing. I had a little Ford coupe and was allowed only five gallons a week, which was not enough for my travels between school and work.

So some of my friends and I drove south across the border and bought gas from the Mexican farmers because they were not on a gas ration. The gas was even cheaper than ours, so we made out okay. We also filled several five-gallon cans for some of our friends back home. We tacked a small profit on top of it, enough to cover our cost of driving down there and for us to eat a good Mexican meal.

But the best benefit of going across the border was visiting some of the Chinese families with teenagers. Because we were from the States, the parents of the teenage kids would normally go out of their way to treat us well, especially those with daughters. I must say, many of the girls were quite attractive, having that exotic Latin-Chinese touch. Most all of them spoke three languages, Chinese, English and, of course, Spanish. The families were generally well off, most owning restaurants, grocery stores, and property. The kids were always enrolled in the best private schools.

One of the things that we kids always got a charge out of was that we each had names representative of the country where we lived. The Chinese Mexican girls giggled and could not get used to calling us by our Anglo names, like Thomas, Robert, Edward, James, and Henry. Likewise, we got a kick out of calling them by their names: Juanita, Conchita, Rosita, Jovita, Maria and other Latina names. We'd also have fun dancing with them. They taught us the cha-cha and rumba steps, and we, in turn, taught them the latest jitterbug steps. It was fun and we always watched our manners and were proper. The brothers of the girls were also friendly to us, and, at the same time, they were very protective chaperones for their sisters.

As the years went by, a number of the Chinese Mexican kids ended up marrying the Chinese American kids, and from my recollection, all happily married with family, and not one divorce that I know of.

I must admit, I was one time smitten with a girl from Ensenada, a seaport town about 60 miles south of Tijuana. I met her at a community social event when she came with one of our local girls while she was visiting San Diego. Her name was Roberta Chee. She was quietly charming, and spoke English and Chinese with a Spanish accent. I found her to be so fascinating and interesting as we danced and talked about each other's life, about our families and about our hobbies. The night went by so quickly.

I learned that Roberta's father and mother immigrated to Ensenada from China in the 1920s and established themselves in the grocery business. They did quite well and also had extensive real estate holdings in town.

I did visit Roberta in Ensenada a few times, bringing a couple of my buddies along to help with the driving and, of course, to meet the younger sister. As time went on, we both agreed that we liked each other and that we would remain only good friends. Obviously, that was the right thing for us since I was only 19 and she was 17.

A few years later, she married a nice Chinese Mexican fellow, an accountant, who was in charge of the accounting department of a large fish cannery firm in Ensenada. For both of us, that was part of the maturing process.

XII. The End of an Era

AGES 50 TO 55

Mother Ah Nuing with children. L to R sitting: Wellman, Helen, Ah Nuing, Albert, Herbert; L to R standing: me, James and Allen.

CHAPTER 38

Rolling the Dice

IN 1974 PRESIDENT RICHARD NIXON RESIGNED FROM THE PRESI-
DENCY UNDER THE CLOUD OF THE WATERGATE SCANDAL, AND VICE
PRESIDENT GERALD FORD ASSUMED PRESIDENCY. IN 1976 FORMER
GOVERNOR JIMMY CARTER OF GEORGIA, ONCE A PEANUT FARMER,
WAS ELECTED PRESIDENT OF THE UNITED STATES.

WITH MY AGE CREEPING UP IN THE 50S, I TOOK GREATER care of my health. I had good stamina and remained active playing tennis at least twice a week. While so many of my friends seemed to be slowing down, I still had plenty of energy and the desire to stay fully engaged in business and all my other activities.

We bought a town. In the spring of 1979, I got a call from my friend Phil, who stated that he was in a bad situation on a real estate transaction. As he explained to me about a year earlier, he and a group of potential investors formed a partnership to purchase 140 acres that encompassed the little border town of Tecate, also known as Tecatito. At that time, Tecatito had a population of about 150 and was located on the American side of the U.S./Mexico border. On the Mexican side there was another town also called Tecate, with a population of 75,000.

Phil's dilemma was that the deal had been in escrow for about a year and as the leader of the group, he had put up the necessary deposit funds to tie up the transaction. After a number of escrow extensions, Phil was having problems getting the rest of the investors to put up their share of the money. In two days at 5 p.m., the escrow would be cancelled and his deposit forfeited. He wanted to save his deposit.

In desperation, he asked me whether I would be interested in taking over the deal so his deposit could be returned to him. He explained the details of the deal to me. I asked him to have his office send me the plat maps and escrow papers to study that evening.

After reviewing the maps and escrow papers, I saw some possible potential in the property. I immediately called my brother James and related the situation confronting my friend Phil. We decided to drive out to the property for a physical inspection that morning, about 35 miles from downtown San Diego.

When we got to the little town of Tecatito, we saw that it had California Highway 188 running right through it to the border crossing into Mexico. The 140 acres set around all that area, except for a grocery store and about half a dozen other small businesses. Around the outskirts of the area, there were a few scattered homes. The terrain of the land was level to rolling, nothing too steep. It was a pleasant surrounding where one could walk right across the border into the much larger town of Mexico's Tecate.

My brothers and I always felt comfortable in dealing with the Mexican people, both socially and in business. This property intrigued us enough to move toward working out a deal with my friend Phil.

When we returned to town, I called Phil to say that we would take over the deal, provided the sellers would give us two weeks to raise the funds for the purchase. It so happened that in reviewing the escrow papers, I noticed the name of Byron White, an attorney friend who was one of the principals of the selling group and was handling the legal aspect of the deal. I called him to share our interest and discuss the extra two week extension that was needed. It was granted, and we closed the deal within the two weeks. It was a very good deal.

As the years went by, we sold parcels of land to the United States government to expand its border crossing facilities. We also sold some to the State of California's Transportation Department for their truck crossing inspection program. With these funds, we paid off the balance of the mortgage, helped upgrade the Tecate Mutual Water Company system and loaned funds to some of the other family partnerships for their projects. We also derived some income from the rental of land for storage and parking.

In hindsight, what I could have done was ask Phil whether he wanted to join us as a partner to purchase the property. But at that point, I guess all he wanted was his large deposit back, and he was lucky that we made it happen. He was a good guy. When I was a State Assemblyman I had him appointed as a commissioner on the State of California Real Estate Board when Governor Reagan's office asked me for a recommendation for such an appointment.

Ironically, hindsight is always full of wisdom.

ONE OF THE PLEASURES I HAD each early morning was to read the newspapers, notably the *San Diego Union, L.A. Times, San Diego Transcript* and the *Wall Street Journal*. Generally I was able to finish reading them within an hour. One article that caught my eye was an article in the *San Diego Transcript* reporting that the Federal Communication Commission (FCC) in Washington was planning to allocate a new television station in San Diego, named Channel 69 under the UHF frequency. Applications for the station frequency would be accepted the following year.

I didn't know too much about ownership and investment in television other than what I occasionally read about a television station selling for tens of millions of dollars or more. Those big dollar numbers were out of my league but owning a TV station from the start up intrigued me.

A couple of days later, during a business meeting over lunch, I asked an attorney friend of mine, Forrest Chu, as to whom he might know that had knowledge about applying for a TV permit from the FCC for a television station. He referred me to a former classmate that worked in that field who had his office in Hollywood. I contacted his friend, Attorney Ken Browning, and I shared with him my interest in applying for the permit for a new television station in San Diego. He explained that his main role in television applications was to help with proposed programming and other essential items that made the application more viable for acceptance. He told us we needed an attorney in Washington, D.C., that was completely familiar with the application process, and suggested we contact Tom Carroccio.

I did, and within a week he flew out to California to meet with me along with Ken Browning. I was impressed with Carroccio's track record working with the FCC, the people he had as clients, and his professional strategy to work in such a formidable and bureaucratic system as the FCC.

After the second day of meetings, Carroccio and Browning laid out some of the criteria that we had to meet in submitting the application. They were extensive, including the names and background of each investor, other funding resources, the ethnic makeup of the group, an outline of the type of programming, references, business experience, etc. "Enough material that could well amount to 500 pages," said Carroccio, "and the cost can run from $200,000 to $500,000. Plus it'll take from a year to two years before the permit will be issued. For sure there will be several other groups that will be vying for the application as well."

I knew we would have competition and that the wheels of government worked slowly, but I was a little surprised about the length of time it would take, and the amount of work required to apply. We would need ultimate patience to work in that environment of bureaucracy, and, hopefully, we wouldn't have to spend $500,000.

Shortly after our meeting, I discussed the application with my brothers and we decided to move ahead on it. In consideration for diversity among the proposed investors, I had only two of my brothers on board with me, plus my Caucasian son-in-law Will, three African Americans, two Latinos, and three other Caucasians, amounting to twelve total investors. Funds were raised among the investors, with most of it deriving from the Homs.

In time, there were 13 applicants for the permit including us. Through the process we were able to obtain a copy of the other parties' applications. I'm sure they had ours as well. It gave each of us the opportunity to evaluate our opponents' strength and potential to obtain the TV permit. Our attorney's evaluation was that about half of them were weak and of the other half two were stronger, including ours.

As we went into the second year of the application, cost continued to accumulate for us as well as the other applicants. It came to a point when I thought it might be a good time for all 13 applicants to get together to discuss where we might have some common goals such as buying each other out or merging to form one entity.

I asked my attorney to contact the attorneys for the other applicants and see whether they would consider meeting to discuss each other's needs and interests. Obviously, the permit process was costing much more than each of us anticipated. The good news was that everyone agreed to a meeting. It was held at the U.S. Grant Hotel downtown in a private conference dining room. Everyone showed up with their lawyers.

I chaired the meeting. After four hours of discussion, with the lawyers doing 90 percent of the talking, mostly rebutting each other, it became obvious to most of us that we could be there for two days and still not get anything conclusively done. During a recess, some of us investors got together and decided that we should give the lawyers the rest of the day off, like going to the beach in La Jolla or the movies, and returning in the evening at about 8 p.m. At first, the lawyers were apprehensive and were reluctant to leave. However, we assured them that they were still under the clock as if they were working while they were out, and no agreement would be made without their final review. Meanwhile, we investors talked among ourselves.

By 8 p.m., we had an outline of an agreement as to who would be considered to be bought out and who was strong enough to stay on. When the lawyers came back, we needed more time and suggested they go to a movie or wait outside in the restaurant or bar and return at 11 p.m.

By 11p.m. we had an informal agreement, subject to the finalization by our respective attorneys. The general outline was that nine of the 13 applicants would be bought out with dollar figures given, and the four remaining, of which we were one of them, would merge into one entity. The attorneys did an outstanding job in working out the details.

I must say that was one of the most intense and hard-driven negotiations I have ever participated in. But it was worth it, for with the change in structure and only one qualified entity applying, the FCC granted us the permit within six months.

We named our new entity San Diego Television, Inc. and I was elected chairman. Jim Harmon, an investor and experienced television station manager, became president. His job was to pull all the necessary parts together in order to open the station within a year. Harmon was a partner with his sister, Helen Alvarez Smith. Later, after the opening of the station, they bought out the other two remaining partners making them the majority interest holding. In spite of that, they asked me to remain as the chairman.

In about eighteen months we opened for operation with quite a bit of fanfare. A new television station for San Diego! We were the headlines in all the news media. At the opening, there was ribbon cutting, speeches, congratulations, entertainment, and lots of food.

The station operated successfully for several years until we suffered an unfortunate consequence by the action of OPEC, the coalition of countries that supplied the majority of the world's oil needs. They did a shocking thing. They raised the oil prices so high that it triggered world inflation, causing the banking systems to raise their interest rates to as high as 25 percent. By so doing, many businesses went broke and we were badly damaged as well.

As a result, we sold the television station to the large media conglomerate, The Chicago Tribune, after a bidding war that consisted of several other large companies. The price paid was more than we had expected, enabling us to pay off all bank loans and distribute the profits to the partners. It turned out to be a very lucrative venture. Today what was Channel 69 is part of the Fox network, carried on all cable/satellite transmission under Channel 5.

I learned a lot. I learned that as hard as we might try to have the feeling that we were in control of the direction of a company or a situation, there was always another force, an outside element that could come along and alter that course, a force that could affect us immensely. Luckily in this case, with the TV station, it worked out very well for us.

AN END OF AN ERA. In November, 1981 my second mother, Ah Nuing, passed away. At times, she was also referred to as our stepmother. But mostly we children acknowledged her as our second mother, and we were taught to call her Ah Nuing. I never really found out what the words meant but that wasn't important, Ah Nuing was just fine.

As I became older, especially when I became a father, I often wondered if Ah Nuing knew that my father, a widower, already had five sons ranging from one to eight years old, when he courted her. I mentioned that to Dorothy and she, having a close relationship with Ah Nuing, asked her about that. Ah Nuing told Dorothy, "Yes, I knew he had five young sons, was a proud and hardworking man with his own business, and well respected by the community. He was well educated and could read and write English, too. I saw pictures of him and some of the sons. I was proud to marry such a man."

Dorothy related that Ah Nuing then paused, shook her head, and said, "But I never knew that life in America would be so hard. And so many poor people. Everyone in China said that America was so rich that you wouldn't have to work and you could just enjoy yourself. That is not so." Dorothy said she then reminded her that the world in the 1930s was in a major depression and that was the reason life was so hard.

Ah Nuing did say that America was indeed the land of opportunity. She had seen her children move on to become successful in many professions. She had 33 grandchildren and a week before she passed away at 76 with colon cancer, she wanted to see her first great-grandchild, my oldest daughter Nora's newly born girl, Camille. Ah Nuing held the baby tenderly and smiled, then looked up at the rest of the family and said, "So lucky. A new generation!"

One of the more rewarding times for me with Ah Nuing was when we had the Far East Trading Company import store that she managed. I looked forward to taking her to Los Angeles twice a year for the wholesale gift show where she personally did the buying for the store. Dorothy always came along. Three hours up and three hours back gave us time to talk about a lot of things.

Ah Nuing talked a lot about the business, about the children, her friends, her cooking, and the family gatherings. But one subject she would always get emotional about, even to the point of wiping her eyes, was when she spoke about being the luckiest person in town. She said her friends constantly referred to her as being so lucky. They said something in their Chinese or broken English, "With 12 children now so successful, like in business, banking, medicine, law, science, and government, you are number one lucky and a well deserved mother."

In expressing how lucky and proud she was, she also said something I had never been aware of during the earlier years after my father's passing. She confessed that in trying to raise all 12 children, she might have shown too much preference and favoritism towards her own seven, and in turn was too severe with the five older boys. Her greatest fear for years was that the older boys would abandon her and the seven younger ones.

I expressed to her the best way I could that the abandonment thought never occurred to any of us older boys and that Dad told us about our responsibilities to help hold the family together. Aside from that, when the children were quite small, the older ones helped take care of them. I think that was a powerful bonding situation that occurred and has sustained us throughout our lives. Again, I gave Ah Nuing assurance that the thought of abandonment never entered our minds. For a brief moment, I thought I saw relief in her face because she got it off her chest by confessing about having such negative thoughts.-

Now being older and a father of six, having gone through hard and good times, I often think back about Ah Nuing. I think about the overwhelming situation she faced in coming to a new land, a new culture, the language barrier, a ready-made family of five rambunctious boys, racial discrimination, and loads of other things adjusting to an entirely new life. Under those circumstances, I think she did pretty well.

CHAPTER 39

A Mexican Fiesta

A FTER AH NUING PASSED AWAY, MY BROTHERS AND SISTERS NO longer got together regularly at her house each Sunday for dinner. This was the weekly event that Ah Nuing looked forward to and joyfully prepared food days in advance. Nevertheless, we continued to get together, the whole clan, at least three or four times a year at either one's home or at a restaurant. We still do even today.

One time, Dorothy suggested that maybe we should do something different. "How about an outing with the whole family at some remote place with a lot of fresh air and open space? Like a resort!" said Dorothy. I thought that was a great idea. Something different. Especially for the young kids, of which there were quite a few. As a matter of fact, at times it was even hard to remember all their names.

I ran this by my siblings and it was a unanimous, "Let's do it!" With that consensus, Dorothy was appointed to find a location for the event to extend over a long weekend starting Friday afternoon through a Monday holiday. She worked with some of the other sister-in-laws and found that the resorts required reservations a year in advance in order to accommodate that many people, and the prices were much more than we were planning to spend.

Then in the interim, something good happened. Dorothy and I happened to be invited to a Coldwell Banker Commercial Realty's company retreat. The weekend invitation was given to us because of my personal relationship with the manager of the company from having worked together on some of the civic matters.

The retreat was held at the Hacienda Rancho Veronica, a 2,500-acre ranch resort in Mexico that was owned by the wealthy Bustamante family in Baja California. The Bustamantes were a prominent family in Mexico with real estate holdings and large businesses as well as involvement in governmental affairs. Señor Bustamante had a love for the art of bullfighting. At the resort ranch, he had set aside an area away from the main hacienda where he built a bullring. He bred fighting bulls there and trained young men who wanted to be bullfighters. It was in a beautiful setting among the oak and pine trees and had all the necessary facilities to promote his program for bullfighting.

A couple of times I visited the bullring area to watch some potential bullfighters train. They were mostly young athletic types and a few were middle aged. I was told some of those were frustrated dreamers who never made it to actually do any fighting but still had the illusion of making it one day. Most of the bulls for the trainees were young and hadn't grown big sharp horns yet. I also watched some of the more advanced trainees working with the mature bulls and that was scary. I'm not sure why in the world one would want to be a bullfighter to make a living. It must be the human instinct of man against beast. Or maybe the glamour of it, and the wealth and stardom that comes with it. In hindsight, it may not be that much different between bullfighting and high risk drivers of the Indianapolis and other high power auto races that take place around the world. That's pretty dangerous, too.

I am an admirer of the writings of Ernest Hemingway. In a number of his interviews and stories he describes his fondness of bullfighting, especially those that he frequented in Spain. Knowing his love for bullfighting, I attended at least three professional bullfights in Mexico, two in Tijuana, and one in Guadalajara. In a way, I wanted to see what he saw in it that made him such an aficionado. After sitting through three of them watching a man tease, beat up, and eventually kill the bull, I concluded that I still loved Hemingway's work but we sure differed about what was entertaining.

The resort area where we were staying was built along the lines of traditional Spanish/Mexican architecture with a hacienda motif and lots of beautiful tile work. It had all the modern conveniences: tennis courts, swimming pool, basketball court, workout room, and a spacious social hall with large traditional hanging chandeliers.

The grounds were well maintained with hiking trails through the many wooded areas, a horseback riding arena, and two lakes where one could go boating and fishing.

We were thoroughly impressed with the resort, its many amenities, and the outgoing courtesy of the management and staff. Added to that, the price was amazingly reasonable, due mostly to the weak *peso* to the dollar. After our short stay there, Dorothy and I decided this would be an ideal place for our family event, so we took a bundle of Hacienda Rancho Veronica brochures to share with the family.

After we got home, we sent a cover letter with a colorful brochure to the relatives explaining what we saw and experienced at the resort. The response that came back was enthusiastic and unanimous, "Let's go for it!" The trip was booked for the middle of summer when the kids were out for school vacation. The logistics of putting together a retreat for 60 people, including a bunch of kids of various ages, was challenging. Dorothy and I were the main coordinators with the help of other family members.

A few of the Hom women planned for each family to put on a talent show or skit of some kind. Another night was reserved for Hom family history, facilitated by the elder members, accompanied with a slide show. Each night we would enjoy mariachis entertaining us before and during dinner. There were more than enough activities at all times for those who wanted to remain active.

The ladies were forever concerned about not having good healthy food available, so they had our brother Albert bring a pickup load of fresh fruit and vegetables from David Produce. Needless to say, that was a wise thing to do, as the outdoor activities kept everyone hungry most of the time. Teams and games were organized by the younger brothers, George and Johnny, with prizes awarded to the winning individuals or teams. On top of that, some of us went hiking and horseback riding. The resort cooks were kept busy from early morning all day long, even preparing late night snacks for us. They were happy to do this, as we assured management that we would provide them with an adequate gratuity for their extra work.

Coming to Baja California ended up being a great experience for the younger generation, as many had never traveled to Mexico before. Crossing the border between the U.S. and Mexico during that time did not pose a problem for most people. Mexico wanted more American tourists to help their economy. Americans, going back to the states had no problem either, as long as they spoke fluent English and had a driver's license to show if asked for an ID.

But it wasn't always that way. There was one period, for about a 60 year span, when most of the people of Chinese descent had to have an official U.S. permit in order to return to the States, because of the 1882 Chinese Exclusion Act which excluded Chinese laborers to enter. However, my being a student of Chinese history in America, I judge it was more than just an economic means of protecting the white working class. I think it was the fear of and not understanding the culture of the industrious Chinese people that led to Congress passing that act. Fear breeds prejudice.

It was in 1943, after 61 years, when Congress voted to remove the Chinese Exclusion Act, due mainly to the friendship established between the two countries as Allies together in fighting Japan in World War II.

After four fun-filled days of activities and bonding between families, it was time to pack up for home. At luncheon before leaving, young and old family members were given the opportunity to share their thoughts about this retreat and what they learned from it. The comments were all positive, and the only real negatives were that some had sore butts from horseback riding and sore arms from too much tennis.

The one sad moment of the outing was on the last day. Just before leaving, a group of the teenage boys wanted a last splash in the swimming pool. While horsing around, one of them, Nathan, slipped and hit his head hard on the tile floor and was knocked out completely. We could not revive him and we began to panic. He was loaded into a car and hurriedly driven to a hospital in San Diego, which was about 90 miles away. Naturally, we were very concerned and anxious about Nathan, so while going home, we were all pretty subdued. The first thing Dorothy did upon arriving home was to call Nathan's parents to learn the latest on his condition.

The good news was that he had been revived and was almost back to normal, but with a big headache. That evening Dorothy and I shared some thoughts, that considering the types of activities and how hard people played, we were lucky that we only had one casualty. Dorothy then said, jestingly, "On the other hand, those that did a lot of horseback riding, with sore butts, might dispute that. " And I said, rubbing my butt, "Yeah!"

About 25 years later, Dorothy and I revisited Hacienda Rancho Veronica Resort while we were on the way home from a visit to Mexicali, Mexico. I was thinking that maybe the Hom family might again have a retreat there.

The Hom Brothers at Hacienda Rancho Veronica, Mexico. L to R: Albert, me, George, James, Herbert, John, and Allen.

To my disappointment, it wasn't the same. Upon arriving and entering the normally guarded gatehouse, I noticed that it was in a rather dilapidated state. The paint was peeling and one of the windows was cracked, and weeds were growing in the flower pots. There was no gate man to welcome us as before and the large colorful Hacienda Rancho Veronica sign was now faded and needed retouching. In driving further into the resort, I noticed the landscape was not kept up, and the array of flowers that had beautified the grounds no longer existed, nor were the cobblestone and tiled walkways well maintained. There were cracks and broken parts here and there.

The biggest change was the large clubhouse. Instead of bull fighting decor, it had become more Americanized with posters, paintings and photos of off road vehicles. The bar was catering to a large group of off roaders, mostly from north of the border. Many were singing along with the mariachi band, the only thing that seemed familiar. Everyone seemed to be having a good time.

Later I ventured out to the area where the bullring was located and likewise, found it had deteriorated quite a bit. The building that housed the potential bullfighters was also neglected. All about the surroundings, there were off road vehicles and motorcycles climbing up and down the hills along the many trails they had carved out.

Although the resort had deteriorated, I must say that it was hustling and bustling with people and activities. Before leaving, I visited the registration office and chatted with one of the office employees and asked about the change in the venue and how it was going. I was told, "Si, *Señor*, the original resort was not doing so good and losing a lot of money. This is much better financially for us. We have more workers now and at better pay!" I guess one can't argue against that. In any event, I'm grateful our family had the good experience of enjoying the beauty, activities, and ambience of the original resort.

THE YEARS BETWEEN 1978 AND 1982 were challenging years for America. There was a major recession and interest rates soared as high as 25 percent, and the American embassy in Tehran was stormed by the Iranians, holding 52 Americans hostage for 444 days.

This was also the period when California Governor Ronald Reagan decided to run for President of the United States.

When Reagan first announced his candidacy for president, the rest of the nation saw him as an actor who happened to win an election in wacky California, a place of fruits and nuts. According to early polls he trailed far behind the other strong candidates. But I knew he would sway the rest of the country once he began stomping for votes on the campaign trail, just as he had when he ran for governor.

That is exactly what happened. Reagan won by a landslide vote, beating an incumbent, President Jimmy Carter. He also won overwhelmingly in electoral votes, garnering 470 when 270 would have been enough to win. President Carter, in my opinion, was not a bad or ineffective president, but his communication skills were simply not strong enough to compete with a great communicator like Ronald Reagan.

I have often thought of Reagan and his outstanding ability to communicate since I first met him in 1965, when he was contemplating a run for Governor of California and he invited me to meet him in private for 30 minutes to discuss the issues confronting California and San Diego. Before going into that meeting, I had already decided to support San Francisco Mayor George Christopher for the Republican primary. After those 30 minutes with Reagan, I changed my mind and shifted my support to him instead.

I share this story because from the very beginning of my childhood, when I was able to do some thinking, probably at about age three, I enjoyed communicating with people. It got me, most times, what I wanted and I was praised, as well. Sometimes I even got a pat on the head, too. The only language I spoke was Chinese until I went to public school at five and learned English by immersion, just by listening and speaking English with my friends and teachers at school.

I believe it is crucial to communicate well in our society today. So much in life today is so instant; to get it right the first time is important. I tell that to my kids a lot. Say it the right way, say it clearly, and say it with understanding of the person to whom you're talking. Yes, Dale Carnegie said that many times, "Say it right!"

One of the things I regret very much is that over the years I have lost a lot of my fluency to speak Chinese. I do believe that in the future of the world economy, there will be three major languages that will dominate international transactions: English, Chinese, and Spanish. It'll probably be in about 25 years, but that's the direction the international community is headed.

WITH THE RECESSION TAKING ITS toll on a number of businesses in town, a minus became a plus for us. One day James called and said, "Tom, the City of San Diego recently decided to restrict large truck parking in our produce market area, no more overnight parking on the public street right-of-ways. We need to find a parking lot somewhere for our trucks within 90 days."

The next day I picked up James to scout around an area that might lend itself for that purpose. I figured it would have to be a parking lot of at least 30,000 sq. ft. After checking several potential locations, we found the prices to either rent or to purchase too high, or the location was not convenient enough.

The following day we checked other locations and still didn't find anything suitable. On the way back to David Produce, James noticed a small sign on one of the buildings of the Western Metal Supply Company, located only three blocks from our company. The Western Metal Supply Company happened to be one of the oldest and largest wholesale hardware dealers in southern California, established in 1904, with buildings and lots covering almost three city blocks. The sign said, For Sale, Call Home Federal Savings.

I just happened to know the president of Home Savings, Kim Fletcher, and the executive vice president, Gordon Luce, from working together on the improvement of the downtown district. In addition, they were strong supporters when I was involved in politics. That day I called Gordon Luce, and he said, "The Western Metal Supply Company is in bankruptcy and is in the process of liquidating its assets. If you're interested, I'll have one of the boys bring down the particulars on the properties as well as the keys."

I said, "Yes, bring them down; we'll be waiting in front of the main building!"

As we waited in front of the impressively large four-story red brick building, we were contemplating what the total property might be worth and what it might eventually sell for. We were concerned it might be too big of a deal for us to handle, or the down payment would be more than we could afford. Shortly, within half an hour from my call, a man brought down the keys and information on the property.

James and I studied the floor plans of the complex of buildings, the land coverage area, and other particulars. The total complex consisted of several huge warehouses, some with large loading docks. One particular structure caught my eye. It was a much older building than the rest, built in 1886. It was formerly used to build horse carriages and later used as a livery stable, and then finally as a storage warehouse. It consisted of 20,000 sq. ft. of space, with huge open wooden beams and rafters, which included a mezzanine that had a catwalk bridge and a wide open area to look down on the main floor. The most interesting thing about this building was that the super structure was built without nails or metal bolts. In its place, wooden pegs were used. Quite unique.

The total square footage of building floor space of the whole complex was 115,000 sq. ft., plus 40,000 sq. ft. of empty fenced yard space.

In its report, the property was appraised at $1.2 million dollars. After a review of the information and inspection of the buildings, we decided to make an offer. We made it for $700,000 plus $140,000 on another half block owned by a subsidiary of Western Metal Supply Company, with a six month escrow. To our pleasant surprise, Home Federal Savings accepted the offer. And they also offered to finance it for us as well, with a 15 percent down payment.

Indeed, it was a pleasant surprise, not only the financing part of it, but also with the six month escrow, which would give us enough time to turn this white elephant into a revenue producing entity.

With the purchase of all this vacant property, I really had my work cut out for me. I had to start figuring how to structure a revenue producing program to make the mortgage payments and to pay the taxes on it, as well as alterations that would be needed in order to rent it out. At the same time, we would have to form a new partnership in order to get the necessary funds together to close escrow.

Also, the six month escrow gave us ample time to do the planning on how the complex of buildings would be used. After we made the necessary security deposit on the purchase, Home Federal Savings was nice enough to provide us with the keys and combinations to two large walk-in vaults in the main building.

We really did not have any particular need for the vaults, but upon opening them, we found boxes of business records and historical photos and public articles of the Western Metal Supply Company dating back from near the very beginning of the firm. Along with that, there were various old time office equipment and paraphernalia from the early 1900s. As someone who loves history, I found them to be extremely fascinating and fun to go through.

Discovering all this, especially the photos of the old 1886 carriage warehouse, gave me an idea. I immediately thought of the famous old Pike Street Market in Seattle, a thriving marketplace, the historical 1742 Faneuil Hall Market in Boston, and the Farmers Market on Fairfax Avenue in Los Angeles, all of which I had visited. I said to myself, "Why not a similar operation for the historic carriage building?" So that was it! We'd design a farmer's type of operation in the carriage building, which would be the centerpiece for the complex of buildings. From there we could expand if we needed to. That would be, as they say, "the tail that wags the dog!"

I hired an architect to help lay out some of the improvements we would need in order to meet city code, to add some stairways to the mezzanine, and to layout the floor plan to place the concessionaires. The anchor for the concessions would be several retail produce markets, and various ethnic restaurants, meat and seafood markets, flower shops, jewelry and various novelty shops.

At the end of six months, with the partnership and funds all gathered, escrow closed. In that interim we had commitments to lease out about 20,000 sq. ft, to several antique stores, and several offices to small businesses. Upon the closing, we went ahead and converted 30,000 sq. ft. into mini-storages, which we named Downtown Mini-Storage. It became very popular with small businesses and residences due to the low rates we were able to charge because of the low cost of the property purchase.

Within a few more months, we leased one of the larger buildings to a general contractor, and also leased to other tenants, such as an auto storage company, the City of San Diego, and the University of California, San Diego.

Because of the sale of the large parcel of properties of the Western Metal Supply Company, an iconic company of the past, the news media ran several stories on our purchase. It was in these stories that I was able to share what we planned to do with the properties, which included a farmers market to be named Farmers Bazaar. Shortly after, I was flooded with calls from a great number of people wanting to open a concession in the Farmers Bazaar. By the time we opened for operation, which was about six months after the close of escrow, we were fully leased and had a waiting list of applicants wanting to move in.

By Grand Opening day, we had a crowd of hundreds of people waiting to get in to shop in this old, rejuvenated carriage warehouse. The crowd was enormous throughout the day and the following weeks, until it mellowed down to something more sensible, but still very busy with a steady flow. It helped by opening earlier and closing later, and also by staying open seven days a week instead of six.

Obviously, with the success of turning the white elephant into a good investment, we found that the operation of the Farmers Bazaar was especially fun and rewarding. A few headaches here and there, but overall, they were minor.

After 10 years of successful operation of the Western Metal Supply properties, a tragedy occurred that was most unforeseen. The Farmers Bazaar caught on fire one afternoon and was totally destroyed, with the fire spreading into several other buildings, burning about 50,000 sq. ft. of structure into a heap of ashes.

I was first notified of the fire during a bank Board of Directors meeting in La Jolla, about 20 miles away. When I was called and was told that the fire was out of control, I immediately left the meeting. Going to my car, I could see dark bellowing smoke rising in the direction of downtown. I knew then that the fire was big and hoped to God there would not be any casualties.

After an investigation of the cause of the fire, it was reported to me that it was due to some faulty wiring. I had some doubts about that, for we had the carriage building completely rewired and city approved before we opened for business. All and all, I didn't question it, for I was more than glad that no one was seriously injured. The insurance covered a good portion of the damages, both for the tenants and us, but like in most cases, not enough to fully compensate for the total loss.

In my interview with the news media, I was asked, "What are your plans now for the future of Farmers Bazaar?" I didn't mean to sound dramatic or poetic, but I did say, "From the ashes, there shall rise a Phoenix!" What I really meant, was that I planned to rebuild the Farmers Bazaar in one of the other large warehouses. That dramatic quote turned out to be good PR. I got a lot of responses from Farmers Bazaar customers that expressed their condolences due to the fire and at the same time congratulated me for moving ahead with the new Phoenix.

With all stops out we proceeded to build another Farmers Bazaar in another section of the complex of buildings. The new site was larger than the former location, and was all on one floor. In designing the new floor plan, I couldn't help but think of the mezzanine with the catwalk we had at the destroyed Farmers Bazaar. I thought that was so neat. I'm sure some of the regulars would miss it, too, as many would stand on the catwalk and view the colorful market and take photos of the activities below.

The new location with the added space provided even more variety of different types of stalls, and also for greater income as well. This helped make up for the loss of income from the buildings that were destroyed by the fire. Aside from that, with the new added space, we were able to charge more for rent, as we had many eager applicants. With respect to our original tenants, we made it a point to keep the same rental rates as before for five years.

As the years went on, like all things, it eventually came to pass that the forces of change would take place. Downtown San Diego had been on a major program to redevelop the area through the government program of Urban Redevelopment. At the same time, the Major League Padres baseball organization was in need of a new baseball park, because the facilities at the San Diego Stadium were inadequate for its future goals. A number of major cities had offered to build a new state of the art baseball park if the Padres would consent to move to their city. The offers were enticing for the team.

The polls showed that the Padres were an important part of our cultural well being in San Diego and the citizens wanted to keep them here if it did not affect the tax roll.

The city fathers had to make a decision, to build a new ballpark to keep the Padres here, or to let them go. Naturally, with the Padres being part of the San Diego fabric for over 40 years, it was decided to keep them here. Therefore, the City Council and Mayor voted to establish a relocation committee to find a suitable place for a ballpark and to devise a financial plan for the Council to consider. Because of my experience in helping build the San Diego Stadium in Mission Valley, now known as Qualcomm Stadium, I was one of the people the Mayor asked to serve.

After a thorough search throughout many parts of the county to find a new location, it was finally down to three areas of which downtown San Diego was one. At that time, our family had become major property owners in the downtown redevelopment area and it concerned me. Because of that, I decided that I should resign from the relocation committee to avoid any possible conflict of interest that might come up in the event downtown became the final choice.

Ironically, after another year of research and studies, the committee zeroed in on the exact location where our Western Metal properties were located. Since the properties were located in an Urban Redevelopment zone, they could be condemned and purchased by the Redevelopment Agency to be used for a "higher and better use," in this case, a baseball park for the San Diego Padres.

I had mixed feelings on losing our Western Metal properties through the force of eminent domain, and yet it was for a good cause. Our original long range plan for the properties was to develop it into high rises of offices and hotel buildings along with some commercial sites and open space. We were resigned to the fact that the people of San Diego wanted the ballpark. In addition, the financing of it would be partly through the Redevelopment Agency, which could make it happen without it being on the tax roll. We accepted that as a good deal for San Diego. After several meetings with the Redevelopment Agency and the Padres, we negotiated a price that was fair for both parties.

The negotiated price did give us a decent return on our investment. With the funds, we went on to invest in other projects, as we normally did when one of our investments sold.

After completion, the Padres' ballpark was named Petco Park. In appreciation of our past ownership of the Western Metal properties, and our cooperation in working with them in acquiring the Western Metal properties, the Padres honored the David C. Hom Family with a bronze plaque that reads "Hom Family Plaza" in the Palm Court of the ballpark. They also gave us complimentary tickets to the games, up to 100 at a time, for our Hom family gatherings in the panoramic view seats in the exclusive area that is located on the rooftop of the multi-story historic Western Metal building that had been completely remodeled to accommodate large groups. At other times we were given private boxes, as well, that seated about 25. This went on for several years.

It's a good thing I wasn't in public office then, because I wouldn't have been able to accept all these freebie tickets!

CHAPTER 40

I Likee...

DALE CARNEGIE WAS RIGHT ON WINNING FRIENDS AND INFLUENCING PEOPLE.

A FEW YEARS EARLIER, I WAS ASKED TO JOIN A BUSINESS GROUP, known as San Diegans, Inc. It was an organization that had limited members, up to a hundred, and the members were in the top tier of their organizations, mainly in businesses and in the professions. This included companies like San Diego Gas & Electric, Bank of America, First National Bank, the Copley Press, Coldwell Banker Commercial Real Estate, large law firms and a number of larger manufacturing firms that had an interest in promoting a better and more vibrant downtown San Diego.

At that time I was the vice chairman of the BSD Bancorp, a bank holding company that included the Bank of San Diego, of which I was also vice chairman. After about three years with San Diegans Inc., where I served two years on the board of directors, I was elected to the position of vice president. As a traditional progression, this would lead me to the next position as president the following year, and then chairman of the board.

That process of filling these positions was always challenging because they had a high local profile. The news media always gave it good coverage. It was an organization that was highly regarded by the community and the local government. Our various proposals to the government as to what might be the best way to create a bigger and better downtown, were generally backed up by well researched reports by outside professional firms, such as well known architects and accounting firms from the Big Five.

I know that being a leader, one goes through a process of both praise and criticism. Mine was no different. In my case I had two antagonistic fellows that always harped on me and would criticize my leadership and viewpoints. Other than that, I got along very well and had good support of my viewpoints and opinions with the membership at large.

In trying to understand what the problem was with these two fellows, I thought of my science teacher in high school, who said, "To solve a problem, you must first pin point what the real problem is. Once you know that, then you can work towards solving it." In their criticism of me, especially in open meetings, I concluded that the first critic, Ross, was unhappy because he felt he was more deserving than I to fill the leadership position. He was better educated, went to the best schools, and had several successes in the business world. Realizing that, and knowing what his problem was, I made an effort to include him in some of the more important issues we were advocating for downtown. One of them was that San Diegans Inc. had bi-monthly meetings with the Mayor, the City Council, and members of the Centre City Development Corporation to discuss downtown issues. As president, I normally took the lead at these meetings from our side and reported back to the board of directors. I, instead, asked Ross to take that lead and report back to the board. He was most appreciative of that and did an excellent job. I complimented him on that, especially the way he handled the tough questions that were asked. Overnight the antagonism evaporated. Later on he did become president of San Diegans, Inc. and made a good leader.

As to the other fellow, named Byron, I made it a point to study his short biography that members submit when they become a member of San Diegans Inc. I found that he was born and raised in Alabama, served as a young officer at the end of World War II in Asia, in Japan, China, and the South Pacific. At that time the Asian people were down and out, struggling to survive. After returning to the States, he went on to earn his law degree, did well and was now with a prominent law firm as a partner. He lived in an exclusive neighborhood in La Jolla.

As part of my analysis I thought back to an occasion where I was at one of the committee meetings to lay out a procedure to enhance our traffic flow downtown and to recommend for the city traffic engineer to review. The committee chair asked if there was anyone who would like to add anything to the proposal. Byron got up and said, "Yes," and went up to the proposed outline and suggested a couple of changes. After looking at them, I thought they were smart changes. After he made those proposed changes, he looked at me and said, in Pidgin English, "You likee ... or no likee?" I knew he said it partly in jest, but behind it was a subtle insult to my ethnicity disguised as a jest. There were a few groans and light laughter.

I sensed it was awkward for the rest of the members, so I responded by saying, "I velly much likee!" The room responded with a big roaring laugh. Then I went on to say, "Yes, Byron, I really do like it!" Then we all applauded. Yes, his proposals of changes were readily accepted by the committee.

From then on, Byron became less and less antagonistic, and by the time my term as president was nearly over, we became friends. I was once again reminded of what dear old Dad said in dealing with people: "First have people respect you for your character, and what you are and who you are, and from there they can learn to like you, and after that, they can even come to love you!"

I can't say Byron ever learned to love me, but I do believe he did come to respect me, and we did become good friends.

XIII. The New Immigrants

AGES 55 TO 65

一只兔子崎岖的心路历程

Working with others to achieve the American Dream.

CHAPTER 41

Fatso

IT WAS THE YEAR 1985 WHEN SOVIET RUSSIA CHOSE MIKHAIL GOR-
BACHEV AS THEIR NEW LEADER.

ONE MORNING, JUST FOR CASUAL ENTERTAINMENT, I WAS browsing through the newspaper classified ads to see what people were selling, not wanting to buy anything. I found their thought-provoking headings and their descriptions very interesting.

"EUREKA! YOU'VE FOUND IT!" was one of the ads that caught my eye. "Your dream will come true. A beautiful twin crew 32 ft. Owens Cruiser to make your own vacations, fully equipped, immaculate condition, and going for a bargain! Family separation. Honeymoon is over." Curiosity got the best of me, so I circled the ad and wondered if I should call just to find out what a boat like that would sell for. I knew full well I wasn't the sailor type, and I didn't care much for swimming, either. I was only good at swimming for about 50 yards because I had to when I was a Boy Scout going after a merit badge. Water, as far as I was concerned, was for drinking and bathing. So I set the paper on the coffee table and left it at that.

The next morning during breakfast Dorothy brought the newspaper with the circled ad to me and said, "Tom, I didn't know you were interested in buying a boat. How nice! How much is it selling for?"

A bit surprised with her positive tone, I responded in a matter-of-fact way, "Oh, it's nothing. The ad caught my eye and I was just curious. We don't need a boat, and I don't think we can afford one with kids in college and other needs. Aside from that, neither you nor I ever cared much for boating ... other than enjoying large cruise ships, but owning a boat is something else."

With Dorothy's cheerful manner, she replied, "Don't forget, deary, I'm from Hawaii and the sea has been part of my heritage and bloodline. Let me call and check it out for you!" What could I do, she was already walking towards the phone in the den with the ad in hand? So I thought, oh well, I'd like to know more about it, too.

After about 15 minutes, Dorothy came back to the kitchen and said, "Guess what, Thomas. (She called me Thomas whenever she wanted to make a point of importance.) I had a good talk with the man selling the boat. He and his wife are separating and will need to sell it as soon as possible. He is willing to lower the price from $25,000 to $22,000 for a quick sale. I asked him if he could do better. He said if we could pay cash he might do a little better, like $20,000. I asked him if the boat was free and clear and no money owed on it. He said yes. So I offered him $18,000 subject to final inspection and to your approval. He hesitated, and asked his wife and she approved. See, I made no commitment. It's subject to a final inspection and your approval. And the boat has a cute name, 'Fatso!'"

"Yes, dear," I said, knowing that we were already halfway into buying it ... subject to my approval and the final inspection. What did I know about boats?

I did feel a little better when she reminded me that if we got it, we could entertain business clients on it and depreciate part of it and charge off some of the expenses for business promotion. Also, it would be a good thing for the family as a gathering place. Plus, I could cook up some of my favorite dishes in the galley at these gatherings. Since cooking was one of my hobbies, I liked that idea. Well, since owning a boat had all these advantages and Dorothy liked it, then I knew if it passed its final inspection I'd approve.

So in preparation to checking the boat over, I lined up one of my friends who was in the brokerage business for boats to inspect it for a fee. He checked the boat over, went through the paperwork on its maintenance, and declared that the boat was in ship-shape condition. He also said that the market price for a boat like that was about $26,000. That even made me feel better, like I knew what I was doing.

For a silly fleeting moment I thought, "Hey, I can really make several thousand dollars on it by turning around and selling it!" By this time all our kids knew about Fatso and rallied around me as a great caring father buying a boat for the family. Plans were already being talked about for bringing their friends onboard for a cruise around the bay. With the kids jumping up and down with such great anticipation, how could I even think for a moment of reselling it? At this point I was resigned to the fact that we would have a boat in the family.

Prior to consummating the deal with the boat owner, he let me take the boat out with a boating friend for a trial run. We sailed around San Diego Bay where he showed me how to use the two throttles of the twin screw engines doing some turning, backing up, sharing the versatility of it. After a couple of hours we came back in and he backed the boat into the slip with ease. I said to myself with cocky sureness, "Hey, this is really duck soup! I can do this. What's so hard about handling a boat?"

A little later I learned handling a boat was not like driving an automobile, where you can have quick and fast results. With a boat, it is anticipation and judgment with gradual results.

It was a couple of days after I closed the purchase of Fatso the boat that the seller offered to take me out for some lessons on boat handling. Returning after an hour or so in the bay, he let me be in charge of backing up into the boat slip. In so doing, working the twin throttles, and with some water currents pulling the boat sideways a bit, I got confused and started to panic. As I did, I started pushing and pulling the throttles every which way, gunning the engines, and went out of control, hitting two other boats that were docked in their slips. Quickly the seller neutralized the throttles, and calmly took over and maneuvered the boat into our slip. As he was doing this, he said, "Remember, Tom, always remain calm and learn to anticipate."

Upon docking, with my hands still shaking, I wrote two notes with my phone number to put on the boats that I had hit, explaining what happened and that I would be responsible for any repairs. The next day I heard from them with one explaining that he saw no damage, but a scuff mark that could be painted over. No problem, he said. The other saw some damage and would get an estimate for the repairs. My boat insurance took care of that. Luckily, I had good people to deal with. In all this, I had learned a couple of lessons: never ever be cock-sure of yourself, and there is a big difference between confidence and cock-sure.

Soon after taking ownership of the boat, I bought several books on navigation and knot tying. Sea navigation was totally new to me, but knot tying was familiar to me from my Boy Scout days, so that part was easy. Dorothy and I enrolled in a class sponsored by the U.S. Coast Guard, teaching sea navigation safety, right-of-way for different kinds of ships, the meaning of the buoys, color schemes, landmarks, seaman vocabulary, and such. After several classes, we took a number of written tests. Lo and behold, I passed and got a certificate stating that I was a worthy captain. Dorothy passed with an even higher score!

In due time after learning from my mistakes, and working alongside friends with boating knowledge, I started to really appreciate the ways of maritime life. It was a culture unto itself. I was constantly entertained with all this new knowledge. I regularly took the boat out with the family and friends cruising outside of the large San Diego Bay area into the open waters of the Pacific Ocean, and taking it out to explore the shorelines of the Mexican-owned Coronado Islands. One of our favorite destinations was to visit the quaint Mexican seaport town of Ensenada, about 100 miles south of San Diego. It was about a five-hour trip along the peninsula shoreline of Baja California where we would see colonies of seals and schools of leaping dolphins on the way. Great sights!

Ashore in Ensenada, we would end up in one of the many excellent seafood restaurants, especially those that specialized in abalone steaks. That, along with good Mexican beer and mariachi music, would hit the spot as a day well spent.

Along with the fun times cruising about, I think perhaps the best times were when Dorothy and I had the kids together and I'd prepare a fancy meal in the galley, then we'd enjoy it during the late afternoon while the sun was about to set, creating an array of brilliantly colorful clouds in the horizon.

In the first few years we used Fatso fairly frequently. Each year we got together to give it the once over, like sanding and re-varnishing the woodwork and dry docking it to scrape the bottom and apply a new coat of paint to it. During those early years, I had no problem in getting the kids and their friends to help. But later, it was a bit difficult mostly due to the many other activities they had. And, of course, some were in college and had their studies to do. I imagine some were excuses too. I understood, for I did some of that when I was a kid.

After about 10 years of owning Fatso, I used it less and less, as my business had expanded and tripled in size. With my added workload and more frequent out of town meetings, I thought of selling the boat. I kept it for an additional year, because my fourth daughter Jennifer liked to use it, often doing her college studies while relaxing on Fatso. After her finals, and since I hadn't taken it out for over a year, I put Fatso for sale in the classified ads for boats.

I had several calls the next day and met with prospective buyers at the boat site. Of the several prospective buyers, I was impressed with a family of four teenage boys and their father who was an airplane mechanic. I could tell the family was in love with the boat when they first saw it, especially with the four boys climbing all over it with plans as to how much fun they were going to have with it. The father inspected the boat from top to bottom and declared to me that the engines were in need of some repairs, especially needing an overhaul. I readily agreed with him, as I never really made any major repairs on the engines since I bought it.

I had it for sale at $15,000, and the father offered me $10,000. I returned and said, "Make it $11,000 and it's yours. I know you'll have to rebuild the engines, so that might be fair." He accepted the terms and was happy about it. His boys then began whooping it up.

I felt happy with the deal, especially knowing Fatso was going to a family that would really enjoy it. In retrospect, owning a boat had taught me a lot about loving the sea and all the beauty it provides.

MY REAL ESTATE BUSINESS CONTINUED to grow and as I said earlier, I brought my hard working son-in-law Will, who married our first daughter Nora, into the firm as a partner. During its growth, we divided the operation into two divisions: One, the real estate brokerage business that consisted of an associated sales staff of eight to ten; and the other being the real estate development division specializing in developing and building apartments, shopping centers and industrial buildings. Under this division, we also had a general construction company contracted to work some of our projects.

With Will handling the real estate development division, I had Dorothy manage the brokerage department. She was efficient and worked hard, and was well liked and respected by the sales force. For years, Dorothy had her real estate sales license but never took time to study for her exam for a real estate broker's license. Although Dorothy had only a sales license, I felt her knowledge of real estate business was superior to all those she supervised day to day. Proof of that was that they often came to her for advice about how best to structure a deal, resolve problems, or mitigate issues that often came up about sales transactions. Because several of the sales associates were already brokers working under her, we thought it was only good business sense for her to get her broker's license as well.

When Dorothy decided to take the exam for her broker's license, she enrolled in a night class at San Diego City College. The broker license course was for eight weeks, twice a week, from 6:30 p.m. to 9 p.m. It was my job to drop her off and pick her up. So instead of going home and coming back again I decided to go to the college registrar's office to see which courses I could take during the time of her class. An art course in watercolor came to mind. I could always learn something new.

While going through the catalogue of different courses, I ran across a course titled, "How to Read Music and the Basics of Playing Piano." I stopped and thought, "For years I have encouraged my six children to continue their piano lessons, the one instrument that can be found everywhere in the world." Yes, that's what I'm going to do, take piano lessons! Our daughter Phyllis was an accomplished pianist. If I could someday play only half as good as her, I mused, I'd be very happy.

So I enrolled and learned to read music again. I had forgotten most of it since I first learned it in the 7th grade at Memorial Junior High. The course was fun and educational, for I had always loved music. In fact, for years Dorothy sang alto and I sang bass in the sanctuary choir at our church.

Playing the piano, my new hobby, became equal in fun and pleasure as my love for painting and art. With the six kids now out of the house, I had the baby grand piano to myself, generally practicing every day, mostly in the late evenings.

After the course was complete, I took two piano lessons from a private teacher, but quickly found that it interfered with my work schedule too much. My evenings were pretty scheduled, too. Dinner was with the family, which Dorothy held as sacred time. Later, I had meetings to attend at church and organizations I belonged to such as the Masonic Lodge, Optimist Club, and others. So in order to further improve my piano playing, I relied on books for beginners. My favorite was *Piano for Dummies*, which became my bible for piano playing as well as for music theory. I practiced mostly late at night, and as the years went by I was told I had become a fairly accomplished pianist. I use that word "fairly" rather loosely.

It had gotten to the point that I enjoyed playing so much, that whenever Dorothy and I traveled, I would pack a couple of music songbooks along. I found wherever we went anywhere in the world, we'd find a piano. Music, the great common denominator, was always fun to share with others.

Maybe it was due to my interest in the piano and learning more about music theory that I then became interested in playing the accordion. When we were traveling in Buenos Aires, Argentina I came across a large music store that had a huge display of accordions. On the spur of the moment I bought one. Now I play the accordion, too, but not nearly as well as the piano, my first love.

IT WAS IN THE 1970S when a great number of Asian refugees were immigrating to America through the sponsorship of the U.S. government. As a consequence of the Vietnam War ending, many of the Vietnamese, Laotian, and Cambodian people who fought on the side of America were given asylum to come our country.

A great number were brought to the San Diego area, where they initially were encamped in tents for the first few months at the 220,000 acre U.S. military base, Camp Pendleton. Like most refugees and immigrants in the past, such as the Chinese, Japanese, Mexicans, Irish, Jews, and others, they were poor and eventually ended up in the older and poorer sections of town where rents were cheaper and the neighborhood had seen better days. In this case, many of them moved to the older section of East San Diego, into the vicinity around University Avenue and Fairmount Avenue where many stores, apartments, and homes were vacant and were in need of repair.

I have seen a pattern of neighborhood transformation created by immigrants from my experience as a real estate person. Originally, sections which had one time flourished and had since become old and depressed experienced a new resurgence and energy brought on by new immigrants. These areas would turn into a thriving place again such as a Chinatown, a

Japan Town, or a Korean Town followed by an increase in property values. The pattern is not uncommon, especially with the metropolitan cities in America.

As a real estate person, I saw an opportunity, both for turning the area around and making it into a good investment. My company at that time, the Tom Hom Investment Corp., had some capital to invest so we bought several parcels of properties at below market prices since the owners were anxious to sell and move on. One was a rather large, boarded up property, formerly a Chevrolet car dealership on the highly traveled University Avenue with the properties located on both sides of the street. We also bought a boarded up former Bank of America building also on University Avenue. In the surrounding area, we purchased land with some old uninhabitable houses, which we had removed and built 58 family apartment units.

With the commercially zoned properties on University Avenue, we built three separate shopping centers. Seeing the progress of the new construction generated enthusiasm in those immigrants who wanted to work the American Dream they heard so much about. I was pleasantly surprised that even before construction was complete, we were deluged with inquiries about how to rent space for a business.

I really enjoyed working with these eager potential tenants who were mostly Chinese and Vietnamese. They were so anxious to do something in the way of being their own boss and to work together with their family members. There were a number of people who were formerly in business in Vietnam and lost everything when the new Communist government took over. I could see that they were experienced and understood the nuances of running a business. There were applicants for Asian grocery stores, restaurants, seafood markets, coffee houses, bakeries, and lots of other specialty businesses that fit the cultural environment of the area.

By the time we had the shopping centers finished, we had most of the units rented. It took only a short time to rent the remainder after completion. Because some of the proposed tenants were not able to raise the necessary funds to start their businesses, I helped by directing them to the U.S. Small Business Administration to get them a possible loan. Dorothy made time to help them fill out their loan applications, talking to them slowly in broken English so they could understand. There was something about Dorothy in her warm, caring Hawaiian way that made it easy for people who did not speak English to feel comfortable with her.

Since most of these new immigrants came with nothing of monetary value, it was a major challenge for most of them who wanted to go into business to find capital. Normally, they would either: borrow from friends or relatives; borrow from a lending institution; or get a government-backed loan through the bank.

There were several applicants who were formerly successful in business in Saigon, from where they quickly had to evacuate, leaving everything behind. Two young men in particular caught my attention when they came to fill out an application. Before doing so, they inquired about the lease terms, the ratio of parking available, the possibility of an option for a lease extension later on, the amount of an upfront deposit, and so on, speaking in fairly good English. Their knowledge of all the questions to ask impressed me. It impressed me more when they asked to see the floor plans of the shopping center, and in so doing they picked a potential location, the largest unit, and started to discuss between themselves about where the checkout stands would be, the produce and meat departments, and so on. This went on for fifteen minutes. I just listened. I was also impressed with their knowledge of the grocery business. Their discussion told me that they were formerly in business, and were most likely successful at it. That day they turned in their application and I said I would evaluate it.

I had the office check their credit rating. We found no listing at all, probably because they never bought anything on credit before. Later they told me they paid cash for everything. That was pretty normal where they came from. I checked further about them with other people in the immigrant community. The result was high praise about their honest and hardworking large family. I approved the application and had a lease drawn up for their review.

In starting their business, which required putting up a large deposit, buying numerous types of equipment, permits, inventory, and much more, they ran short on cash. By this time I had become more than just a landlord, I became a friend who wanted to help. The two young men reminded me of my own family with the father running a successful business, raising a large family, all working together.

So with that sentiment, I directed them to the bank where I was the vice chairman, The Bank of San Diego, to apply for a loan. I vouched for them and they got the loan. It really wasn't that big of a loan, but to them it was large and the key to their way of making the American Dream come true. In a short period of a year with their whole family working and helping, and good merchandising, they became very successful. Their loan term from the bank was to be paid off in five years, but they paid it off in just 18 months.

It's deals like this that made me feel good about being in business. It helped fortify my view that there were good, honest, hardworking people who didn't have a hidden agenda. This counter-balanced some of the scoundrels that I would occasionally run across, with lies and phony schemes, out to only make a fast buck.

I decided long ago that the experience of having the good as well as the bad parts of business had its merits. Experiences in having positive and negative business dealings gave me the opportunity to better judge the good from the bad. That's part of life's lessons.

CHAPTER 42

Ready for Donny-Brook

A
S I MENTIONED EARLIER, DOROTHY'S ETHNIC BACKGROUND
was Chinese and Irish, Chinese on her father's side and Irish on her
mother's. It was in the spring of 1985, when she got a call from a
friend at City Hall, who said, "Dorothy, this is confidential. There is a new
owner of the downtown block where the old historic Chinese Mission is
located at Market and First Streets, and the plan is to tear down the building
and build a high rise there! I thought you should know!" Dorothy being
a history buff, evidenced by her work to save all the vintage buildings in
downtown to help form the Gaslamp Quarter, and also a board member
of what is today the Historical Resources Board for the City of San Diego,
was incensed and shocked that the historical Chinese Mission building
would be destroyed. On this rare occasion, it really got her so-called Irish
up. That was one of those times I didn't tease her about it because I knew
this historic church building was something really special to her.

"Tear down the historical Mission building?" Dorothy responded loudly,
not being her normally calm self, and added, "Not over my dead body!"

Some years earlier the old Chinese Mission became the Chinese Community Church that was sold and the congregation relocated to a new
church building. Following that, the old Mission building was designated
as an historical site. It was also designated that any new structure or new
development around it was to incorporate the historic Chinese Mission
building in it.

By this time I could see—and hear—Dorothy's Irish temper coming out.
She stamped her feet a couple of times, and then asked her friend, "Who is
doing this development and when can I appeal the waiver of the historical
designation before the City Council?"

"In about four weeks," he said, "and that's when the developer will present his plan to the City Council and ask for the waiver of the Mission building's historical designation. All this has already been approved by the Planning Department." Then he went on to say, "Dorothy, I'm calling you as a friend, and you don't need to mention my name." She thanked him and hung up. She stamped her feet a couple of more times, took a deep breath, and tightened her lips, getting ready for an all out battle. If I didn't know her mother, whose name was Patricia Dunaway, I'd worry about her. Rarely did Dorothy let her temper flare up like that. Mostly her Chinese side, nurtured by her traditional Chinese grandmother in Hawaii, would prevail, by keeping a cool and collective calmness in situations like this. I knew the Chinese Mission building was special to her, so letting steam off once in a while was to be expected.

Dorothy right away went to work lobbying the Mayor and each City Council member to nix the waiver of the historical designation of the Mission building. By the time she finished presenting the importance to retain the historical designation, she strongly suggested that the developer incorporate the building into the development. She contacted several of the historical societies of various cities in San Diego County for support as well. Within one week she and others had a petition signed with over 500 names supporting her position.

Two weeks later, apparently Dorothy's efforts were beginning to take effect because the developer, a person whom we knew, contacted Dorothy to have a meeting and included the director of the city's planning department to try and resolve the problem of the historical designation. A meeting was set up, and I tagged along to lend support, as though Dorothy needed it.

As the meeting started out, each party gave their pitch and concerns regarding the development project. After about an hour, expressing the pros and cons, the developer suggested something unexpected: he would consider paying for the cost of relocating the historical Mission building to another site of our choice. He would pay up to $40,000 for that relocation move, and it would have to be done within six months. We were to get our own contractor to do it. We could then rehab the building as we pleased and then put it to a good new use. That proposal was a surprise. While that offer of $40,000 was generous, we didn't know if that amount would be adequate.

And also where would we move it? We didn't have any land we could put it on. I suggested that we be given a month to work on it, and meanwhile ask the City Council to postpone the public hearing on the waiver for a month.

Dorothy was not only vitally interested in historical buildings and sites, but also historical relics and history. For that reason she and her good friend, Sally Wong, an attorney, worked together to start the Chinese Historical Society of Greater San Diego and Baja California. In its formation, Dorothy suggested that Sally be its first president, as she spoke several dialects of Chinese, could read and write it, and was steeped in Chinese culture as well. The Society was an immediate success and a Chinese museum was temporarily opened in a section of the lobby of the newly restored historic Horton Grand Hotel, in the former Chinatown area.

In the evening after the meeting with the developer, Dorothy, Sally Wong and I had dinner together to discuss the surprising proposal made by the developer to relocate the Chinese Mission building. Frankly, after a lot of discussion of the pros and cons, we got pretty excited and agreed this proposal had a lot of merit, and could be a good thing for the permanent headquarters of the Chinese Historical Society & Museum. If we could put it together it would be an outstanding and positive effort in providing the greater community with more knowledge about Chinese American history in San Diego and still retain the significance of the historical aspects of the old Mission building.

We had our challenges cut out for us. Our initial dilemma in accepting the developer's proposal to remove the Mission building from the present site was not knowing where we could store it. And after storing it, there was the challenge of raising the funds to buy the land on which to place the building and then have it rehabilitated. We discussed this at length and decided that we would need to take this to the museum board of directors.

During the board meeting, like all important undertakings, it was discussed at great length. In time, it was obvious that this was a good deal for us and we should support the proposal. A formal vote was taken and passed unanimously. Following the vote, President Sally Wong said she wanted to suggest something that should help this along. She said, "Dorothy and I discussed this earlier and agreed that this undertaking would require a great deal of work and communication with City Hall, especially with issues such as the timing, land acquisition, zoning, special permits, variances for historic buildings, the storage site and so on. I'm not familiar with working with City Hall on matters like this." And she went on to say, "I have a suggestion. Tom Hom, our former City Councilman who already knows many of the key personnel at City Hall, should take my place as the president because he can be more effective in representing our Society in getting this done."

I already knew about President Sally's thinking since Dorothy told me, but I wasn't sure I'd take it on. However, after seeing the enthusiasm of the board for Sally's suggestion, I decided to accept. That's how I became the second president of the organization. And I didn't even solicit it. I had my work cut out for me.

First we needed to notify the developer that we accepted the deal. Next, we needed to find a contractor to move the historic Mission building. And, of course, in moving it we needed to find a location to store it. In so doing, it would give us time to figure out the permanent location where we could set it down for the rehabilitation. And then we would have to raise the funds to do it all.

Well, first things first. I contacted the developer about our decision and he was glad to hear that we would go along with his proposal. Next, we met with the president and staff members of the Centre City Development Corporation (CCDC), a subsidiary of the City of San Diego's Redevelopment Agency, which I served on as a board member when I was on the City Council. I knew they had vacant land in and near the old Chinatown area. In wanting to help, CCDC agreed to let us use an empty lot they had in Chinatown on 3rd Avenue to store the historic building.

We followed up by seeking bids from several moving contractors. After their review of the Mission, they all declined to bid because it was a non-reinforced concrete block building and posed the potential of falling apart during the move. Too risky they said, and our maximum of $40,000 would not even come close in covering it. One of the workers of the moving firm, a Mexican American fellow, told me afterwards that he had a cousin in Tucson, Arizona, who could probably move it, as he specialized in moving non-reinforced buildings. I got his telephone number and called his cousin who came out to meet me the next day. He surveyed the building, checked the location where it was to be moved to, and then with a shrug, said in Spanish, "*No problema!*" So in two weeks he was in San Diego with his crew and equipment for the move.

This was a family operation, and it was amazing to see how they worked together, with cables and long iron rods, running every which way, tying everything together. In about two weeks they had the building on wheels and rolled it through heavy downtown traffic to the storage location. The great thing about this is that he did it all for $37,500 which was below our budget, and did such a good job. Not one concrete brick fell off the building during the move.

After the move, the following week was Super Bowl Sunday. In appreciation of the San Diego cousin for his referral, I bought a case of Corona beer, sodas, and a big assortment of snacks and took it to his house for the family to enjoy during the Super Bowl game, along with $200. He was surprised. He graciously thanked me for the drinks and snacks. But he refused to accept the $200 because, as he said, "It was for the church and the new museum." What a kind and wonderful man!

While the church building was being stored, we devised a plan and timetable to have it moved to a permanent site in the old Chinatown area. From my previous knowledge of the California Redevelopment Law, a certain amount of money from the Tax Increment funds, money raised by increased property assessment values in the redevelopment areas, must be returned to that area and help fund programs for cultural development.

With that in mind, we again approached CCDC with our plans and requested assistance in acquiring a site for our future museum. After a lengthy discussion, CCDC said, "Give us a couple of weeks to analyze your proposal." As we left the meeting, I felt there was great enthusiasm from some of the staff members because our project was for cultural development, which was one of very few proposals submitted in recent times.

We met with CCDC again in about three weeks, and the response was very positive. CCDC would help provide a location for us, pending final approval of the location site and the detailed plans for the building's restoration. They had three proposed sites in the Chinatown area for our consideration. There were other conditions for us to meet. We were told that we must raise all the necessary funds amounting to $400,000 for the rehabilitation of the building. We thought that was a very fair offer. At that time, we never really figured how we would raise that kind of money, but we knew that we would. And later we did, thanks mainly to our fundraiser chair, Dr. Alex Chuang, who solicited a great many contributors, with a number of them being quite generous.

Of the three sites in Chinatown for our consideration, we picked the largest one that had good exposure, on the corner of 3rd and J Streets, with an old abandoned warehouse on it. The other two sites were smaller and situated in the middle of the blocks, so we passed on those. Instead of buying the lot, which we could not afford at the time, we proposed that we lease the lot instead for 55 years. This would free up our capital to do the rehabilitation of the Mission building to remodel it into the museum. CCDC accepted this on the premise that cultural enhancement was badly needed in the downtown area and this would be a forerunner and driving force, hoping that others would follow. It also gave credibility to the revitalization of this older section of downtown as well. This proved to be correct, as years went by. Many new buildings were built and older historic buildings restored in the area with property values going up tremendously since.

I didn't say anything at the time when we chose the corner lot at 3rd and J Streets for our museum site, but I was born on that exact corner in a two-story brick building in 1927. Because the site was the best of the three, the largest and with the best exposure, I felt it was justifiable in picking that one. At first, I felt a bit self-conscious about this, but we did the right thing, regardless.

Within two years, funds were raised, the building rehabilitated, and in the outside area, a courtyard and a Chinese garden with a running stream and fish pond were completed. Shortly afterwards on January 13, 1996, the grand opening event with government and foreign dignitaries, along with members and friends, celebrated this hard earned completion. Along with the ribbon cutting and speeches, the ceremony was capped off with the traditional lion dancers. The crowd amounted to several hundred, so in order to accommodate such a large event, the street on 3rd Avenue was closed to through traffic.

On reflection, all this couldn't possibly have been done without the help of government, the generous contributors, and the many volunteers of the Chinese Historical Society & Museum. This was a good example of the public sector working with the private sector. After three years as president of the Society, I knew the board was well fortified with capable people, so I chose not to run for another term. My personal philosophy was that an organization, in order to vibrantly grow, needs to change with fresh new leadership periodically.

The San Diego Chinese Historical Museum has grown significantly, and now is a major landmark in the Asian Pacific Historic Thematic District. It has become one of the focal points for visiting public and private schools, the general public and others to learn more about Chinese culture and Chinese American history along with the ethnic diversity of our American society, especially in San Diego.

CHAPTER 43

The Golden People

WITH ONLY ONE OF OUR SIX CHILDREN LEFT AT HOME IN the late 1980s, Dorothy and I became near-empty nesters. That was Cindy, our youngest daughter, who eventually graduated from UCLA with a degree in communications. After graduation, while at home with us, she was given an internship with KNSD-TV Channel 39, NBC, working and learning the ins and outs of broadcasting and at the same time took a special course in that field at San Diego Community College. Shortly afterwards, she applied and got her first real television job at the CBS television station in Yuma, Arizona, a community of 50,000 that doubled during the tourist season in the winter. Cindy was elated with the job, giving her firsthand experience and getting paid for it. She started as a field reporter for the daily news, and soon enough, with her shining personality became an anchor for the news. Later her journalist experience included opening up the station in the early mornings and taking part in other aspects of a TV station's operation. All this experience fared well for her future.

After three years working in the dry desert climate of Yuma, often noted as one of the hottest spots in the country, Cindy was hired by the national syndicated news program, *Inside Edition,* with CBS in New York City. This program had an average viewership of about 10 million, a super big difference from Yuma. At *Inside Edition,* one of the most helpful people to Cindy was Bill O'Reilly, who was then one of the anchors for the show. He helped her adjust to the big time environment, including interviews with high profile people, such as Jackie Chan, Donald Trump, and Muhammad Ali. She adjusted well and later at times would do some fill in as the anchor.

Working with *Inside Edition* required Cindy to do a great deal of traveling to cover stories. Upon returning from one of her trips, she was pretty tired and decided to go to bed early. However, a colleague insisted that she attend a party with him. Cindy reluctantly accepted. That evening she met a young man, Brian Metcalfe, originally from Connecticut, who was working in NYC. He had MBA degrees from both an American and a French University and spoke French fluently. That evening turned out to change both of their lives. Later they became engaged.

To celebrate the engagement, Dorothy and I flew to New York and drove to Connecticut with Cindy to meet Brian's parents, Richard and Joan Metcalfe. We were greeted most warmly and graciously, just the way I had always imagined New England people to be. During our visit, we shared a lot of our family histories together, especially the lives of both our Cindy and their Brian. Later we had dinner at grandmother Metcalfe's home, a charming elderly businesswoman who worked in the family's business of glass installation. One could see she was the matriarch of the Metcalfe family.

The evening went quickly and very well. We felt our youngsters were well-matched and our blessings were with them. Later, being engaged and wanting to travel less, Cindy decided to leave *Inside Edition* and took a position as an anchor for the news at *E! Entertainment* network in Los Angeles. Shortly afterwards, Cindy and Brian married and settled in San Marino, outside of Los Angeles.

Cindy was the last of the six children to marry. Interestingly, all six of the children married persons who are not of Chinese descent. It seemed a bit odd at first, considering that much of their upbringing had so much association with the Chinese culture, like attending the Chinese Community Church and the influence of Dorothy's rather strong Chinese upbringing. But on the other hand, what was important was that all the in-laws were nice, good, caring people. One other reward was that all of our 13 grandchildren are intelligent, caring, and exotically beautiful. I don't think I am too partial on that for many others have said so, too.

That reminds me of what bestselling author James Michener said when he introduced his historical novel *Hawaii*, 25 years ago: "In the 21st century, America will see a new group of people emerge. I call them the Golden People, the fusion of the Asian and other races in our nation."

CHAPTER 44

Minus 1

I N THE SUMMER OF 1992, WHEN I WAS 65, DOROTHY AND I VISITED China. It was our fourth trip there. The country was huge, like America, with so many places to visit and things to see, we only saw a fraction of it. One day, following an extensive all day tour, our tour guide asked our group of about 20, "Is there anything else you'd like to see before going back to the hotel? We have enough time to spare for a couple of hours, before our dinner and show event tonight!"

In a flash, Dorothy, who was a health and alternative medicine advocate, quickly raised her hand and said, "Yes, I would like to see a Chinese hospital and learn something about the Traditional Chinese Medicine that we hear so much about!" Spontaneously, the group enthusiastically supported that suggestion. Seeing that a great number of our tour group was made up of senior citizens, I could see why.

The tour guide said, "Good idea! I'll see what I can arrange." He immediately got out his cell phone and made several calls, and within a few minutes he had made arrangements for us to visit one of the larger, well-known hospitals in Beijing.

Within 20 minutes we arrived at the hospital, a huge complex of white multi-storied buildings with an expansive and well kept landscape made up of tall trees and flowering plants. We were impressed. As we drove up to the covered entry, there was a middle-aged gentleman who spoke fluent English waiting to welcome us. He was our guide and also a practicing doctor with the hospital.

As we entered the lobby, the doctor pointed out that on the left side there was a pharmacy for Western medicine, and on the right side there was a pharmacy of Traditional Chinese Medicine (TCM), made up of herbs and Chinese medicine. We asked who decides to go where, the Western or Chinese pharmacy? He said, "It's the patient's choice. After choosing, the doctors will work with the patient for the health treatment."

That's interesting. Some of these things I already experienced. Growing up in a bi-cultural environment, both Western and Chinese, I have seen on many occasions the Chinese families adhere to both types of medical treatments depending on what the health problems might be.

The doctor was very gracious and accommodating and took us through the Western and Chinese pharmacies, explaining its working systems. He also gave us a tour of the operating rooms and the cafeteria, and introduced us to some of the Western and Chinese trained doctors. In meeting the Chinese trained doctors, the tour group was very interested in learning more about TCM and bombarded the doctors with questions. Because of this intense interest, our guide doctor said that he could arrange a lecture by several TCM doctors to give us background on that subject. We were escorted to a conference room, where four doctors gave us lectures on the ancient art of Chinese medicine, all touching on different areas of treatment.

After a most interesting presentation on remedying and treating health issues, we were asked if any of us had any health problems. I immediately raised my hand, and several others followed. I said, "I have a concern about my prostate, with a Prostate Specific Antigen (PSA) reading hovering between 4 and 5. I have been told that is fairly high and taking Western medicine hasn't helped reduce the reading. Is there a traditional Chinese remedy to lower that?"

One of the doctors stepped forward and replied, "I have just the herbal medicine for you. Please see me afterwards." Then he turned to one of the nurses, speaking softly to her, and then she left the room.

Following, there were a number of other questions, but one woman in particular sitting next to me, a retired nurse from Louisiana, complained that she had an acute back problem for the past 10 years and nothing had helped, including surgery. One of the doctors suggested that she come in the next morning and he would try and diagnose her back problem. The next morning she went to see the doctor and upon diagnosis, he treated her with acupuncture that day and the following two days. On the fourth day in Beijing, our tour group left to fly to Xian and on the plane I asked this woman how the acupuncture treatments worked out for her. She smiled, got up from her seat, bent forward, backward, and then made circular movements with her upper body, and even shook her rear a bit, and said, "See, four days ago I couldn't have done this without massive pain, and now I'm completely pain free. First time in 10 years, I'm pain free. Hallelujah!" A bunch of us applauded and congratulated her.

As for my PSA reading, the doctor gave me a plastic jar of 1,000 small black herbal pills, to be taken six at a time once a day. The total cost was $30. He said when I ran out, I could reorder by faxing the label to the hospital and they would send the pills. After I received the pills, I could then send them the money. That seemed pretty fair ... and incredibly trusting, I thought.

When we got on the bus for the hotel, I took out my bottled water and took six pills. I continued to take those pills every day throughout the trip and at home. After two months, at my annual physical checkup, which included the PSA test, I got a call from my primary doctor, who said, "Tom! I've got good news for you. Your latest PSA test reading is now minus 1! Isn't that great? Just keep doing what you're doing!" I was elated to hear that, but I didn't have the heart to tell him that I'd been taking those Chinese herbal pills, because I didn't know whether he believed in that or not. I know a great number of Western trained doctors were skeptical of TCM. Personally, I believe there is a place for both.

The important thing is that it worked for me. Ever since, and that has been about 22 years in taking those herbal pills, my PSA readings have been between minus 1 to not over 1. And instead of sending for the pills from China, I found a Chinese herb store in San Diego for the same thing at $40 for a year's supply.

All of this I owe to Dorothy for suggesting that we visit a Chinese hospital on the spur of the moment. I call this serendipity!

xiv. Blindsided

AGES 66 TO 75

一只兔子崎岖的心路历程

Campaige Place—one of our projects.

CHAPTER 45

The Bad and Good Times

IN 1993 THE NEW PRESIDENT-ELECT BILL CLINTON WAS SWORN IN
AFTER BEING ELECTED WITH 43 PERCENT OF THE POPULAR VOTES
AND 360 ELECTORAL VOTES, WHEN ONLY 270 WERE NEEDED.

THE COUNTRY WAS IN THE THIRD YEAR OF A DEEP DEPRESsion. Unemployment was up to 15 percent, banking interest rates were high, and the real estate market was slow with many of the development firms either closing shop or in bankruptcy. From what I read in the Business Section of the local newspaper, business failure in this field was up to 75 percent. It was a tough economy and it affected us as well.

During the busy years prior to the recession we were developing and building shopping centers, apartments, and buying a number of commercial buildings in town and hundreds of acres of vacant land for future development. Fortunately, we always tried hard to abide by the principles of keeping our banks informed and maintaining good relations with our bankers about our cash flow and financial statements, while meeting payment obligations on time and informing them of our business activities. Because of this, bankers worked with us in rolling over loans and even providing new loans as well. At times, the loans might even be at lower interest rates and payments to be readjusted up when times got better.

The principles of prudent banking relations came mostly from our family's involvement in the banking business. James had been chairman of the South Coast Bank in Orange County and Allen, co-founder and board member of several banks in Los Angeles County; I was the vice chairman of the BSD Bancorp, a holding company of three different banking corporations. Education and up-front values are always great assets in doing business.

In spite of all the planning and the precautions made, sometimes the forces of circumstance are beyond us and we have no control over them.

One of our major financial losses was working toward the development of a new wholesale produce terminal. At that time, the wholesale produce houses, located in the San Diego downtown area at lower Sixth Avenue since 1885, were mostly in older and make-shift buildings which were no longer accommodating their growing needs. Aside from the cramped area and inadequate parking area, streets were way too narrow to service the huge 18-wheeler semi-trucks. For these reasons and more, the produce operators were very interested in moving to a new location. They needed a new produce terminal with loading docks, one level floor space for a forklift operation, and a sufficient parking area for semi-trucks to maneuver in and out.

Because I was familiar with most of the produce owners, I was asked by them to look into the feasibility of creating such a produce terminal with all the amenities to go with it in order to have an efficient, cost savings operation.

In so doing, we checked out several locations and finally picked a location not far from the border of Mexico in the new industrial area called Otay Mesa. A lot of land was available there selling for a reasonable price. The zoning was in place for industrial use and had excellent freeway access. With this information, we ran it by the committee composed of the produce men. They liked the location and accepted it. They liked it partly because much of the winter produce is grown in interior Mexico where the growing season is opposite from ours and produce is shipped to the U.S./Mexico border, and from there shipped throughout different areas of the United States. With our new modern terminal facilities close to the border, this would be a good drop-off area for the San Diego market and other markets, especially in the western part of United States.

In its then present status, much of the produce was shipped directly to the produce terminals in Los Angeles and then they sold to the San Diego market. The reason it was shipped to L.A. was because they had the facilities and the capacity to handle all the high volume of produce coming in every day. San Diego did not. In our new terminal, we would be able to easily compete with L.A. and expand the growth of the industry.

The produce committee was enthused with the concept, and wanted to go into the next phase. In so doing, it was decided that our firm would develop the project and have it financed. The produce owner operators would buy stall sections structured along the line of a commercial condominium where they would form a board to run the total terminal facilities.

This type of ownership structure had been commonly done in other regions of the country, such as the produce terminal built for the Boston produce markets when they had to leave downtown Boston where they had operated for over 150 years in the congested Faneuil Hall area.

Shortly thereafter, we hired an architect and finalized the contract to purchase 26 acres with a deposit. We then met with the San Diego Trust & Savings Bank which agreed to finance the project based on our *pro forma*.

Meanwhile, unknown to us or anyone else in San Diego that we knew of, the Mexican President contacted Washington, D.C., to inform the U.S. government that Mexico was planning to expand the airport in Tijuana. Tijuana borders the U.S. adjacent to the Otay Mesa area where we had planned to build our produce terminal.

Mexico wanted to have a feasibility study done for a joint bi-national airport between Mexico and the U.S., similar to the bi-national Basel BSL Airport between France and Switzerland, the Salzburg Airport bordering Germany and Austria, as with some others.

This was at a time when the City of San Diego was in the early stage of making plans for the expansion of San Diego's Lindbergh Airport with only one landing strip, located adjacent to the highly urbanized area of downtown and on the waterfront since 1925. Expansion of the landing field was not feasible because of the constriction of the land area. The San Diego expansion would mainly be creating more terminal space and some improvement on the single landing strip.

The proposal from the President's office in Mexico City was referred to the Secretary of Interior in Washington, D.C., and in turn referred to the Federal Aviation Administration (FAA), and then the Mayor and City Council of San Diego. From there, American officials met with the Mexican airport authorities to look into the feasibility of such a plan. After several meetings, a preliminary plan was initiated with a number of optional plans of how a bi-national airport layout would look if the proposal moved ahead.

It covered several thousand acres expanding into both sides of the border.

Later, to my dismay and disappointment the proposals of the layouts all took in the property that we had for the produce terminal. I was surprised that they would extend as far as they did, and my objection to several officials did not have any effect. At that point, it was more of an international issue. I never felt so helpless as to what I could do to alter the layout plans.

Meanwhile, the news media gave the proposed plan prominent headline billings. The feasibility study went on and as it happened all the time on new and large projects, it would become very controversial. And it did. People said, "Hell, we in the U.S. will probably end up paying for most of it! What about health and safety matters? We have different standards! The people are nice but it's still a mañana culture!" There were some positives expressed as well, but the negatives were the loudest. The ongoing controversy on both sides of the border spawned a number of organized opposition and support groups as well. Meanwhile, the international feasibility study for a bi-national airport continued.

The repercussion of all this was that the majority of the signed-up produce operators were no longer interested in the new terminal project since they didn't know if and when this issue would be resolved. I agreed, but not happily, and returned their deposits. San Diego Bank & Trust informed us they could no longer finance the project because of the possibility of condemnation of the land for the airport, and also because of the lack of support of the previously signed-up tenant-buyers of the project.

About three years later, the bi-national airport concept was dropped mostly due to lack of support from the American side of the border. Meanwhile, my produce terminal project went up in smoke and we lost a good sum of money. The deposit on the land, the studies made, the architectural plans, attorneys, and other expenses came to a rather sizable loss.

Aside from that, we were sued by the seller of the 26 acres we had in escrow for not completing the purchase. The matter went to court and it ruled in our favor. But we still lost a hefty amount. That was a good example of being blind-sided by something beyond our control.

ONE DAY I RECEIVED AN IMPRESSIVE red and gold envelope with an even more impressive card inside inviting both Dorothy and me to a ten-course banquet at a famous Chinese seafood restaurant in Monterey Park, a city in Los Angeles County. The invitation indicated that the host was the special representative from France for Remy Martin Cognac, an iconic producer of excellent champagne, brandy, and other spirits since 1724.

The event was about three weeks away on a Wednesday. It so happened that the day following the banquet, Dorothy and I were leaving on a trip to China. So, as intriguing as the invitation was, I suggested that we simply reply with regrets. But Dorothy felt this invitation was not just an ordinary event but something very special.

So before sending our regrets, she called several of our friends in Los Angeles and asked if they knew of this event by Remy Martin. None did.

So she called the RSVP number in care of a Miss Jean Lee. "Miss Lee," Dorothy said, "today, we just received the invitation to the Remy Martin banquet. We live in San Diego and it just so happens that early on the next day my husband and I are leaving for China. This event sounds so special. Can you tell me something about it?"

"Yes, certainly," Miss Lee responded. "This event is indeed special. Remy Martin Cognac in France has decided to host a special banquet such as the one in the invitation in three major areas in the United States, one in New York City, one in San Francisco and the third one in the Los Angeles area. By all means if you and your husband can make it, you will not regret it." Lee went on to say, "Among the guests will be 500 of the most distinguished people in southern California, Chinese-American leaders from all walks of life along with high public officials such as the Mayor of Los Angeles and others. The list is all special guests! I hope you do come!"

Hanging up the phone, Dorothy exclaimed, "Tom, this is a one-of-a-kind event! I don't think we want to miss this!" And she went on to describe her conversation with Miss Lee.

With some skepticism, I replied, "Yeah, but what about China? We have to fly out early the next day. We can't miss that!"

Dorothy, forever the optimist as well as a major problem solver, said, "What we can do, dear, so we won't miss the plane, is have everything packed and ready. After we drive the three hours from Monterey Park, we'll wash up, tidy up things around the house, then go directly to the airport early and wait there. That way we won't miss the plane for sure. Besides, the flight to China is 13 hours long. We can sleep all we want then."

I knew that plan would be a bit taxing but seeing that Dorothy really wanted to go, I muttered, "Okay, okay, we'll go!" Secretly, I thought that was a pretty good plan.

Well, the party was really something! The restaurant was exclusively reserved for this one event and decorated in the theme of ancient China. I thought it was presented very sophisticatedly down to the waitresses and waiters in specially designed attire. The cocktail hour was superb with excellent hors d'oeuvres served with Moet & Chandon champagne.

After the cocktail hour, we were seated at our assigned round table of ten. By that time, it seemed half the people were a bit tipsy from the festive atmosphere and champagne. The master of ceremony greeted everyone and made about two dozen introductions, and to my surprise I was one of them as the former City Councilman and Deputy Mayor of San Diego and a California State Assemblyman. I surmised the reason for that was because at that period of time, Chinese in these positions were a rarity. That's probably because the Chinese then were probably too busy making money and raising a family.

Next, the special French envoy from Remy Martin welcomed us and told us the reason for such a grand party. He said in his French accent, which reminded me of Maurice Chevalier, "This party is to say thank you to all the Chinese people in the world. Wherever they are, the Chinese are our best patrons who consume over 60 percent of our vintage product. This includes China, Hong Kong, Taiwan, and wherever the Chinese population is, such as in New York, southern California, and the San Francisco Bay area." He continued to say a few other complimentary things about the Chinese and shared a brief history of Remy Martin that was founded in 1724. Funny, when he got through, I thought he even looked a bit like Chevalier and I almost expected him to sing. Maybe it was the champagne.

The dinner came next. Without describing the whole thing, I thought this was one of the most elegant dinners I had ever experienced. We had many courses, all beautifully and delectably prepared and served, such as a whole braised abalone for each person, sautéed shark fin, lobster in curry sauce and other delightful and savory dishes. Aside from wine served with our dinner, each table was provided with a bottle of Louis XIII Cognac.

During the dinner, the restaurant manager came by our table and chatted in Chinese with one of the people, apparently a friend. After he left, the friend leaned forward and whispered, but loud enough for all of us to hear, "The Remy Martin people are really going all out for this party. They're paying this restaurant $2,500.00 for each table of ten. And the Louis XIII Cognac, which Remy Martin is providing retails for $1,600.00 a bottle." We were all impressed. But more so when they immediately brought us another bottle of Louis XIII Cognac after we finished the first one.

It was a fun evening and the party lasted until 11 p.m. We had a plane to catch so we left immediately after thanking the host.

On the way back to San Diego after driving about 20 miles, I really thought the wise thing to do was to stop off somewhere and rest a bit before going on. The drinking and food made me sleepy. Dorothy, too. So we stopped off at a Denny's Restaurant parking lot and took a nap. We meant to nap for an hour, but slept two and woke up in a near panic that we overslept. We got home at 6 a.m., later than expected due to an accident on the freeway. We quickly loaded up the luggage and drove to the airport against crawling rush hour traffic. Under pressure, we parked the car in a parking lot that seemed like a mile away and ran. When we arrived inside the terminal, the plane was loading the passengers. Thank goodness, we made it. Luckily, there wasn't time-consuming Homeland Security screenings and inspections back then, otherwise we would not have made it.

On the plane Dorothy apologized for causing all this anxiety by insisting that we go to the party. "What!" I exclaimed. "And miss all that? It was worth it!"

She smiled, leaned over, and pecked me on the cheek. Then she whispered, "Now you can sleep all the way to China."

IT IS SAID THAT ALL GOOD THINGS come to an end. Perhaps yes, and maybe no. I like to think in the family of my father, David Hom, it was no ... at least, not yet.

To put it in that context, David Hom started the wholesale David Produce Company in 1920, and it continued until its closing in 1996, due to the retirement of the siblings who took it over when father passed away in 1943. The company ran for 76 continuous years as the oldest wholesale produce firm in San Diego.

But the good things did not stop there. As far as I could see, it continued onto the next generation. Father had twelve children and during our growing up period, at one time or another, we all had worked at the produce company. Some worked during and after school and vacations, and others worked fulltime until their retirement. Working there in the environment of a cosmopolitan atmosphere, with mixed races and languages, each and every one of us gained a practical sense of what the real world was about— understanding, getting along with people, bi-cultural appreciation and, of course, learning the basics of business. And then there was the art of negotiation, which we had to do on a daily basis. Because the price of fresh items such as produce was dictated by daily supply and demand, we learned how to best negotiate our sales so that both parties ended up as winners.

During those early years after Dad passed away, the primary source of income for our family of twelve kids and Mother was through the David Produce Company. Some of the older ones who served in the military during World War II and the Korean War qualified for the GI Bill for a college education but had to forego that opportunity in order to stay with the company to help support the family's financial needs. And, of course, one of the main priorities was also to save money for higher education for the younger siblings. Some went on to college early and later helped provide financial assistance to the younger ones, who in turn went on to college as well. Most of the brothers and sisters ended up in the medical field, chemistry, teaching, and law.

I don't know or recall, after nearly 100 years, that any of the offspring from David Hom and his two wives ever committed a serious crime or was sent to prison. Knock on wood!

Yes, I can honestly say that the good times continued on, and, admittedly, along the way there were a few bumps here and there, but overall, God and America have been good to the David Hom family.

IN 1998, WE HOM SIBLINGS decided to establish an endowment fund for charitable giving through the San Diego Foundation. The fund was named The Hom Family Fund in honor of our parents. In establishing the fund, we donated 800 acres of land in San Diego County which was sold and the proceeds became the principal of the Hom Family Fund.

Income generated by the charitable fund is directed to education, science and medical research, health and human welfare, arts and culture, historical preservation, the environment, civic engagement, and faith based organizations. Our motivation in directing donations is to benefit society as a whole. All the siblings agreed that our giving back to society was reciprocal. Society had been good to us. You sow, you reap, and you give back.

WHAT ABOUT THE SINGLE PEOPLE who work for minimum wage? Downtown housing was a problem for them. These were the people that worked in the restaurants as dishwashers, waiters, busboys, janitors, bellhops, maintenance, and the like. Many ended up living in the downtown area in old hotels, some as old as 75-plus years that no longer met the health and safety building code standards. They lacked adequate heating, air circulation, proper fire escape exits, along with loose floor planking, peeling walls, outdated electrical wiring, and other items that made these types of buildings unsafe. Most had become shoddy and hazardous and were always a potential fire hazard.

This problem was especially acute during the 1990s in downtown San Diego due to the fast rate of demolishing these older substandard hotel buildings, eventually replacing them with the Horton Plaza regional shopping center, gleaming high rise hotels, office and commercial buildings. This was done through the redevelopment program of the Centre City Development Corporation of the City of San Diego. All this was a worthy cause, for it renewed the central downtown area, raised the tax base, and, equally important, in time it provided once again a thriving downtown that was clean and much safer.

But like so many things, doing something good can also cause some unintended negatives. And that negative was the once affordable living accommodations for the single minimum wage earner were no longer available. It created hardship for many of them, causing some to even end up homeless.

In time the city fathers recognized the situation resulting from the redevelopment program and created an Ad Hoc Committee to look into resolving some of the housing problems of these minimum wage earners. After a thorough study, the committee came up with a Single Room

Occupancy (SRO) ordinance. That ordinance allowed a special building code for SROs with specifics to house single residents. It included all health and safety measures such as fire sprinklers and heating, but would deviate from some of the highly strict building code for the downtown area. Each living unit was basically a studio with a number of amenities, such as security, a small cooking area, heat, overhead fan, a TV, bed, bathroom, some furnishings and weekly maid service. It was modest but clean and safe. The ordinance did not require air conditioning because of the mild weather of San Diego.

In creating the new building code ordinance for SROs, the City was adamant that any buildings to be razed for an SRO must first have its history reviewed as to whether it had historical significance relating to San Diego. The San Diego Historical Resources Board would determine that. If it did have historical significance, then the building would be either rehabilitated and preserved, or integrated within a new project.

I thoroughly agreed with that approach since seeing how rehabilitating the Gaslamp Quarter had paid many economic and social dividends to the community. An historic site became even more important as time went on.

Because much of our interest was downtown, we decided to look into the matter of the SRO ordinance. In so doing, we decided to build an SRO on one of our properties on Park Boulevard near Broadway. This was among the first SRO projects based on the new ordinance. It was called Trolley Court and consisted of 185 units with underground parking. Being among the first, we got a good amount of coverage by the news media. The reaction to all this was very positive. There were few negatives, very little, but enough to hear them argue that we were building living units for the low end of riff-raffs. Sadly, I thought that they would think that way. After all, San Diego was a big city, sixth in the nation, and to be truly a cosmopolitan city it needed a diversity of people—the movers and shakers, business people, workers, artists, shopkeepers and everything else for an active downtown. They needed workers of all kinds including lower-end ones.

Within three weeks, all of our units were spoken for and we had a waiting list. It worked out very well for the single person. Our tenant make-up was about 25 percent women and the rest were men. We found that having women as part of the tenant base added a bit of civility to the place. Overall, it seemed to help keep most men more gentlemanly and courteous with less cussing, too.

Based on the success of Trolley Court, we decided to build another SRO on a property we had downtown that spanned a block that had an operating gas station on it. After clearing out the gas station, we built a larger project with 300 units called Peachtree Inn. This site was a little more complicated than the Trolley Court site due to the gas station usage for many years. We discovered that the gasoline storage tanks had leakage. It was an obstacle and in order to remedy the situation, we had to remove the contaminated soil and haul in fresh, clean soil.

After the completion of Peachtree Inn and successfully renting it, we were presented a number of awards from local and statewide organizations for building affordable housing based on this new concept of providing for the needy section of society.

Shortly, we heard that Las Vegas had a program to build affordable housing in their redevelopment area for the prior 10 years, but had not been able to successfully launch a project. Seeing the potential, my partner Will and I met with the City Council and Planning Department staff about building an SRO project. This resulted with our building a 319-unit project named Campaige Place located just four blocks from City Hall. New Las Vegas Mayor Oscar Goodman joined us in celebrating the Grand Opening. The positive publicity ended up with a photo of the project on the front cover of the national *Affordable Housing Finance* magazine.

Our next stop was Phoenix, also in need of affordable housing for single modest income workers. There, we built 302 units, also naming the SRO Campaige Place, in the redevelopment area located within walking distance to the new downtown sports arena and the U.S. Airways Center, home of the NBA Phoenix Suns.

One of the things that the family established long ago was that our investments in different areas would be in separate entity partnerships, as some wanted to invest in one, and not in the other. And later, as in the larger projects such as some of the SROs, we included partners outside of the Hom family. This worked out well because by the 1990s a number of the siblings were at retirement age and further investments were not a priority for them.

After 15 years of developing SROs with several partnerships, we accumulated a sizable number of units with over a hundred employees managing and maintaining them. Thank goodness for modern technology with its computers and high tech communication systems. We were able to keep abreast of the widespread areas of our investments and oversee them well. Even then there would be some occasional breakdowns, but they could be quickly remedied by our in-house technicians.

However, one area we were not able to overcome was the devastating real estate bubble bust starting in 2008. We lost two of our larger projects in Las Vegas and Phoenix. These cities were among the worst in the nation to be affected by the recession. We tried hard to overcome the real estate crises in these two cities, but just couldn't do it. It was a major loss.

CHAPTER 46

It Was Just a Back Pain

I N THE YEAR OF 1999 AT AGE 73, I EXPERIENCED MY MOST MAJOR crisis. I know in our lifetime we all go through major crises, but there is always one that stands out as the most major.

The crisis was building up and I was not aware of it, nor were the children, and not even Dorothy, who always had a particular sense of pending situations.

In hindsight, probably the first indication of the coming crisis was in October 1999 coming home on a bus from Mesquite, Nevada, with 30 of our golfing friends. On the way home Dorothy, who never complained about pain, said to me in a soft voice, almost whispering, "Tom, I don't know whether it's me or the bumpy road condition, but my back is aching." I immediately knew it couldn't be from golfing because Dorothy didn't golf. She and a couple of other non-golfing wives came just for the ride and to enjoy the Nevada outdoors. One of the wives gave Dorothy an Ibuprofen pain relief pill and shortly afterwards the pain went away. I never thought anymore about it.

A few days later, the pain occurred again and she said to me, "Tom, I think the pain is a strain on my back muscle. I think I strained it rolling out the trash barrels to the alley." I thought that was a bit strange because one or the other of us had been rolling out the trash barrels for years and had no problem. And then I mischievously jested, "Yeah, I think maybe our old age is catching up with us. At our age we've got to be careful about lifting and moving things that are too heavy! That's what we have Emilio, the yard man, for." She chuckled and said she needed the exercise.

Two weeks later on the second Monday of November 1999, Dorothy went with me to Tecate, California, for the Chamber of Commerce's monthly meeting where we were both members and she was the secretary. On the way home from the meeting, with a sense of desperation, she moaned, "Tom, I think you better take me to the hospital right now. I think something is wrong!" With that tone of voice and knowing Dorothy who seldom complained, it had to be something more than just a back pain.

It was about eight in the evening and we went straight to emergency at Kaiser Hospital where we were members. When we got there, like all emergency units, it was crowded. My feeling was that Dorothy's situation was extremely urgent. I told the front counter nurse that Dorothy's problem was serious and we wanted to see a doctor right away. In spite of Dorothy's condition, she was somewhat embarrassed to see me cutting through the line of other people needing care. And she responded, in a groaning, murmuring voice, "No, no, I'll wait!" The nurse detected my desperation and saw her condition and immediately went to talk to the doctor. Within a few minutes, Dorothy was escorted in and I went with her. I was thankful. Hopefully, the people who were waiting understood.

The doctor heard about Dorothy's physical problems, such as the acute back pains, not having a bowel movement for three days, and the continued body weakness, then he examined her. After about 20 minutes, his diagnosis was that she perhaps had a back and upper body strain, and her bowel movement problems were due to a blockage and something else I don't remember. Subsequently, he gave two prescriptions, one for the body pain and the other to precipitate her bowel movement. In addition, he asked the nurse to refer this information to Dorothy's primary doctor and suggested that further tests be done immediately.

From there we went to the pharmacy to fill the prescriptions, which Dorothy took immediately. Later that evening her pains were partially relieved and a few hours later she had her first bowel movement in three days. The following day I contacted the primary doctor and an appointment was arranged for the next week.

Meanwhile, in spite of Dorothy's growing weakness, and with the help of the pain pills, she still insisted on going to some of her community events such as the inaugural naming of the new panda from China at the San Diego Zoo. As a board of director for the San Diego Library, Salvation Army, and Maritime Museum of San Diego, she felt she must continue to attend those meetings, too.

Because of her growing weakness either I or one of our daughters, Nora or Gayle, would help her along. She refused a wheelchair. Remarkably, in spite of Dorothy's discomfort and weakness, her spirits were always high and cheerful.

After a series of tests were taken at the hospital, two more weeks of tests were recommended. By this time, the family was becoming more and more concerned about Dorothy's deteriorating condition.

A week later, after the second series of tests, on December 3, I got a call from Dorothy's primary doctor. He asked me to come to his office to discuss the test results. On the way to his office, I was both apprehensive and hopeful about the outcome of the tests, but mostly I was worried.

Upon arriving at the office, the doctor, who was also a good family friend, greeted me solemnly and had me sit down. He right away began explaining the series of tests, and said, "The result, Tom, I'm sorry to say, is that Dorothy has an advanced case of ovarian cancer. It has spread throughout and it'll be a matter of time until she'll die from it."

I sat there in disbelief, shaking my head. My first question was, "How long, doctor?" I was hopefully thinking that there might be some area of treatment that was available that could postpone the eventual death for some years, or even a miraculous recovery.

The doctor, responding with compassion, was direct. "Tom, it'll be one to two weeks." And he added, "I understand if you want to get a second opinion." This was a double whammy shock! I left his office confused and depressed.

Driving back to my office I had to think how to best tell all the children about this tragic news, and how it would affect them. So many things were going through my mind. We had been married 48 years, which didn't seem so long. I thought about how terrible life would be without Dorothy. After all the positive things she had done for me, how could I make up for the times I may have been unkind and impatient with her?

When I got back to the office, I called all six children and told them to come to the office at 4 p.m., as I had the doctor's report to share with them. None of them asked me what the results were. I am sure they detected the seriousness of my voice saying they would be there, except the youngest one Cindy, who lived out in Pasadena, California, and would join us on speakerphone. At the gathering of my five daughters and son, and some with their spouses, I told them pretty much what the doctor said. As expected, the one to two weeks to live was shocking to them. We all agreed that a second opinion should be arranged immediately.

That evening the children and I gathered with Dorothy to tell her of my meeting with the doctor. With a great deal of reluctance and sadness I told her of the findings of the recent tests by the doctors. The hardest part was to tell her that the doctor said she had only one to two weeks left to live.

In spite of the sorrowful news, Dorothy looked at us with a half smile and said in her weakened but clear voice, "Don't you all feel so bad. I've known it was something like this for some time. We all have to go sometime, sooner or later. This just happened to be sooner. I am not afraid." At this point, some were crying. And she went on to say, looking at our daughters, and with some vigor in her voice, "I want to say to you girls, and for you to know, that I don't want your father to live alone. I want you to help him find a nice woman to marry when I'm gone!"

What Dorothy said might have been a surprise to the children but it was not surprising to me. Knowing her, she was always one to not have anyone feel sorry for her. Secondly, regarding her remarks about another woman, it dates back to many times and many years of telling me that scenario. She would say that should I go before her, which is what she expected, as women usually lived longer than men, she would spend the rest of her life caring for the grandchildren. She would be happy with that. And if she should go first, I should marry again, for I'm not the kind to live alone. And then she would add to that, "And it better not be just some floozy after your money! Otherwise I'll come back and haunt you!" That night I cried. The last time I cried was in 1943, when my father died.

Four days later Dorothy was taken to the Perlman Medical Offices, affiliated with the University of California at San Diego Health System for the second opinion. They were waiting when she arrived. After about an hour of examination and reviewing tests and records, I was told by the doctor that Dorothy's case was too advanced for them to be of any help. This was expected, but we felt we still had to try for a second opinion. From there, with prior arrangement, we took Dorothy to the San Diego Hospice.

After a few days at the hospice, having visiting family members and friends, Dorothy's pains became more acute and she was then put under heavier sedation. When the doctor told us that her demise would be within 24 hours, the children and I spent the last day with her. Reminiscent of her Hawaiian background the children brought some flower leis and some Hawaiian sheet music. We sang to her, not knowing whether she was conscious enough to hear us. Later, holding her hands and leaning over close to her, I alone sang softly to her some of our favorite songs that we used to sing together. After a few songs, I detected drops of tears coming from her eyes. It was a very sad moment for me, but it was also a moment with a great sense of fulfillment knowing that she knew I loved her dearly. Dorothy passed away on December 11, 1999, nine days after the doctor's report to me.

We had a graveside service for Dorothy at the Greenwood Cemetery, with just our children, the grandchildren, and the families of my siblings and Dorothy's relatives. Following, in the afternoon, a Memorial Service was held at the First United Methodist Church which had seating for 1,200. Our church, the Chinese Community Church, could only hold 300. The attendance was large, perhaps over a thousand, which included a wide spectrum of people such as family, friends, government officials, business and professional colleagues, and many others. For me and the children, and those that knew her, that was an end of an era.

HOW DOES ONE START LIFE OVER? So many people wanted to help me heal from this tragic loss by bringing food, inviting me out, advising me how to cope with my new life, and many other well intended offers. Naturally, the best help came from family members, my children most of all. The first two weeks, each of the children's family would take turns staying overnight with me. I personally did not think that was necessary, but they meant well and were concerned for my well-being.

I took it upon myself to keep busy, like working overtime at the office, doing watercolor painting, golfing, and jogging. In spite of my intensive activities, there was not a time when I didn't think of Dorothy. I even made it a point to go to the bookstore to get a book on how to cope with losing a loving spouse and how to adjust to the grieving process. It helped, but it mostly reminded me to just use good common sense. And also trust in God.

With the number of organizations to which I belonged, I was kept busy. The days went by fast, but nights were especially lonely. It was strange going to bed without Dorothy. I knew in time I would adjust, but I would never forget.

One of the areas where I relaxed and which I enjoyed was my involvement with the San Diego Watercolor Society, where I could be creative as well as exhibit some of my paintings. Painting and working with other artists, and serving on a committee to open and close the office and art gallery on certain days, were good diversions for me.

During Easter, four months after the passing of Dorothy, I decided to take my children and their families for a vacation to Hilo, on the Big Island of Hawaii. Dorothy's Uncle Robert had a new five-bedroom vacation home on two acres there. He had invited us to visit there several times, but we were not able to take him up on it. But this time, I did, with the whole family of 21, including the grandchildren. Flying to Hawaii during the peak time of Easter, the fares were about double the regular price, but the cost wasn't important. This was to be the first time since Dorothy's passing that we could get away together to heal, and what better place than Hawaii?

It was a wonderful break for all of us. It was a whole week of beaches, exploring, waterfalls, luau, volcano, horseback riding, hiking, dining out, shopping, and helping Uncle Robert create a rock garden with all kinds of tropical plants and trees. It was a great, fun week. During all this time, we often thought of Dorothy, knowing that although she wasn't there physically, she was there in spirit.

This Big Island trip for the family was our fourth trip to Hawaii. The other three visits were to Honolulu, Oahu, where we enjoyed the sandy beaches of Waikiki. Honolulu is a major city and the state capitol of Hawaii, with skyscrapers, lots of nightlife, and outstanding restaurants. The Big Island of Hawaii is practically all rural and reminded me a lot of what Oahu must have been like 100 years earlier. It was a great new setting and environment for the children. Everything was so pristine.

WITHIN THREE MONTHS AFTER I became a widower, word got around to friends in church and elsewhere about Dorothy's parting words to my five daughters, "I don't want your father to live alone. I want you to help him find a nice woman to marry again!" Some of my friends meant well telling me that certain women might be available. But I wasn't interested and, perhaps, would never be. As time went on, I received several invitations for dinner and was invited to escort women to various events, like the theatre or social parties. I turned down most of these sending my regrets "due to a prior engagement."

Almost every one of the invitations was from women who were fine people and had known Dorothy. I never thought of myself as a lady's man or that attractive of a person to get that kind of attention. I venture to think that many of these invitations were simply due to sympathy. I did, however, accept a few of them for their company, home-cooked meals, or to go out to dinner, and once as an escort to a symphony.

On a couple of occasions, I asked two different artist friends from the Watercolor Society out for dinner. One of them later invited me to spend a couple of weeks at her château in Nice, France, where we could paint. She was a nice person, an attractive divorcee, and a prize-winning artist. I told her I could not go due to prior commitments. Besides, my daughters had never met her and didn't think it was a good idea.

By then I was beginning to think my daughters were really taking Dorothy's marching orders about finding a wife for me pretty seriously.

At this stage I never felt that I had to set a timetable for meeting a woman that would fit my idea of a new wife. I really didn't know what that criterion would be. One thing was for sure, though, I knew I could not set an unrealistic standard that she would have to be like Dorothy. Clearly, that would be setting myself up for disillusionment for no two persons can be alike. Therefore, I needed to set a new standard with an open mind that a person could be different from Dorothy, but yet good.

Aware of Dorothy's marching orders to marry again, many of my friends started introducing me to their single lady friends and relatives. Since I'm not such a prize catch, these meetings normally ended up being just friendly and "glad to have met you."

I was even urged to go to a huge five-day golf tournament with over 300 participants, sponsored by the Chinese Federated Golf Association (CFGA) to be held that year in Tucson, Arizona. I was told that there would be many single women participating, so I should go and meet some of them.

Since our San Diego Chinese Golf Club was affiliated with the CFGA and most of our club members were going, I decided to go too. Besides, I never played golf in Tucson before and the four courses that we would be playing were among Tucson's best. Aside from that, desert courses are different from our California ones, so that would be a challenge too. I loved that!

Tucson was only about 350 miles from San Diego, and instead of flying, I rode with my brother Herb and his wife Deanna. The drive was only about five hours, passing through mostly desert landscape. I liked that scenery, as I have painted desert scenes a number of times before. I saw great beauty in it.

The golf courses were indeed in top shape, so much well-trimmed greenery in a desert setting. The first two days of the tournament, playing in the heat of mid-90s wasn't too bad. On the third day, the temperature shot up into the 100s. After that game I was exhausted and dehydrated so I didn't even bother to go partying as I did the earlier two days. I then questioned whether I really wanted to play the next day, the fourth round. After taking a shower, having dinner and a beer to relax, I thought I better not be a party pooper, I better play. And besides, I had already been posted to be part of a foursome the next morning, scheduled to play at 9:07 a.m.

That day it was still hot, but somehow or another I got my second wind and did pretty well. That evening was the final blowout, a party at the greyhound racetrack, which was one of the popular attractions in Tucson. There was food galore and an open bar. It was quite an event, along with wagering on the greyhound races. Since I'm not much into betting, I spent my time socializing and meeting new people. Most of the golf groups were either professionals, business people in well secured jobs, retired, or like me, semi-retired. Ages ranged from the 40s to greater maturity.

During the course of the evening, with efforts by a number of my self-appointed matchmaking friends, I met a number of single ladies: two medical doctors, a dentist, three or four doing research of some kind, and others. In the atmosphere of party gaiety, I didn't detect any of them to be on the prowl of looking for a husband. They were friendly and having a good time, and so was I. Some cards were exchanged, but no one followed through and neither did I.

CHAPTER 47

Serendipity

I WAS BECOMING MORE CONSCIOUS OF THE FACT THAT SOONER OR later I needed to settle on a course of life that would be more meaningful. It so happened that while I frequently turned to my stacks of diaries, over 50 years' worth of them for reference, I came across a page dated April 27, 2000, and it read as follows: "I am continuingly making adjustments to my life. Clearly, it's not the same as before. Things are changing and I am not sure where it is leading. I keep myself busy, but seemingly with no great aim in life. I know things will get clearer as time goes by, so I need to keep going, be patient, and things will fall into place." This was five months after the passing of Dorothy.

Three weeks later, with an urge to just get away, and not having seen many of Dorothy's relatives in Honolulu for a long time, I decided to take a trip there and visit for a couple of weeks. I made reservations to fly over on June 1, 2000. I told the children I was going, and asked them to set up a schedule to feed my German Shepherd and to check the house.

A couple days later, daughter Nora called and asked, "Dad, how about taking Gayle and me to Honolulu with you? We want to go and see our uncles and aunties, too!"

"Sure, why not. I'll get the tickets. It'll be fun. Meanwhile," I said, "Nora, make the arrangements for the hotel in Waikiki!" So I made the decision to bring them along, and it was probably one of my better decisions in a long time.

After a five-hour flight on a Friday from San Diego to Hawaii, we checked in at our hotel in Waikiki, and immediately called some of the relatives to say hello and set up a time for dinner the next day. The following day, the girls spent their time at the beach, while I visited the famous U.S. Army

Museum at Fort DeRussy in Waikiki. That evening we had dinner with
relatives in Chinatown, where the food was plentiful and always good. It
was a wonderful evening, especially listening to the relatives share so many
stories about Dorothy in her younger growing-up days.

When Dorothy and I used to visit Honolulu, on Sundays we would
normally attend services at the well known Kawaiaha'o Church, one of the
oldest and largest churches in Honolulu, dating back into the mid 1840s,
started by early Christian missionaries from Boston. They always had a
beautiful service there.

On this particular Sunday morning, I somehow decided to attend another
church, the Judd Street United Church of Christ, where Rev. Harold Jow
once served. He also formerly served as pastor at our San Diego Chinese
Community Church, the church that I attended since I was four years
old, starting in church kindergarten. Perhaps because of that sentiment I
decided to go there instead of the usual church.

I invited the two girls to go with me, but Nora had an appointment to
do something else, so Gayle went with me. The church was not especially
large, about the same size as ours in San Diego, with an ethnic makeup of
mostly Chinese descent and about 35 percent of various other groups. The
total service was conducted all in English like our church. It was structured
along the same line as ours, with a praise band, choir, and similar hymns,
and it felt very familiar. The manner of worship was also very similar to
ours, along the lines of the Congregational Church who were the original
founders of our respective churches.

After service, as at most other churches, there was a coffee hour, where
church members met and greeted each other over refreshments, cookies,
and cake. I introduced myself and my daughter Gayle as San Diegans and
friends of their former pastor, Rev. Harold Jow. I also shared that Rev. Jow
and I worked together for many years on a missionary program, called
East West Christian Outreach. He was president and I was vice president.
We worked in cooperation with the Ministry of Religion in China, visiting churches and seminaries and sharing American praise music and the
word of God.

It was then that the gentleman I was talking with pointed out a lady
a few feet away with her arms loaded with folders and books, and said,

"That lady over there went on one of those missions. You might want to meet her!" I then turned and walked over to her, extending my arm for a handshake and boldly, but pleasantly saying, "Hi, I'm Tom Hom from San Diego. I'm a friend of Rev. Harold Jow and also the vice president of East West Christian Outreach. I understand you went on one of the mission trips not long ago!"

She gave me a quizzical look, the kind that said, "Who is this guy, so bold, with an in-your-face introduction?" She also glanced over to my daughter Gayle, and I sensed that she might have been thinking that Gayle was my young, attractive trophy wife. I then introduced Gayle as my daughter, one of five daughters and the second oldest. Then, with a friendly smile, the lady introduced herself as Loretta Lum, a member of the church. She went on to say, "Normally I'm not able to make the after-church social hour due to meetings, but today I'm here greeting new people to our church since my meeting was canceled." Now with a broad smile, she said, "Yes, I did go on the wonderful mission trip to China with the San Diego group. And how is Rev. Harold Jow?"

I responded enthusiastically, "Rev. Harold Jow is a special guy, a dynamic leader, and full of enthusiasm for the China missionary program. I consider him to be one of the most admired men in my book." She agreed. We continued to talk, mostly about her mission trip to China and about our respective church work and our families. By this time I noticed that she had an exceptionally warm personality with a smile that made her eyes twinkle.

We talked on and I mentioned that my late wife Dorothy, also from Hawaii, passed away just last year and that she had graduated from Roosevelt High School before moving to San Diego in 1950 for college. She responded and said, "I'm sorry to hear that about your wife. You know, it'll take a while to heal. And I understand. I lost my husband, Ben, a number of years ago, and yes, it'll take some time."

From those few remarks, I detected a woman who had a sympathetic heart and understanding as to what life was all about. All this time Gayle was there with us, once in awhile joining in the conversation. She asked Loretta about her life, what kind of work she did, and other personal questions that only a woman can ask another woman without being too intrusive. Loretta told us she was a retired school librarian and most of her time was devoted to church work and also serving as an officer in the retired teachers association.

We visited for about 20 minutes, and as we were about to depart, I said, "By the way, Loretta, can you tell me what there is around town that a guy can do without going to the tourist places? Something more local rather than touristy." She gave me a contemplative look, which triggered the thought that she might think that I was looking to her as a tour guide, which had never occurred to me.

She replied with an inviting smile and said, "If you want something local, I'm in charge of a program to feed the homeless at the Rescue Mission in downtown this coming Tuesday. We'll be cooking for about 150 at the church and will take the food to the Rescue Mission and serve it there." She went on to say, "All this is done by volunteers and we can use more help. We start preparation at the church kitchen at 3 p.m. and serve at 6 p.m. You're welcome to join us!" That wasn't my idea of a local event. I was hoping for a suggestion like a college or high school chorus presentation or a community street fair or the likes of it. I thought she might even be kidding.

That afternoon, back at the hotel, I mentioned to both Nora and Gayle, "You know, that lady Loretta, she seems pretty nice. I wonder if she would consider having dinner with us." I thought we could either look her number up in the phone book or call the church. Before I could think further, Gayle reached into her purse for her cell phone and said. "I got her number, Dad. I can call her and ask, or you can."

For a fleeting moment I was mystified as to how she happened to get her phone number. She must have gotten it when we were leaving. And, how did she realize that we might use that number later? My only conclusion was that children were probably more intuitive than we realized when it came to knowing their parents. I always thought it was the other way around, parent over child. Apparently, it's both ways.

I suggested that she call, as I didn't want to appear too aggressive, being that we just met that morning. Gayle dialed the number and Loretta answered. "Loretta," said Gayle, "it was a pleasure meeting you this morning. If you are free tonight, my sister Nora and I and my dad would like to invite you to dinner at Sam Choy's." Sam Choy's was one of the best restaurants in Honolulu.

Loretta replied, "Oh, I can't. I already invited my son Jonathan and his family over for dinner."

Gayle replied, like she was on a crusade, saying, "Loretta, we're staying in a hotel and we need to take all our meals out anyway, so tomorrow we'll be going to Alan Wong's for dinner. We'd like to have you join us then." Alan Wong's was considered to be the best in Honolulu and among the finest in America. Loretta accepted, but only if it could be at 7 p.m., as she had a meeting to attend earlier. Later I briefly wondered whether she accepted because of the high rating of the restaurant, or she was looking forward to enjoying our company. I rationalized, probably both.

Loretta arrived at Alan Wong's at 7 p.m. like she said she would. By this time, my daughters had sensed that I had at least a peripheral interest in her, so they cordially greeted her with that openly friendly aloha spirit. Over dinner there was a lot of discussion about our families, what the kids did and where they were now. I did manage to get a few words in here and there, but the three of them seemed to have so much more to talk about so I mostly listened. I knew all of my six children had the gift of conversation like their mother Dorothy, so all this was interesting.

During the two hours of dinner and learning more about each other, my daughters periodically, and subtly, referred to me as a man of many accomplishments, such as an artist, chef, musician, politician, successful businessman, among other things. I was slightly embarrassed, and I tried to downplay that by saying something like, "That is only through the eyes of my children." A couple of times Loretta looked at me and smiled as if she was thinking " Is this guy for real?"

The next day on Tuesday morning after a late breakfast, I wanted to see Loretta again before we left for San Diego, so I decided to take her up on the local event of feeding the homeless. I had Nora and Gayle drop me off at the church to help with the preparation of the food.

When I arrived there several people were already working on the preparation, with Loretta leading the work force. She seemed surprised that I actually showed up to do this kind of activity. Actually, kitchens and cooking were not new to me, which I did not tell Loretta, as I had previously owned several fast food Chinese restaurants, where we also did outside catering for up to 1,200. I grew up helping my mother cook some of our family dinners as well, and also had cooked for the church luncheons of 150 to 200 people.

Loretta put me to work peeling potatoes and carrots, chopping lettuce, washing pots and pans, wiping down the counters and sweeping the floor. The main dish for the homeless was curry chicken. She also had me cutting chicken to bite size pieces. Several of the ladies saw me cutting the chicken very fast, easily and orderly, and asked me to show them how to do it. I did. And I thought to myself, this local activity is turning out to be pretty fun.

After all the preparation and cutting, the curry chicken was cooked in two large woks. When the curry chicken was done and ready to be transferred into large pots to be taken to the Rescue Mission, someone shouted out from the back of the kitchen, "Hey, we forgot this big pan of uncooked chicken for the curry. We gotta have it otherwise we'll be short!"

One of the volunteers said, "Just bring it here and I'll throw it in with the rest in the wok, and cook it up!"

Being somewhat of an experienced cook, I knew that you never added raw meat to meat that was already cooked because of the potential to develop salmonella, bacteria that created food poisoning.

So I spoke up, explaining that mixing raw meat with cooked meat had the potential of food poisoning. I suggested that we cook the raw chicken in a separate pot and after it was cooked, mix it in with the other cooked chicken in the wok. The other volunteers agreed, so it was done.

Afterwards, when all the food and materials were packed into the vehicles and ready to leave for the Rescue Mission, Loretta came over to me with a warm smile and a sigh of relief, and said, "Tom, I see you are sort of a take charge guy, aren't you?" I took that as a compliment. I shrugged my shoulders, and said in a whispering voice, "Oh, it was just a spontaneous reaction."

After a church service of prayers, a sermon, and some hymn singing, the homeless gathered in the social hall for the dinner. I helped serve and after everyone was served, the servers and kitchen crew sat down among the homeless to have dinner with them. Within a couple of moments, Loretta tapped me on the shoulder and whispered to me whether I would rather eat in the kitchen or in the office. That question puzzled me. I said, "I'm fine right here." At that point, some of the kitchen crew were bringing out their ukuleles to play and sing Hawaiian songs, which I loved. Why leave?

Later I asked Loretta why the offer for me to eat in the kitchen or office, and she said that she thought that I might be uncomfortable eating with the homeless. I was silent for a moment, took a short deep breath, and said, "Loretta, I have absolutely no problem with the homeless. I grew up in the wholesale produce markets where my dad had a business and there were always homeless about, some nice, others drunkards, some thieves, and some were even friends ... so in the dining hall I was not at all intimidated. I was quite comfortable." With that, I sensed she felt she had misjudged me. That's okay, for at the end it came out for the better, showing Loretta that I was not a picky person and above it all.

After cleaning the dining hall and loading the pots and pans to take back to the church, I called Nora and Gayle to pick me up. While waiting, I had a chance to visit with Loretta. In our conversation, she asked when I planned to return to San Diego. I said tomorrow. She appeared surprised, and replied, "You mean, today is your last day here and you chose to spend it with us cooking and serving the homeless? Why, that is very nice of you!"

"Loretta, you may recall, I told you I was looking for something to do here that is locally oriented and without a touristy atmosphere. After thinking about it, I thought cooking and feeding the homeless at the Rescue Mission was about as local as you can get. That was fun and worthwhile. Besides, I didn't even see one tourist there in the whole dining hall ... except me. And that doesn't count!"

She laughed. Just then Nora and Gayle pulled up in their car. I quickly gave her my card and asked her to look me up whenever she visited San Diego. When I got in the car, Nora asked how the day went, and I answered, "Somewhat unusual, but most rewarding, and I found out there is something special about Loretta. What you see is what you get. Purely a good person!"

The next day in San Diego, when I went to my office, I opened my email, as I normally did. To my surprise, I got a message from Loretta. It was short, but to the point. It said, "Tom, thank you for your help in feeding the homeless and the poor, especially on your last day in Paradise. Mahalo, Loretta."

Although brief, it was a most welcomed message. I really hadn't expected to hear from her, but since I did, I wanted to answer back. In spite of the other emails pending, which were probably a hundred or so, I answered hers first. The other hundred didn't seem so important.

That was the start of an email romance, if one can call it that. We exchanged messages, many of them. Some were short, but most of them were long, talking about family and our experiences in life. We also wrote about our favorite places to where we had traveled and our impression of the culture and foods we liked best, the things people talk about as they are getting to know each other.

Early on, I found out that she was much better educated than I was. She had two Master Degrees in Education from the University of Hawaii, while I had only a high school diploma and a number of evening college business classes. My education was largely from the school of hard knocks.

But overall, we had more in common than not. She came from a large family of eight siblings, with five girls—she being the fourth—and three brothers. Her parents were immigrants from China. Both of our families started out with very little money and managed to build a comfortable living. She and I believed in a strong and viable public school education, free enterprise, helping the needy, and other important issues—in spite of the fact that she was a Democrat and I, a Republican. Our values were pretty much the same, except we may have had different ways of achieving them.

It came to a point where sending emails back and forth wasn't enough, so I decided to start calling her and we would talk, sometimes for an hour or so. Generally, we would set a time for the evening call. The phone calls worked out better, as verbal communication was much easier for me than writing, and much more intimate and pleasant.

After knowing Loretta for a couple of months, I sent her a framed reproduction of one of my watercolor paintings, a scene of a number of the participants preparing for the Chinese New Year lions dance, titled "Getting Ready."

When Loretta received it, she called and said that she was both delighted and surprised with the beauty of the painting, and that she didn't know I had such talent. By that time I had the courage to invite her to San Diego, where I could show her around and introduce her to more of my family. I offered her the option to either stay at my six-bedroom house or I could arrange for her to stay at a hotel. I promised that there would be a lot of things to do and see.

Loretta expressed her fondness of San Diego, where she had visited a number of times, sharing that her son Eric was once stationed in San Diego after he graduated from the Naval Academy. While there he also attended the Chinese Community Church, where he sang in the choir. I also sang in the same church choir, and it clicked in my mind that I knew Eric. Eric was very much involved in our church and attended many events of our Hom family activities. What a remarkable coincidence.

With this common and indirect relationship, Loretta accepted the invitation to come to San Diego for a visit. Instead of staying at my home, she opted to stay at the Hilton Hotel where she had stayed before. That was fine. I respected her more for that. After all, staying with me could have created a scandal.

After two weeks here in San Diego, Loretta and I got to know each other better and I became more and more fond of her. Since the passing of Dorothy, I'd had the chance to meet many nice women, either through introductions, various civic events or invitations, but I found Loretta to be the one-of-a-kind that I would want as a wife. My children sensed that as well. After all, it was Dorothy's marching orders to find a nice wife for me. Loretta easily met their approval.

The following month I went to Honolulu to meet Loretta's mother and siblings. I had the opportunity to meet them after church at her mother's house, where they would regularly meet on Sundays for lunch. When I met the family, they were nice, cordial and welcoming, but I also sensed that I was under a certain amount of scrutiny, as to "Who is this mainland fellow coming to pursue our sister, and what kind of a person is he?"

I felt that was fair and good, after all, having been in politics, business and everything else, that came with the territory. It turned out to be a very pleasant afternoon. Each of Loretta's siblings was friendly and discreet in inquiring about my background. We talked a lot about both of our families and I think that was an important link as to who we were in many ways. I was especially impressed with Loretta's 97-year-old mother, who had a sharp mind and a warm personality and came from a family of nine children. We both understood the culture of large Chinese families, and I think that helped her evaluate me favorably.

After two weeks in Honolulu, I returned to San Diego, and a few weeks later Loretta followed on December 20, 2000, to spend the holidays with me. By this time, I had already proposed marriage to Loretta and we decided not to announce it until Christmas Day, when we had my Tom Hom clan over for our traditional Christmas dinner. The children knew that eventually we would be announcing an engagement, but didn't know when. After we made our announcement, they all enthusiastically applauded and the champagne that I had put aside for this occasion was uncorked for several rounds of toasting. The Tom Hom clan was happy for us, as they had all come to love Loretta.

A few days later, before the New Year, Loretta and I went to Scottsdale, Arizona to meet with her children to announce the news of our engagement. Her four children, three boys, who were engineers, and a daughter, who was a financial planner, were there with their spouses and children. Over dinner, the official engagement was announced, and Loretta's family, like mine, expressed great happiness and applauded to that.

Even so, I did, sense a bit of apprehension from Loretta's daughter. That was understandable. She had not known me long enough. After all, I was new and a former politician and there was a lot she didn't know about me. But in a short time, Sylvia and I got to know each other better and our relationship turned out to be great. I think cautiousness is just being prudent, which is always good.

With our coming marriage, Loretta and I felt it was important that we should have the consensus of approval from our children beforehand, as it would set a positive tone for both our families in the coming future. And as time went on, this proved to be entirely correct, for the children of both our families have become very good friends, spending vacations together, visiting each other, sharing intellectual matters, and being part of an extended family.

IN JANUARY 2001, NEWLY ELECTED President George W. Bush was sworn in. That year was also a new chapter in our lives. We married at my church, the Chinese Community Church, on February 17, 2001, with both our families and a few close friends in attendance. We decided that this time around we wanted to keep the wedding small and mostly family oriented. We only invited about 125 people, about 80 from my family side, and the rest from Loretta's side, plus a few close friends. When I say small, it's really relative. When my oldest daughter Nora married, there were about a 1,000 guests, and then my second daughter, Gayle, had 800. And with the rest of my other four children, their weddings were also much larger than ours. Those were the days during my active political and civic involvement. We were quite happy to be the smallest of them all.

Following the wedding, we had the reception and dinner at a rather nice Chinese restaurant, in a private room decorated for this special occasion. Along with the good food, champagne flowed for the toasting and speeches of good wishes were made, praising the sterling character of both the bride and groom. I thought that sterling character part probably applied more to Loretta than to me. But that was okay; it was my wedding day and I accepted those compliments. For entertainment, we had a Mexican mariachi band that played very festive music, replete with trumpets, guitars, fiddles, and lots else, with a Latino ranchero beat and singing. While we commonly had mariachis at Hom family events, this was a new type of music for those from Hawaii, and they really seemed to enjoy it.

We didn't go on our honeymoon right away like newlyweds normally did. We waited a month later, due to some plans that were made before Loretta and I met. It happened that Loretta earlier had made plans for a 14-day cruise with two of her close teacher girlfriends to visit Southeast Asia, China, and Japan. Since Loretta was the one who initiated the tour, she did not want to let her friends down and cancel.

So before our wedding, after discussing it, we decided that she would still go on the cruise, and I would join her, enabling us to celebrate our honeymoon together with her friends. It would be a different kind of honeymoon and I didn't mind, nor did Loretta or her friends. It all worked out fine, with everyone having a great time. When I think about this arrangement, I chalk this up to older people solving a problem that younger people would see as a dilemma and almost impossible to accept.

With our marriage, we wanted to start out fresh in a new setting, so we decided to buy a new house. We loved the present old stately and classic two-story home, with its six-bedrooms and a full basement, set on a third of an acre, but it was way too big for the two of us. We wanted a new beginning with something smaller with only one story, as I was then 74 and she was 67, and climbing stairs and major housekeeping would not be part of our future.

In house hunting, we looked at dozens of homes and checked out new subdivisions. We finally settled on a new tree-lined gated community in Chula Vista, located near Otay Lake. We were impressed with it, and bought a four-bedroom, three-car garage, one-story house, with enough space to spare to take care of visiting guests. Before moving, we had to get rid of the monstrous amount of things my family had accumulated at the old house. At the end, we gave over 100 large boxes of items away, like books, appliances, clothing, artifacts, plus furniture and anything else we wouldn't need at the new place. The hard part was choosing what to keep and what to let go of, especially the things that had deep sentimental value, and there were lots of those.

In spite of sorting what to keep or give away, we still ended up renting a large storage unit for the extras. Two years later, I decided to empty out the storage, and I still ended up keeping half of it, which I finally put in my third garage. Sorting was not physically tough, but it was emotionally hard work. Loretta and I decided that this would be our last and final house. No more moving.

After we were settled in, we decided to have a housewarming party and invite the children and their families over. Not long afterwards, we had Loretta's family coming from out of town to spend time with us. We also had some of Loretta's former teacher friends as well. All and all, it was a fun time for us, with so many people helping us to adjust to our brand new home and our newly married life.

This has turned out to be a good home for us. The house is large enough for us to have a library of about 2,000 books, a spacious kitchen where I love to cook, and a room where we have my art studio and Loretta's office with computers and files. And then there is the living room, with plenty of space for my grand piano, where I enjoy playing daily. And the yard, about one third the size of our former one, we had newly landscaped and much easier to maintain. One thing we do miss, though, is the fruit trees.

xv. The Ups and Downs

AGES 75 TO 85

一只兔子崎岖的心路历程

Tom Hom, photo by Melissa Jacobs.

CHAPTER 48

The Man Upstairs

IN RESPONSE TO THE SEPTEMBER 11TH TERRORIST ATTACKS, THE
UNITED STATES INVADED AFGHANISTAN IN PURSUIT OF AL-QAEDA
LEADER OSAMA BIN LADIN IN 2001.

I WAS SOON TURNING 75 AND I WANTED MORE LEISURE TIME. AT
that point, I felt more than comfortable that Will, who had been with
me for over 25 years, was more than capable of running the Tom Hom
Group investments. He has had the position of President and CEO for more
than five years and has done an excellent job of it. My role has been mostly
consulting on issues that Will wanted to bounce off of me periodically.

With more leisure time, Loretta and I traveled throughout Asia, Europe,
South America, and other interesting places. On occasion, we took the
whole Tom Hom clan on various trips, mostly to Hawaii or on a cruise.
These gatherings were always fun and also gave us time to bond together.
Heavens! Children and grandkids all grow up too fast!

On one of these travel outings, Loretta said something to me that con-
firmed just how thoughtful and caring a person she truly was. She said, "I feel
so privileged to be sharing this time in your life. You and Dorothy worked
so hard to accomplish so much in business and civic affairs. The honors
and accolades you are now receiving really belong to her as well, and I feel
humbled that I am reaping the benefits." I was touched by those remarks.

Loretta too, like Dorothy, was also an outstanding achiever. In Hawaii
she had been very active in the public education system. She represented
teachers and university professors on the Board of Directors of the National
Education Association, which entailed lobbying for educational reform in
Congress and the White House.

She took leadership positions in her church, serving as board chairperson of the thriving pre-school. She also chaired a committee which worked with the River of Life Rescue Mission to feed and house the homeless. She always gave 110% to everything she did.

I have indeed been blessed with two wonderful, caring, and intelligent women in my life.

IN 2002, JUST AS I WAS BEGINNING to enjoy a more leisurely life-style, I was asked by the minister and the moderator of our church to take on the task of fundraising for our anticipated new church in the Tierrasanta area of San Diego. Our present church was built in 1960, and our congregation had outgrown that location. Many members had moved to a more central location near the Tierrasanta area. They related to me that the fundraiser campaign had been going on for the past three years and it had not gotten the results needed to build the new church.

Aside from that, the church had recently sought out a professional firm that specialized in raising funds for churches. The fundraising firm evaluated our church, taking into account its congregation size, its demographics, and other factors, and estimated that they could help us raise between $800,000 to $1 million dollars. They would charge us 15 percent for the firm's service plus 5 percent for overhead expenses such as auto mileage, reports, promotional literature, etc., totaling a 20 percent share of the funds raised. In addition to the firm's services, church members would be required to have a volunteer committee make personal contact with potential donors under the firm's direction. The amount to be raised was not a guarantee.

The problem was not so much the expense involved, but rather the goal of funds needed to build the new church, which was $2 million dollars. If this amount was raised and our present church sold, there would be adequate building funds. The crux of it all was that we needed to raise $2 million dollars, by far the most we ever had to raise, and the firm could only raise $1 million, at best.

With all this explained to me, they asked me to take on the chairmanship of the fundraising. The minister said, "The last three years in trying to get it done has been frustrating and we are now desperate, and that is why we have come to you!" When he said that, for a fleeting but light humorous moment, I thought to myself, "Hey, now they're scrapping the bottom of the barrel by asking me." But I knew that wasn't the case, because the church had known that I was actively involved for many years in fundraising programs such as Stewardship Fund Drives as well as being the finance chairman when our present church was built in 1960.

Being just re-married and now at a more advanced age, I was hesitant, so I told them, "I'll have to think about it, and I need to discuss it with Loretta. Can I let you know this coming Sunday at church?"

As they were leaving, the moderator, Devin Chin-Lee, turned to me and said, "Tom, by the way, my Uncle Felix said that if you take this on, he will be the first to donate, and that will be for $150,000 towards the campaign." I knew Felix well, had grown up with him, and knew he was good for it. I was impressed.

That evening, I thought about the meeting and the many dedicated people in our church. like the trustees, deacons, Sunday school teachers, Ladies Guild, and others. They were dedicated in so many necessary ways, but few in the fundraising area. I probably had more experience in that area than most because of my background. After talking things over with Loretta, I decided to accept the task.

The next morning, when Loretta and I arrived at church and were walking through the patio area, my friend Felix came up to me and said in a soft, friendly voice, "Tom, I know you've been asked, but if you take on the new building fund drive, I will donate $150,000! I want that to be treated as being anonymous."

That touched me. I assured him that I would take the job on and thanked him for his great generosity. Before church service, I notified the minister and moderator that I would be happy to take on the new building fund drive. I used that word "happy" because I wanted people to know that I was enthused about my new role in this important fund drive. But deep down, I can't really say that I was happy to take on this responsibility; what I really felt, at that point, was that it was my Christian duty.

During church service, the minister announced that I was asked to serve as the fundraising chairman for the new building and that I was happy to accept. With that, there was a loud round of applause, as I think the congregation felt there was someone who was at least willing to take it on and also enthused about it. The minister asked me to say a few words, for which I really had not prepared, but I thought I would announce the anonymous donation of $150,000 along with a few other thoughts on organizing the campaign.

I first talked about our goal of $2 million dollars, the importance of all getting involved, including the children, regardless of the size of the contribution, and that this fund drive was for Jesus Christ. I talked a bit about the fund drive that we did when we built our present church over 43 years ago when our congregation was much smaller and now that we're larger, we could do it proportionately much easier. I announced that shortly I would form a committee and ask for volunteers. In closing, I shared the news about the anonymous donation of $150,000. There was a loud and enthusiastic applause. I felt that was a good kick off.

As I was leaving the podium, member Dennis Avery stood up, while his wife Sally Wong sat by his side, and announced in a firm and pleasant voice, "Tom, thank you for taking on this important fund drive. My wife and I would like to add to that anonymous donation an additional $300,000 donation!"

That caught me by complete surprise—joyous, absolute surprise. The applause was thunderous as everyone stood up to thank the donors for their unsolicited and spontaneous contributions. Imagine, I said to myself, $450,000 total, just like that. As I left the podium, walking to my seat at the pew, I was thinking, "I'm glad I used that word 'happy,' it sure helped carry on the enthusiasm for this drive." And, truth be told, it ended up that I was really truly happy, too.

The next day I started mapping out the timeline we had to follow in order to meet our building schedule. For the past two years, our building coordinators, Roger Lee and Emma Hom, had been working with the architect and getting the necessary construction permits from the city. In order to coordinate this in a timely manner, I figured we had a window of six months to raise the $2 million dollars needed.

The six months were broken into two parts, with two months to form the committee, plan and organize the publicity, highlight the tax benefits in giving, create a list of friends outside of the church family who might contribute, draft a newsletter to report progress of the fund drive, print pamphlets, present a rendering of the new church building and other details. The balance of the four months was devoted to the actual kick off of the campaign, outreach through personal contacts, do mailings, and hold rallies.

In the interim, between the planning and the kick off, some of the people were already starting to make their contributions. One, in particular, occurred during a planning meeting when there was a soft knock on the door. It slowly opened and Kay Fung, a pastor's wife, poked her head in and softly said, "Can I come in with Ellen? She wants to give you something."

"Of course," I replied.

When they entered, Ellen, a gentle quiet women, handed me an envelope and said in her broken English, "Me and husband like this for the church." I thanked them and they left.

I resumed the meeting, but within minutes someone spoke out and said, "Tom, aren't you gonna open that envelope?" By the looks of others, they too were interested to know what was in the envelope.

So I opened it, and lo and behold, it was a check for $250,000 made out to the church building fund. We were all shocked and most certainly pleasantly surprised. It was contributions like that, especially before the kick off, that really motivated the committee to work harder and enjoy it even more.

After the planning was done, our first priority was to get the fundraising brochures in the mail to all the potential donors. We followed up with a newsletter especially designed to keep everyone up to date about the progress of the campaign, sharing who donated and why they were supporting the fundraising drive. This information and other news helped promote a bandwagon effect.

That was evident when one of the church members called me up and said. "Hey, Tom, I just got a call from Paul Tchang, and he wants to know how come no one has yet contacted him about the church fundraising! He wants to have lunch with you and me!" The next day we met Paul Tchang for lunch near his office, in a modest little Chinese restaurant. During lunch he asked a few questions about the church, and after we were about through eating, he said he wanted to make a donation of $100,000. That just about floored both my friend and me. On top of that, he also insisted on paying for lunch as well.

Another instance of unsolicited generosity occurred on a Hom cruise with 67 family members. Over lunch brother Allen and I were talking about sports, and then he changed the subject, and said, "Tom, I heard that you're trying to raise money for a new church building. How much are you trying to raise and what's the single largest donation so far?"

"The goal is $2,000,000 and so far the single largest is a generous $300,000," I replied. Nothing else was said and we went back to talking about sports.

To my surprise, a week after the cruise, Allen sent me a check for the building fund for $315,000. With gratitude and a bit of curiosity, I called to thank him and then asked why the odd figure. He replied, "Tom, I was going to make it $350,000, but I decided that I needed a new car, so I made it $315,000."

That's Allen, forever generous. Contributions like this have been given many other times without anyone asking.

It was because of big donations like these, along with the many, many medium and small donations, that we hit our goal of raising $2 million dollars three weeks before the end of our campaign. We didn't stop there, so by the time our campaign ended three weeks later, we raised an additional $500,000. We now had funds totaling $2,500,000, a half a million dollars over our original goal.

By tackling the fundraising ourselves, we saved the church the 20 percent fees and overhead costs of hiring a professional firm to direct the fundraising for us. Instead, the final total cost to us, by doing it ourselves, came to about only 3 percent, and that was mostly for printing, postage, and other necessary items. The volunteers did the rest. It is amazing how much talent there is in a church family.

And when it came to the construction of the new church building, we had a member who was a successful and recently retired general contractor who volunteered to do the contracting for us at no charge. Normally, a contracting fee is between 10 and 12 percent of the construction cost, which in our case, the cost of construction was about $5,000,000. Therefore, his generous no fee contribution saved us about $550,000. Lucky us!

The construction took about a year, and in the interim we sold the old church property. With those funds, along with the funds from our successful building campaign, we were able to finish our church construction, complete with new furnishings, fully equipped, and ready for occupation. Another accomplishment was that the spanking new church, twice the size of our former facilities, was completed with no debt, making it free and clear.

After all this, overseeing the fundraising campaign and having the responsibility of selling the old church, I asked myself, what did I learn? I learned that with any big undertaking, one needed a good plan, which we did have. Secondly, when dealing with people, a plan needed to be flexible. Thirdly, accept the unforeseen, and if it was negative, turn it into a positive. And if the unforeseen was a positive, capitalize on it and build upon that.

This has been very much a part of my life since I was fifteen when my father passed away. Whenever there was a negative, there had to be a positive. That's the law of physics. One just had to look for it. Aside from that, it helped when you worked for a good boss, like the Man Upstairs.

CHAPTER 49

Counting Heads

IN THE YEAR 2006, THE 300 MILLIONTH RESIDENT WAS BORN IN AMERICA ACCORDING TO THE U.S. CENSUS BUREAU.

OCCASIONALLY, WHENEVER I THINK OF POPULATION, I THINK of my family, particularly my father David and mother Yee Kam Yuep who were immigrants married in 1923. Since then to 2013, our clan—my father's 12 children, five from my mother, and seven from Ah Nuing—with all of our offspring, come to a hefty 133 individuals. There have been four generations of Homs living in San Diego. Of course, if you count my grandfather, Hom Fung, who arrived in San Diego in 1884 and eventually returned to China, there have been five generations that have lived here.

Of the 12 siblings, our ages ranging from 90 on down to the 70s, two of our brothers, George, an orthodontist, and Paul, a physician, have passed away. In birth order George was number eight, and Paul, number twelve, the youngest. Both of them left a big mark of kindness shown by their concern for others, especially for those that needed help the most.

George had his orthodontist office in the same building as my real estate office where we would see each other and talk almost every day. He had an excellent practice consisting of two types of clientele: those who could afford to pay for his professional service, and those who could not afford to see an orthodontist. He would make a personal effort to seek out those people who could not afford dental care and braces, offering his professional services for free. He felt strongly that a good, healthy set of straight teeth had a lot to do with one's personal outlook and confidence in everyday life. This applied to children as well as adults. Consequently, he maintained about 15 percent of his practice as *pro bono*.

As for youngest brother Paul, he left a legacy of touching the health and welfare of thousands. When Paul graduated from University of California Hastings College of Law, he joined the domestic Peace Corps, VISTA, which sent him to Texas and Mississippi to help the poor with their legal needs. After two years of working on legal matters, he came to the conclusion that the work he was doing was helpful, but what they really needed was more access to healthcare for their families. These were families from poor communities and included people who were White, Black, Latino, Asian, and recent immigrants.

Since he wanted to become more useful to serve the poor, Paul packed up his briefcase and decided to go back to school and get a medical degree. He enrolled at the University of California, Davis, and in a few short years he became a doctor, which was not a surprise to the family because Paul was probably among the brainiest of all the siblings. He excelled especially in academic matters, passing the SAT examination with a perfect score, attending college at age 16, and receiving scholarships to both Stanford and UC Berkeley.

After he graduated with his medical degree, he was asked to teach at the medical school part time. Eventually, his fulltime job was with the Sacramento Health Department working in the Epidemiology Department, later, becoming the head of that department.

While working these two jobs, Paul started a free clinic in the impoverished area of Sacramento in a modest building freshly painted by volunteer students and staffed by volunteer nurses and doctors. The health needs of the poor continued to grow and expansion was continually needed. This great outreach health program of working with the poor and needy went on for many years, often getting the attention of the news media and recognition by the greater community.

Paul passed away from lupus in 1994 at the age of 53, much too young. He spent more time concerned for other people's health than his own. But in that short time he had done more for the poor and indigent than almost anyone else I know. In commemoration of Paul for his dedication and humanitarian work, the County of Sacramento named a major new health facility after him, the Paul F. Hom M.D. Primary Care Center, located at Broadway and Stockton Boulevard.

When I count the number of years we have lived and the things we have been involved in, such as business, politics, community, church, and other areas, I wonder what has made us what we are today. I am not referring to our monetary worth, but rather, what has made the David Hom family stick together and support each other in times of need.

It probably started at the early stage of our lives, where Father would often preach the orderly philosophy of caring for each other, encouraging the older ones to care for the younger ones, and the younger ones to help when needed and show respect to the older ones. That was the pecking order of working together. This especially turned out to be a lifesaver for our family when Father passed away.

When my brother Allen and I, both high school age, had the immediate responsibility of supporting the family by running the family business, the David Produce Company, there was no question as to "Why me?" It was just accepted. Then James returned from the service to help support the family, along with veterans Wellman and Herbert, and, as the years went by, all the younger ones at one time or another worked at the David Produce Company pitching in. Yes, that was what was taught to us and what was expected of us. I don't recall any real complaints about that, maybe only a small grumble once in a while.

I think it was during this period being responsible for each other and to the family as a whole, that significantly impacted who we are and what we became. On top of Father's teaching, working at the family wholesale produce business offered a good educational foundation for us. It provided us with the opportunity to learn and respect the multitude of cultures represented by the produce employees with their different languages and foods, along with the importance of understanding our differences, and appreciation of our commonality.

As the years have gone by with the children and grandchildren growing in number, and from the Hom family's former wholesale produce business as the base, we have all dispersed into different areas of work and interest. Some of us have ventured into banking, real estate, television, medicine, engineering, teaching, broadcasting, construction, science, government, philanthropy, and other areas. These are careers and activities that my father, during his time, would have found hard to conceive that his offspring could be involved in and be so successful.

He lived at a time when racial discrimination in housing, as well as hiring practices in department stores, banks, labor unions, professional offices, healthcare, and government offices was commonplace. Minorities typically were limited to work as domestic household employees, care-takers, gardeners, and as unskilled laborers, where there were no labor unions involved. The labor unions were the strongest force to oppose hiring Chinese. Hence, in Dad's day, the Chinese created their own jobs, by opening laundries, small restaurants, grocery stores, curio and artifact shops, farming, and selling fruit and vegetables. In time, some of these businesses, with the family working together, would evolve into sizable enterprises, such as Dad's David Produce Company.

Of course, times have changed. Whereas before 60 years ago it was hard for minorities to find meaningful jobs, today most firms and organizations seem to make an effort to diversify the racial makeup of their workforce, which is good. I know that many Asian Americans have gravitated to the medical, scientific, academic fields, and arts and culture, and they seem to be thriving.

CHAPTER 50

The Final Compliment

AT TIMES, DIFFERENT PEOPLE HAVE ASKED ME WHAT THINGS made me who I am today. What stands out foremost? Who were the individuals that helped me along the way? What were the teachings or lessons that I encountered that made me the way I am? And how have I managed to stay so healthy?

I once read that we as individuals can prolong life by doing certain things. Eat healthy, rest well, don't stand when you can sit, don't sit when you can lie down, don't let things you cannot control bother you, treat people as you would want to be treated, don't let anger get the best of you, and do things in moderation. I have tried to live by these truisms.

For our well being and to improve our balance, Loretta and I have taken Tai Chi classes for a number of years. It is an ancient Chinese form of body movement where balance is an essential part, and it has done wonders for us. We have seen a number of stroke victims taking Tai Chi and they say that it has helped tremendously in their physical recovery.

Another one of my practices is that I drink my "health tonic" twice a day. It consists of a teaspoon of honey and two teaspoons of apple cider vinegar in a glass of water. I learned about this from a home folk remedy book written by Doctor D.C. Jarvis. It is a great energizer and it helps stimulate the mind to keep it active and sharp, especially as we age, it helps control obesity, and it also helps control arthritis. I've been taking this since I was 35, and I still do it today at age 86.

On the subject of staying active and sharp, it's just as important to one's well being to stay engaged with the larger community. Today, Loretta and I are actively involved in the Asian Pacific Islander American Public Affairs Association, a national organization which encourages Asian Americans to take leadership roles in civic affairs. Giving back to the community keeps us mentally stimulated and socially relevant.

To enhance my health, I'm also a big advocate of bee products, like bee pollen, a natural antibiotic; bee wax capping to clear sinus problems; and most of all, honey itself. Honey is probably the purest food one can find and it is full of minerals necessary for good health. It is so pure, in fact, that germs can't live in it.

And, of course, I take two little pills from my Chinese herbalist for my prostate.

I better stop here before I start sounding like a healthcare fanatic. Let me just say that I value modern medicine, as well as the natural old home folk remedies. I believe it's a combination of the old and the new, the eastern and the western, that serves us best.

THERE HAVE BEEN SO MANY PEOPLE who have helped shape my life, mentored, inspired, and cared for me, it is hard to know where to start. Likewise, the ups and downs have been many, and I am grateful that I've had many more ups than downs.

The biggest influence of my life was Father. Although I was only fifteen when he passed away, I have tried to live by his teachings. He told us boys to always be a gentleman, although I'm not sure I became one, and the importance of having good character. And it was Father who first made me aware that the kind of laws that come out of city hall are made by the people we vote into city hall. From there, I knew I wanted to be one of those people.

One of the great pluses in my life was the opportunity, as well as the necessity of working together with my siblings in bringing the family from tough times to economic security. We learned a lot working together and from each other.

And then there was my first wife, Dorothy, who I married when she was only 19, giving up her scholarship to the University of California, Berkeley to be with me. When I asked her why she would forego a valuable scholarship, she said, "I found the best, and why should I go out to seek the rest!" I have always tried to live up to her sacrifice in giving up her scholarship. Throughout our lives together, Dorothy was more than a right hand to me, she was, in the words of the popular love song, the "wind beneath my wings." She always gave me the credit for all of our accomplishments. She was, indeed, the better half.

And, of course, six of the biggest highlights are my kids, five daughters and a son. As their proud father I have the right to say all of them are intelligent and attractive with pleasant personalities, and they are also good, caring people, just like their mother. In spite of that similarity, they are remarkably different from each other, for which their mother and I were thankful, as we always felt variety in a family was the spice of life.

I also have my children to thank for helping me find a lovely and charming lady, Loretta Lum, who I married and am blessed to share my life with. Today, the children truly love her enough to introduce her as their mother, rather than "my father's wife" or "stepmother." This is all the more sweeter knowing we have Dorothy's blessing.

Among the most influential people outside of my family was my junior high school principal, William J. Oakes, who always stated emphatically that opportunities were just as great for us immigrant children as anybody else and to not let anyone tell us otherwise. Another instrumental person was Admiral Les Gehres, Chairman of the San Diego Republican Party, who encouraged me to run for office and taught me how to win. Largely because of his mentoring, I was fortunate to serve as a San Diego City Councilman, Deputy Mayor, and California State Assemblyman. Les Gehres was tough, but caring and kind.

A major anchor for me was knowing Jesus Christ since I was four, starting with Sunday school at the Chinese Congregational Mission (now Chinese Community Church). Also, being a Mason for 55 years taught me appreciation and respect for other religions and people of different races and cultures, and that basically people are good.

IN MY EXPERIENCE, GOOD OR BAD, there is usually a valuable lesson to learn. I believe lessons are the tools to understanding and compassion. It becomes part of character building.

The following are some lessons I've learned in life:

- The main thing in life is not security. It is courage.
- When one door closes, another will open.
- Life is full of twists and turns and in time true righteousness usually wins out.

- In life, one needs to adjust constantly, and the way to do that is to remain flexible.
- Whenever there's a negative, there has to be a positive. That's the law of physics. Look for the silver lining.
- Do not take life for granted. Cherish life.
- It is crucial to communicate well. Life today is so instant; to get it right the first time is important. Say it the right way and say it clearly, being respectful of the person with whom you are speaking.
- Your words mean a lot, so be sincere, friendly and fair in your dealings with people.
- To solve a problem you must first pinpoint what the real problem is. Once you know that, you can work towards solving it.
- The true art of negotiation is to produce two winners.
- Seeking personal revenge has a way of rearing back at you and can, in turn, make you the victim instead of the victor.
- Experiencing positive and negative business dealings gives one the opportunity to better judge the good from the bad.
- To do well in the Free Enterprise system be innovative and be better than the competition.
- Growth of a good organization must constantly refresh itself with new ideas and new leadership.
- There has been, or there presently is, a mentor in your life. Be open to being mentored.
- Diversity: There is good in every race and culture. It is just a matter of accepting it.
- Value and work with family and community for the benefit of all.
- Always be a gentleman (and gentlewoman).

As the years go by, I shall continue to mark the calendar each year on my birthday. For how many more years, who knows? Yes, we all travel a bumpy road. Overall, I have come to the profound understanding that it is how we live our lives, with a sense of dignity, compassion and gratitude, and respect for all, that really counts. And the final compliment is knowing that others think that the path you have trod is worth following.

Index*

* PI = Photo Insert.